PENGUIN BOOKS

The Angels of Englemere Wood

Karen Farrington is a writer and former journalist whose published work includes titles on social and military history, together with a range of non-fiction TV companion books.

Her most recent work includes the bestselling series of books from *The Repair Shop*. She also worked as researcher for *The Life and Times of Call the Midwife*, the companion to series one and two of the BBC series. She lives in Devon.

T0322137

The Angels of Englemere Wood

KAREN FARRINGTON

PENGUIN BOOKS

PENGUIN BOOKS

UK | USA | Canada | Ireland | Australia
India | New Zealand | South Africa

Penguin Books is part of the Penguin Random House group of companies
whose addresses can be found at global.penguinrandomhouse.com.

Penguin
Random House
UK

First published by Penguin Michael Joseph 2022
Published in Penguin Books 2023

001

Set in 12.42/14.72pt Garamond MT Std
Typeset by Jouve (UK), Milton Keynes
Printed and bound in Great Britain by Clays Ltd, Elcograf S.p.A.

The authorized representative in the EEA is Penguin Random House Ireland,
Morrison Chambers, 32 Nassau Street, Dublin D02 YH68

A CIP catalogue record for this book is available from the British Library

HARDBACK ISBN: 978-0-241-55719-8

www.greenpenguin.co.uk

Dedicated to the girls who passed through Englemere Wood and Grenville House. And to the women who gave them happiness and hope.

Contents

Introduction

There can be no keener revelation of a society's soul than the way in which it treats its children.
Nelson Mandela, former president of South Africa

As the Second World War erupted, an exceptional story began to unfold at a grand mansion called Englemere Wood. A remarkable woman opened its doors to girls from a children's home, to keep them safe from enemy bombing campaigns. Dorothy Peyton was one of the Angels of Englemere Wood, but by no means the only one.

Another 'angel' was in charge of this posse of girls, a woman who devoted her life to those who risked getting crushed by the grinding poverty of the twenties and thirties, obliterated in the churn of the Second World War or falling through the cracks of the chaotic times that followed the conflict. Matron Bailey, as the girls knew her back then, was no soft touch. At times stern, she ran a tight ship and didn't tolerate any infringements of discipline that would jeopardize her tip-top organization. But none doubted the warmth and tenderness she had for the girls nestling safely under her extensive wing, the empathy she had for their various growing pains and the faith she kept in each one, to achieve more and better than they ever believed they could.

Then there were lots of 'little angels' drawn from the welfare system of the era. Most had known desperate poverty, having been born in or around the nine-month-long General Strike or the Great Depression that followed, which exerted a vice-like grip on national economies everywhere. Britain was hard hit as wages slumped and prices soared.

The acute stresses brought about by poor housing, hunger and ill health for those who had already been pummelled during the First World War meant family life was too often endured rather than enjoyed. While some relationships flourished, many others hit the rocks and it was children who came off second best in any domestic rupture.

At the time children were by no means front and centre of the national agenda. They risked being lost in this maelstrom. Their story was seldom told. Children's homes were there to help pick up the pieces when domestic harmony fractured or when there was nothing left to pawn to put dinner on the table. The most fortunate, it turned out, ended up at Englemere Wood. For a few years this rambling house on the western fringe of Ascot was where girls got into scrapes, flirted with boys, delighted in clothes and music, inwardly cursed the endless duties of housework – and even stole when hunger got the better of them.

A lady-in-waiting to royalty, Dorothy Peyton became a compassionate pillar of strength at the very heart of the girls' existence. Together with Matron Bailey, she fiercely guarded the girls from the worst of life's barbs, while offering them the gift of childhood. Through her the girls were introduced to a trio of women – two princesses and a once-notorious socialite – who they would meet for weekly knitting parties. This was the kind of company no girls drawn from the roughest streets of London could have dreamed of keeping and yet, after this experience, when it finally came to performing plays in front of the Royal Family, those same girls barely broke stride.

People in Ascot also took the girls to their hearts, offering limitless help and encouragement. Then there were staff members who helped care for the girls, themselves adhering to Matron's high standards and committed to building the girls' lives back up from their very foundations. Among them all, a chemistry was created, and an unbreakable bond was forged.

The engrossing and emotional tale of how a Waifs and Strays Society children's home arrived at a rural idyll after being evacuated from London to escape the Blitz is one Tom Peyton has known all his life . . .

'The lady who opened her house and her heart for these girls, gave them a glimpse of what life could be like, showed them a world they could not have imagined and fired their aspirations, was my grandmother.

'This is an extraordinary story of social upheaval, against the backdrop of war, where people from radically different walks of life came together to provide a home, a family and to become a community that would continue through the generations. From the fishing folk of north Devon and the back streets of Wandsworth, to knitting circles with Queen Victoria's granddaughters and performing before Her Majesty the queen; it was a journey few could have envisaged. It was an experience they never forgot and one that provided an opportunity for a different type of life, one that they grasped readily and with everlasting gratitude. In this book there are so many memories embedded in the social history of their time and bringing to light a different aspect of the war years, when a little love and kindness gave hope and opportunity to a small group of "waifs and strays".'

Despite the colossal efforts of Dorothy Peyton and Matron Bailey to shield them all, the war inflicted a wounding scar that none of the girls would forget. With spring still sharp outside Englemere Wood's floor-to-ceiling windows and raw with grief at a soldier's death, they clung to the vision of a brighter future by taking a solemn vow. They would, they promised, live better lives in recognition of the love and loss that they had known. It wasn't the start of the story, nor did it end there, but that promise expressed the virtues with which one household in an embattled nation survived the conflict.

Tom Peyton takes up the tale once more. 'This promise became the legacy of a remarkable woman, who instilled in a group of girls a belief in kindness and integrity that still shines in those who remain and their families to this day. Matron Bailey was an old-fashioned, strict but loving woman, whose life's work was looking after those less fortunate than herself, who even after the home had closed and the girls dispersed, kept in contact with them all well into her nineties.'

Matron's surviving charges are now in their nineties themselves, yet they still cherish the links forged at Englemere Wood. As girls they discovered how it felt to thrive and got an inkling about the power of unconditional love, something they would in turn pass on to their own children. As nurture challenged nature, the girls also found friends as close as siblings. The connections formed at Englemere Wood were strong and lifelong.

One of the girls from Englemere Wood is Queenie Clapton. Now in her mid-nineties Queenie walks with a stoop and her step is uncertain. Her eyes still twinkle but age has eroded her sharpness of vision. Yet the passing years have done nothing to lessen the clarity of her mind or memory. Her thoughts often stray into the hallowed realm of childhood – and it's enough to bring her to tears.

For Queenie life at Englemere Wood was little short of idyllic. Everything that came later – a long and happy marriage, four wonderful children – was launched from the platform painstakingly constructed by Matron Bailey and Dorothy Peyton, who inspired awe and affection in equal measure. When she sits in her London home contemplating the past, the tears that fall are not for what was lost in childhood, but what was gained all those years ago.

In recognition of both women, and all they achieved, she has created an enduring network of people linked to Englemere Wood, which includes Tom. 'Even now, Queenie keeps in touch with the "girls" and their families and has been the driving force in completing this book,' he says. 'Her memory is in no way diminished by the passing years and she speaks from the heart about her experiences, always wanting to ensure that the story does sufficient justice to the memory of Matron who made a seminal difference to all their lives.'

Without Queenie, Tom and others linked to Englemere Wood, the quicksand of time would have already swallowed this incredible narrative. Thanks to their efforts, the details of a compelling history have been secured for future generations.

National Registration

At the end of September 1939, three weeks after the outbreak of the Second World War, the British government ordered a National Registration of the civilian population, pinpointing the whereabouts of everyone in the country who wasn't in uniform. The forms asked for names, ages, addresses and occupations. It was a necessary piece of bureaucracy to produce the identity papers and ration cards that were subsequently issued. From it we know the ages and the addresses of everyone involved in this account of life in a children's home during the Second World War.*

Englemere Wood

Mrs Dorothy Peyton, 51
Jack Chandler, butler, 25
Margaret Osborn, housemaid, 51
Doreen Dorgan, housemaid, 15
Ellen Bartlett, cook, 25
George Moore, chauffeur, 40
Elsie Moore, 34
Jean Moore, 5

* Some names have been changed.

The Maurice Home, run by the Waifs and Strays Society,
evacuated to Englemere Wood from Ealing

Staff
Doris Hurford Bailey, matron, 37
Lucy Briggs, first assistant Matron, 34
Doris Sheppard, second assistant Matron, 25
Gertrude Measures, third assistant Matron, 21

Girls
Barbara Phillips, training for domestic duties, 15
Sheila McCairn, at school, 11
Monica Harmer, at school, 11
Jenny Logan, at school, 8

During the war, girls came and went from Englemere Wood. The National Registration reveals where some of them were at the start of the conflict.
Queenie Clapton, at school in Leamington Spa, Warwickshire, 12
Evelyn Siddons, at school in Leamington Spa, Warwickshire, 12
Gladys Raffell, living in London, 2

The wartime residents of the neighbouring property, Englemere House, hadn't arrived when the registration was taken. At the time the Weigalls were living in Buckinghamshire and the princesses in London. Their move to Ascot came almost directly after the process was completed. In 1939 Archie Weigall was sixty-five, and his wife Grace was sixty-three. Princess Marie Louise at sixty-seven was two years younger than her sister Princess Helena Victoria.

Men serving in the armed forces were not included in the registration, so there's no record here of Dorothy Peyton's two sons. However, John Peyton was twenty and his brother Tommy was eighteen.

Most of *The Angels of Englemere Wood* is set in a corner of rural Britain where at first it seemed everyone's lives would remain untouched by the bitter hostilities. In fact, the fighting would deal a hammer blow to them all. But the story begins years before the first shot is fired, with the arrival of daughters into troubled families . . .

1. 'Who do you love the most?'

Children are our most valuable resource.
Herbert Hoover, thirty-first president of the USA

'Then steadily shoulder to shoulder,
Steadily blade by blade!
Ready and strong, marching along
Like the boys of the old Brigade!'

When the bellowed lyrics of the song from the trenches reached the window of a cramped top-floor flat, alarm flashed across Maud Clapton's face.

'Quickly, in here,' she called to her three children, beckoning them from the living room to the single bedroom.

The iron bedstead grated on the floorboards as the four shouldered it wordlessly into position, but the sound wasn't nearly enough to drown out the raucous singing that got louder with every lurching step.

Old soldier Hector – Maud's husband and the children's father – was returning from the pub, fuelled by countless pints of ale. He was a familiar face at The Old Sergeant and The Leather Bottle, but he might also have been to The Wagon and Horses, The Halfway House or The Spotted Dog – or any one of great numbers of public houses within walking distance from their home in Garratt Lane, a lengthy thoroughfare that wound through the suburbs of south-west London.

After he had negotiated the staircase, bouncing between wall and banister, and came into the top-floor flat, Hector realized he was shut out of the bedroom and started banging on the door.

John, Gladys and Queenie were already under the covers behind the blocked door with their mother Maud.

'Dad!' Eight-year-old Queenie began talking but was angrily shushed by her mum. The children exchanged looks. They weren't scared of their father. Every Friday night he returned home laden with sweets, to the delight of the trio. Sometimes he even dished out pocket money. But tonight was Saturday and it was a different story. Eventually the knocking and shouting subsided, and Hector settled into a noisy sleep on the lumpy horsehair sofa.

There was no shortage of money coming into the Clapton household; Hector worked as a dustman and got additional employment on the London Underground extensions that took place between the wars, like the one to the Northern Line nearby. The problem was the swift rate at which money fled the household, into the cash registers of local pubs.

While he drank the proceeds of his hard labour Maud would go out to work in the evenings to put food on the table, leaving her daughters in the care of eldest child John.

If Maud confronted Hector about the money he spent on drink, she risked a back-handed slap. Shocking sights like this didn't trouble Queenie unduly. She was accustomed to seeing her father drunk, and the spats between her parents were commonplace.

After she was born on 2 March 1927, the youngest of three children, Queenie lived in part of a house that stood almost exactly halfway between the overground station at Earlsfield and the newly opened Tooting Bec underground station (then known as Trinity Road), a stone's throw from Streatham Cemetery.

It was tenement housing, with the Clapton family occupying one bedroom and one living room. There was no kitchen, but a washbasin stood on the landing with the stove next to it. The facilities were shared with the family below. At this small square sink hard-working Maud did the family washing, hanging it high above the street outside on a washing line attached to the house across the road, operated by a pulley. With the sulphurous smoke from trains, chimneys and factories in the vicinity settling as smog between tall buildings, the laundered clothes looked grey before they even came off the line.

When their tin bath, hung on a nail outside the large sash window, was retrieved and filled with water boiled on the tiny stove, it was shared by the entire family. After bath night, the children snuggled up on the sofa to enjoy a supper of bread and dripping. Soup was a rare treat.

Living conditions and privacy were improved for those families on the ground floor and in the basement. But the only household toilet was outside in the backyard, used by all and furnished with torn newspaper. In short, it was just the type of housing that the London County Council was aiming to eradicate with its ongoing social housing programme.

However, when Queenie was eight years old, something changed. Perhaps it was when one particularly ugly domestic incident erupted, which attracted the attention of the public assistance committee charged with overseeing the care for children at the time. Maybe there were a string of noisy events reported by neighbours that led social workers to the family's door. It might well have been the final acrimonious fracture in Hector and Maud's marriage.

When she was taken to an unknown room, some kindly women enquired, 'Who would you like to live with, your mum or your dad?' Queenie floundered, knowing without understanding that the earth was shifting beneath her. When she failed to answer, she was asked the impossible question: 'Who do you love the most?' She had no answer to give, for in truth she loved them both.

But everything would be different now. There was no tear-stained farewell with her parents or the brother that stayed behind. She must have felt apprehension, as the future she had assumed was hers, in a meagre flat with her family, vanished. Anxiety surely haunted her dreams, while during her waking hours she was wary and watchful. Children like her had no agency at the time. If she'd spoken up for herself, it wouldn't have made any difference; she knew that. But at least she had her sister Gladys – five years her senior – at hand, a comfort in this crisis.

How had it come to this? Her father Hector's story was not unusual for the era. The youngest of nine children, he worked as a market gardener until he joined the initial wave of volunteers in the First World War, enlisting on 7 August 1914, three days after hostilities began, aged twenty-eight. With thousands of others there was a hectic training schedule, characterized by joyful jingoism, before he disembarked in France on 26 January 1915. His name is associated both with the South Wales Borderers and the Royal Welch Fusiliers.

Serving for the duration of the war, he saw extraordinary step changes in the way it was fought. At the start, he wore a khaki woollen tunic and a peaked hat. On cotton webbing he carried equipment including ammunition, a water bottle and an entrenching tool. His legs were protected by puttees, bandage-style bindings. Weapons in use included Webley revolvers, Lee-Enfield rifles and Vickers machine guns. Horses were a key part of British military thinking, with men in the cavalry regiments still armed with swords to run through enemy soldiers after a charge. The largest artillery gun fired sixty-pound shells.

Hector fought in France during the summer of 1916 in actions that collectively became known as the Battle of the Somme. The battle remains front and centre of public consciousness as far as the First World War is concerned, for the 57,000 British casualties felled on the campaign's first day.

Two years later, and after four spent in the army, he was taken ill with 'pyrexia of unknown origin', a high temperature probably caused by a virus. It's the sort of poorly defined illness that afflicted many men who spent time at the front in the trenches, especially during the winter months. By then he was a lance corporal.

When he left the army at the end of the conflict, for reasons unknown, he was back to the rank of private. He'd witnessed the introduction of steel helmets, Lewis machine guns, creeping barrages and the first tanks. Mighty railway guns capable of firing 850-pound shells had been used on the Western Front, with soldiers from both sides killed on an industrial scale. Hector had seen first-hand the suffering borne by men in the trenches where ordnance had rained down on them, day and night, frustrated that the technology associated with warfare leaped ahead while the front lines remained miserably stagnant. By its end in 1918 it had claimed about 886,000 British lives and the scars ran deep. Mothers, fathers, wives and children were left grieving for men who had often died in squalor, in a war that few understood beyond the clarion call of king and country.

Hector was discharged in March 1919, no longer physically fit for war service. But there's little doubt that he had served his king and country with merit. Apart from the standard array of medals awarded to a long-serving soldier he was also the recipient of the Silver War Badge, also known as the Discharge, Wound or Services Rendered Badge, given to those honourably discharged due to wounds or sickness.

Men like Hector who came back from the front were frequently changed beyond recognition. Leaner – and sometimes meaner – they had experienced terrible events that they could not 'unsee'. Moreover, shocking secrets from the front line were never willingly confided. Damaged physically or psychologically, feeling resentful and rejected, men like Hector were the fathers of children born between the wars.

Five months after he left the army he married Maud Johnson, Queenie's mum, in the register office at Kingston, Surrey. Hector gave his military details by way of job description, adding 'general labourer' apparently as an afterthought. No job title was given for Maud, although it seems likely she was in domestic service. At the time he was thirty-four, while she was twenty-seven, and both had been living near Wimbledon.

After the war women were confronted with a shortage of potential partners and the prospect of living a single life without children. Newspapers dubbed them the 'surplus two million', referencing the way women outnumbered men in the general population.

Those like Maud who did marry may, on the face of it, have seemed like the lucky ones, and these were the mothers of the children born prior to the Second World War. But this was a veneer all too easily shattered if those husbands, like Hector, had been traumatized by their experiences. In a country that had a pub on most street corners, many men turned to drink to self-medicate.

Their courtship had been relatively swift. They lived close to one another in the grid of terraced housing at the outskirts of Wimbledon. At the time they met the country was still celebrating the First World War victory, and that no one was now being sent to the killing fields in France, so the national mood was cheerful. The flat fields of Haydon's Road recreation ground marked the halfway point between their rented rooms, where they could meet to walk and talk. A longer trek would have taken them to Wimbledon Common, first pausing at the war memorial built in 1919 to mark the deaths of local men. And surely they went to Merton Carnival with its jaunty procession that took place in July 1919, a month before they wed. When noisy flashing fireworks filled the sky that night as part of the celebrations, Hector would not have been the only man there fighting a rising panic.

He likely splashed his spare cash on his bride-to-be,

perhaps taking her to Ely's department store in Wimbledon for a pre-wedding purchase when previously she had only window-shopped there. Together they moved to the flat in Garratt Lane, and their son John arrived a year later. Even by then, the promise life held for those short months was all but extinguished.

Years fell away, yet the sombre shadow cast by the First World War always remained in evidence. Hector was burdened by hidden trauma from his time at the front and this soon became painfully apparent to Maud.

Although the government had pledged surviving soldiers would return to 'a land fit for heroes', there was scant evidence of it after the echoes of Armistice cheers had ebbed away. The twenties were marked by industrial strife and the Wall Street Crash of 1929, leaving the thirties a far sadder decade.

Between the wars, when there were always at least a million people unemployed and often more, it wasn't easy for working-class men and women to find and keep properly paid work. And Maud herself was also bearing emotional scars, the legacy of a difficult childhood. She was the third of seven children born to John Johnson and his wife Rosa. Johnson called himself an electrical engineer, and was perhaps a man before his time.

The first central distribution point for electricity was opened at Holburn Viaduct as early as 1882. Nonetheless, this new source of power failed to make the strides that men like John anticipated and gas was still the primary choice for lighting homes and businesses. In late Victorian times electricity was most often associated with oddball remedies like the electric flesh brush, which promised relief from numerous conditions including gout, lumbago and 'impure blood'.

At the turn of the century John Johnson and his children were in and out of workhouses, the last-ditch option and a humbling experience, albeit one shared by hundreds of families at the time. At the start of the twentieth century there were more than 200,000 people inside workhouses in England and Wales, shamed by their pauperism.

It wasn't long after the First World War that electricity became the most popular choice in homes for power. But this came far too late for John Johnson, who died in 1905 aged forty-nine in Kings College Hospital. Maud was just thirteen.

Five years later, Maud was fighting her way out of the poverty trap by working as a servant in Parkholme Road, Dalston, for Sarah and Alfred Warr, a legal clerk. Her sisters Alice and Emily were likewise working as servants. John, the middle child and only son, was in Maldon, Essex, the foster son of Henry and Annie Vesey, and a machine operator in a nut factory. Youngest sister Mabel, aged eleven, was living with her mother's brother Alexander and his family in Stafford.

Another sister, Dorothy, was already dead. She was at the Lambeth Schools Infirmary in West Norwood when she died in November 1907 – a workhouse premises. Shockingly her death certificate reveals she'd had marasmus – or malnutrition – for eight months and gastroenteritis for three days before her emaciated body gave up the fight for survival. Another sister, Queenie, had been a pupil at the same workhouse school. At the time it seemed their mother Rosa had disappeared without trace, as there is no mention of her in the records, although her death wasn't recorded until 1949.

Fast-forward thirty years and by now most families didn't endure the horrors that befell some of their Victorian and Edwardian counterparts. Thankfully Maud's daughter Queenie – presumably named for her aunt – didn't confront the privations that her mother had. The foundation of a society that helped those who could not help themselves had already been laid by the 1906 Liberal government. In short order there followed free school meals, school medical inspections, a children's charter that banned youngsters from begging and established juvenile courts (so children were no longer dealt with as adults), an old-age pension and labour exchanges. Sterling efforts were being made by local councils to improve housing for British families, in the knowledge that better sanitary conditions for young families enhanced public health. Medical science was helping to improve the figures for childhood mortality, and innovation was making domestic life easier.

After Queenie was born the records revealed these radical improvements had had a marked effect, with the average life expectancy in 1931 standing at nearly fifty-nine years for men and sixty-three years for women, an increase of some seven years since 1918. And workhouses were finally shut. But that didn't necessarily guarantee a happy home life. Maud's hopes for greater stability as a married woman were frustrated, thanks to Hector's drinking. The marriage would not endure and Maud – with no role model for mothering – lost custody of her daughters, although her son John, who was already working, stayed at home.

Today most mothers would be left bereft. But Maud,

with the spectre of her own troubled childhood still evident, was struggling. Before Queenie was born she'd lost a baby, and after that she'd endured domestic violence and lived a life of drudgery. Showing a tender side had never worked to her advantage. Having suffered so many devastating blows already, the careworn forty-three-year-old assumed the protective armour of indifference.

This one failed family wasn't an isolated case. In 1935, the year Queenie was taken in by the Waifs and Strays Society, more than 1,000 children were admitted into the care of the charity.

Nor was the society working alone in the field. It was one of many organizations that ran children's homes at the time, including the Daughters of Charity, the Shaftesbury Homes, the Girls Friendly Society and National Children's Homes. Alongside the Waifs and Strays Society, perhaps the most prominent was the chain of Barnardo's Homes, established like the rest in Victorian times to tackle the acute deprivation in families like Maud's.

Alerts about child welfare were raised by relatives, neighbours, schools or the National Society for the Prevention of Cruelty to Children. Only after that did children's homes become involved. While some children committed to children's homes were unwanted, others were orphans. Many, like Queenie, had parents who were deemed incapable of properly caring for their children. Some parents kept in occasional contact with their children through vetted letters or supervised visits.

For Queenie the sudden departure from family life wasn't as shattering as it might at first sound. The kindly women from the society charged with grilling Queenie and her sister Gladys told them they would be going for a holiday – and that was a welcome prospect. Holidays had not been a feature of Clapton family life. Initially, though, their destination was St Mary's Home in Cheam, Surrey. In 1914, when it was built, St Mary's was in the depths of rural Surrey. But by the time Queenie and Gladys arrived, the neighbourhood was in the process of being swallowed up by outer London.

Three storeys high with multiple gables and mock-Tudor beams, St Mary's was an imposing sight for the girls as they made their way up its drive to the front door for the first time.

Queenie paused for a moment and looked up in awe at the façade. In one hand she was clutching a small bag that she supposed had been packed by her mother. Any colour that had once defined the clothes inside had long since been washed out, as they were hand-me-downs from her sister. There weren't many clothes, and they weren't unduly heavy. With the other hand, she clutched Gladys's sleeve. The place was considerably smarter than many of the homes in their road, she noticed. They were heading towards a tall arched doorway that sat inside a substantial porch, which looked like a giant mouth that was about to eat them up. Queenie hesitated.

'Pick your feet up.' The woman from the Waifs and Strays Society, who was close behind them, spoke firmly but brightly, and there was some comfort for Queenie in that.

Construction of the home had been paid for by the Church of England's Waifs and Strays Society as part of a programme to rapidly increase capacity. It was a timely addition, as many war widows would be hard-pressed to support their children. The number of babies born out of wedlock had spiked during the conflict. When rudimentary methods of birth control failed, women faced stark choices: seek a backstreet abortion that would imperil their lives or find more money to feed an extra mouth. A third option was provided by children's homes. Then, hot on the heels of the conflict, came a flu epidemic that, as well as the old and frail, killed men and women in their prime and created still more orphans.

In retrospect they were fortunate that Cheam was as far as they went that day. Girls like Queenie and Gladys had previously found themselves dispatched to far corners of the globe because of a controversial across-the-board child-migration policy, forced to make a new life in a different climate among strangers.

Although support for the policy was ebbing, children were even now being sent overseas by a number of charities, including the Waifs and Strays Society, Barnardo's and other children's organizations supported by both the Anglican and Catholic churches. It didn't matter if they had parents who didn't want them to go.

Some voices continued to call for child migration in the twentieth century, in the belief it would somehow cement the empire. But instead of being shipped off to distant lands, Queenie was among fifty girls at St Mary's who enjoyed three square meals a day and had plenty of clean clothes. At the time homes provided each girl with three nightgowns or pyjamas, three vests, three pairs of knickers, four pairs of socks or stockings, a dressing gown, slippers, three summer dresses, a coat, a raincoat, two pairs of walking shoes, one pair of sandals, two pairs of gloves, one pair of Wellington boots, twelve handkerchiefs, plus other clothes, like cardigans and play clothes, as required.

Sometimes, but not necessarily, the items were new. It was the era of make do and mend and the home kept a supply of clothes that were continually repaired until the fabric could stand no further stitching. Nonetheless, it was considerably more than Queenie was used to having. She was dizzy with the amount laid out on her bed on her first day there. Some of the clothes felt rough, but no worse than anything she'd worn before. It didn't worry her that some were second-hand. She'd often heard the song 'Second Hand Rose' and reasoned it couldn't be such a bad thing if a record had been made. Issued with a number on arrival, all her new clothes were marked with it.

Almost as soon as she walked in the door, Queenie was swept up in the daily household routines, which had the place running like clockwork, so there was little time for homesickness. Every morning when they awoke, Queenie and Gladys knew exactly what lay ahead that day. With an array of mundane tasks to accomplish, the atmosphere was impersonal.

Given the age difference, she and Gladys slept in different rooms for the first time in their lives but encountered each other regularly.

One day, after chores, they met on a landing. Wearing her new set of clothes, Gladys suddenly seemed very grown-up.

'How are you?' Gladys asked, sounding more like a parent than a sister, Queenie thought.

'I'm all right. It's fine here really,' Queenie replied. 'The food is quite nice. I don't much like being called by a number rather than a name, though.'

'You look well enough,' said Gladys, noticing a pink bloom evident for the first time in Queenie's cheeks.

'Yes, I've made some new friends, like Rosie. She comes from London, near our house. She says her sister uses the tram to get to her shop job . . .'

Queenie trailed off as she saw Gladys's eyes were no longer fixed on her own but scanning the stairwell as other older girls from the home approached. After staring at her distracted sister for a moment, Queenie peeled away in search of her own pals, muttering a goodbye.

In fact, both girls were finding that friends were now readily slotting into the gaps left by absent family. Gradually comradeship began to trump blood ties. Only occasionally did Queenie's thoughts turn to having toast and dripping, snuggled up with her siblings on the misshapen sofa at their London flat. But, on the upside, she no longer experienced her father's drunken rages, and she relished an unaccustomed feeling of security.

Then came the holiday Queenie had been promised, deep in the Kent countryside.

Queenie looked blankly as she was handed a sack.

'Look smart,' called one of the sisters. 'Here's some straw. You need to stuff the sack so you've got something to sleep on.'

'Won't it be too hard to sleep on?' Queenie asked, perplexed.

The sister smiled. 'You'll soon get used to it.' The policy of having camping holidays was deeply entrenched at the society and, it seemed, never failed in its transformative effects.

When the sack bulged and, after a pillow had been filled, Queenie dragged the rough bedding into a barn where the rest of the girls were lining up to establish a dormitory of sorts.

Sacks had other uses as well, as Queenie discovered. 'Here, take this,' said one of the older girls, thrusting an empty hessian bag at her. 'We need to fill it with wood for the fire tonight.'

In the end, the girls filled six sacks with wood – and carried even more back in their arms.

Queenie learned to love the smell of campfire smoke and the taste of the food cooked on it, although sometimes it was charred. She felt little enthusiasm when it came to boarding the bus that would bring them back to St Mary's. After revelling in this outdoor environment, many girls from St Mary's and other children's homes joined the Girl Guides, an organization formed in 1910 in response to Robert Baden Powell's Boy Scouts and run by Baden-Powell's wife Olave and sister Agnes. Guides everywhere wore the same uniform, a considered policy by the Baden Powells to mask any differences in social standing. And girls at St Mary's were mindful of their obligation, not only to monarch and country but to each other. Encouraged to do a 'good turn' every day, their thoughts often turned to how they could help fellow Guides. Thus the bonds between them all were strengthened.

Queenie went to a local school – where she never felt ashamed to say she lived at a children's home. Already she firmly believed she was having a better life there than she would have done at home. She was neither envious of children from family homes nor made an outcast by them. For Queenie parental contact was all but lost at this time, although not for want of trying by the wayward Hector.

'Queenie, QUEENIE.' Hector's voice floated from the gateway of St Mary's. Hector had come to visit his daughter at the end of a prolonged drinking session.

A crowd of girls, including Queenie, were gathered at one of the top windows, looking out. They'd giggled after seeing him bump into the red pillar box outside the home and put their hands over their mouths in mock shock as he called out.

Queenie laughed along with them. She wasn't shaken or upset at the sight of her drunken dad, more amused. Inside, a small warm glow was ignited. Her dad was making exceptional efforts to see her, even if he was in no fit state. Nor did the laughter of the girls around her sound judgemental or scornful. Although she didn't know any of their backstories – conversations about their past lives were never shared – they too may well have been accustomed to paralytic parents and their untoward behaviour.

The girls couldn't hear the firm words of the home's matron who opened the door, but whatever was said was sufficient to send him away, his head bent, without a backward glance.

It wasn't the last time Queenie saw her father, though. Curiously a bout of severe ill health brought them together again. In fact, the illness turned out to be memorable for all kinds of reasons.

The condition that affected her so catastrophically remains unidentified. It could have been one of many that descended on children of the era: pneumonia, meningitis, diphtheria, scarlet fever, rheumatic fever, whooping cough or measles. But Queenie can pinpoint precisely when she was in the sick bay. Staff collected there on 30 November 1936, the night that Crystal Palace burned down. The orange glow from the conflagration that illuminated the night sky was visible from a window at the top of the house by her bed.

Crystal Palace was an iconic structure, covering 990,000 square feet, initially placed in Hyde Park, London, for the Great Exhibition of 1851. At the exhibition's close it was decided to resite the palace on Penge Common, Sydenham Hill. There it became a much-loved feature of the landscape, familiar to those who promenaded in the park on Sundays.

No one knows what started the blaze that night – faulty wiring or a carelessly discarded cigarette were touted as possible causes – but two nightwatchmen who did their best to smother the flames were quickly defeated. Although 438 firemen and 88 fire appliances hurried to the scene, the building was reduced to ashes. The fire could be seen across eight counties, and Winston Churchill, on his way home to Chartwell in Kent, was brought to tears by the sight, presciently declaring, 'This is the end of an age.'

As the flames ate away at the iconic London landmark, Queenie was herself experiencing burning temperatures. She became so dangerously ill that staff sat with her day and night to monitor her progress. Despite her feverishness she had spotted them in her room, both confounded by her illness and transfixed by the immense fire that they could observe from the window.

Even when the excitement of the incident had died away one newly arrived staff member was constantly at Queenie's bedside, mopping her brow and encouraging her to sip water. As Queenie fought for survival, Doris Hurford Bailey began to take an interest in the fate of this slip of a girl who lay prone and helpless before her.

'Here, try to drink something,' said Sister Bailey, as she was known to the girls. Propping Queenie's frail form up on a plumped pillow, she offered a cup of water to sore cracked lips. From notes kept at the home, Sister Bailey knew all about Hector and Maud and the spartan childhood Queenie had so far experienced. The child didn't once call out for her mother, she noticed. And there was a fighting spirit in this little scrap that stopped the illness doing its worst, which she couldn't help but admire.

'Hush,' she soothed, as Queenie murmured quietly to herself. 'Don't worry. You're going to be fine. There's nothing to worry about. We are here and we are going to look after you.'

The next morning, when Queenie seemed brighter, Sister Bailey returned to the sick bay once more and sat by her bed. For the first time Queenie registered the twinkle in the eyes that had so anxiously watched over her.

'This is your first children's home, isn't it?' Mopping Queenie's face with a damp flannel, Sister Bailey was smiling kindly as she talked.

Queenie nodded weakly. Feeling more refreshed, she kept her eyes fixed on Sister Bailey, whose gentle voice continued talking.

'And it's mine as well. So we are both new at this,' said Sister Bailey, beaming.

Still groggy, Queenie managed a faint smile, but she began to notice the crisp clean sheets on a comfortable mattress, and the tremendous care that was being taken of her. She hadn't met this woman before but the shape of her glasses, her kindly expression and upright bearing as she departed the room would stay in her memory. As for Sister Bailey, here was a girl she had helped nurse back to health, who thanks to her efforts had survived a dangerous illness. With this one small child, she had made a difference. Her sense of purpose crystallized.

Although she was thirty-four, it was Doris Hurford Bailey's first role in the career that would come to define her. Her title, Sister, did not denote a medical qualification but was the title of an assistant at the home – although since childhood Doris had longed to work in a hospital. Unexpectedly she was forced to shelve her dreams early in life, when she was compelled to become her family's main wage earner.

When Doris was born in 1902, it seemed life was guaranteed to be kind. As the second child of solicitor's clerk William Hurford Bailey and his wife, Emily Jane, she was set to enjoy the privileges of being securely middle-class in suburban London. Doris's arrival came almost exactly a year after the death of Queen Victoria. With the accession of Victoria's eldest son, Edward VIII, the country was gripped by a wave of optimism, not least for the social and technological advances that came thick and fast during the decade in which he ruled. Life would now include powered flight, colour photography, cinema newsreels and the vacuum cleaner.

The family lived in a substantial bow-fronted house, in a

tree-lined street in Leyton, east London, an area whose population had doubled in size every decade in the late-Victorian age following the arrival of the railway. But domestic harmony and financial security were shattered when William keeled over at home without warning. His death on 12 August 1916, aged just thirty-nine, was a toxic combination of a stroke and heart disease. Events that Saturday no doubt eclipsed for a while the horrors across the English Channel, of the First World War, where the notoriously bloody Battle of the Somme was continuing, with Queenie's dad Hector among the combatants. Sanitized accounts of it were being related daily in newspapers.

Still, for Londoners like the Baileys, the conflict could not always be dismissed as distant and seemed to get even closer after William's death. In January 1917 an explosion of some 50 tons of TNT at a munitions factory in Silvertown, just six miles from Leyton, echoed across the capital. It killed seventy-three people and injured 400 more. Doris, her mother and her sister would have not only heard the explosion but felt the shock wave of the blast and certainly witnessed an orange glow that illuminated London as the huge fires sparked that day were being fought. At the time, no one knew what had happened. Government secrecy meant details of events were kept from the public at large and Doris's family joined other Londoners in fearful speculation about just what had gone on at the docks that day, and whether Germany was responsible.

And the war came almost to their doorsteps with airborne Zeppelin and plane raids by Germany against London. Again in 1917 bombs from a Gotha biplane killed eighteen children at a school in Poplar, five miles from the family home, as well as 144 others. Although not the first aerial attack in Britain it was a sensational moment as Londoners realized the fundamental risk posed by this new age of warfare. It wasn't necessarily frontline soldiers who were going to be killed but civilians miles from the war zone, sitting in their homes. In three years a total of 668 Londoners died in air raids and nearly 2,000 people were injured, causing a disproportionate drag on public morale.

The onus of keeping the household after William's death would normally have fallen to the eldest son. But by now Arthur Hurford Bailey was serving as a private in the Queen's Own (Royal West Kents) in France. And in May 1918 Doris, her younger sister Mary and their mum Emily were stunned by grief once more when they learned of his death from injuries sustained in France, aged just nineteen. Serving at the Somme, he was a victim of the spring offensive mounted that year by the German army, a final push for victory that ran out of steam in a few months – but not before the deaths of thousands of men on both sides of the line. Records show Arthur left his mother less than £10.

By any standards, these teenage years were a time of excessive trauma for Doris, left bereft twice in two years. Moreover, Emily had to care for young Mary. So Doris, at sixteen, had no alternative but to financially support them both. For her it was a question of duty and not one she would shirk. Although still young, Doris got a job with a firm in the heart of London, with a steady salary that would pay the bills for her mum and sister as well as herself.

On the home front, women had been fighting and winning battles of their own. After pre-war lives of servitude or domesticity they had become integral components in the country's industrial response. Famously many risked their health handling noxious substances to make ammunition for use on distant battlefields. Women ultimately comprised a third of the country's total workforce. However, there was another shortage caused by the conflict and resolved by women, that of clerks in major city firms, and it was in this direction that Doris chose to go. Until the war, clerks were almost exclusively male. But by 1915 the Bank of England had employed 350 female clerks, while half the workforce at Barings Bank were women. Although some women were employed as typists prior to the conflict, the office had traditionally, like everywhere else, been a male-dominated environment.

The shortage of workers on the home front became particularly acute after conscription was introduced in 1916, the year Doris left school. Efficient and keenly practical from an early age, Doris proved an asset as a clerical worker. In doing so, she abandoned her dreams of nursing, a role she'd longed for since childhood. At the time the nursing profession was still unregulated and the wages for a probationer nurse were poor. Hospitals were also the preserve of women much older than herself. It wasn't until she reached her thirties, after her sister had found independence by training as a nurse herself, that Doris could switch careers and join one of the caring professions.

For years the sight of the barefoot children in thin clothes, hungry and wan, that she encountered on her way to work in London seared into her consciousness. At first she wanted to be one of the country's earliest female police officers, at a time when they were assigned solely on casework for women, children and families. During the war women had volunteered to act as police officers but weren't necessarily welcomed by male colleagues. The landscape changed with the 1919 Sex Disqualification (Removal) Act, the first piece of equality legislation committed to the statute books, aiming to level the playing field for women at work. It stated: 'A person shall not be disqualified by sex or marriage from the exercise of any public function, or from being appointed to or holding any civil or judicial office or post, or from entering or assuming or carrying on any civil profession or vocation . . .'

But equal rights for women remained very much a work in progress. A stereotypical suffragette, branded 'militant' by the establishment, still loomed large in the minds of men hostile to equality. Compelled to have women in the force, the head of the Metropolitan Police, Sir Nevil Macready, made it clear that he didn't want 'vinegary spinsters' or 'blighted middle-aged fanatics' in his force. Still, the Metropolitan Police proved itself a front runner by employing forty-eight full-time women police officers by the late 1920s. Even by 1931 Birmingham had only recruited a few unmarried women, with a minimum starting age of forty-five.

A year later, when Doris tried to join Essex police at Southend-on-Sea, it turned out she wasn't welcome in the ranks either. In her case the refusal was said to be on health grounds. Only then did she turn her attention to the Waifs and Strays Society. Given its strong links to the Church of England and her steadfast faith, it seemed she would be a perfect fit.

The drop in wages that accompanied her career change from city clerk mattered not a jot to her. She joined the society in 1934, just a year after the death of founder Edward Rudolf, with his messages about the critical importance of childcare still resounding in the organization. Thanks to his encompassing principles, welfare was at the heart of every decision made by the society and its staff, with an emphasis on kindness and empathy. Services were to be delivered with as little regimentation as possible. Doris Hurford Bailey arrived just after a new law, the Children and Young Persons Act, escalated protection for children at risk.

And there were other ways the Waifs and Strays Society reflected changing times. In America concerns about child development in the aftermath of the First World War had led to a new strand of medical science. In 1927 eight medical professionals from Britain were sent to the US to learn about the latest findings in child guidance. The following year the London Child Guidance Training Centre was opened, with a view to treating a host of children's disorders, ranging from stammering to bedwetting, truancy, anxiety, overactivity and stealing. The Waifs and Strays Society keenly monitored the centre's work and consulted with Dr William Moodie, who was at the forefront of the new 'science'. As a result, a home was opened in Clapham for boys with challenging behavioural problems.

Material standards were also being pushed up, with unsuitable homes beings closed, unsuitable staff being sacked and children moving to the centre of the picture. There were even staff conferences held in London, providing inspiration and accelerating more progressive attitudes – although it took time for edicts like the one issued in the mid-thirties, saying that children should wear new shoes rather than second-hand ones, to have an effect. The ambition of mixed or family homes was gaining more traction and the rhetoric about unmarried mothers was dialled back. Here at last was an outlet for Doris's caring nature and, with the fulsome support provided by the society, she felt fully prepared for the role.

The Waifs and Strays Society ran a convalescence home in Broadstairs, Kent, to which Queenie was duly dispatched when she was well enough to travel. When she was told she was going to the seaside, Queenie's face lit up. She was still frail and tired, but at last there were signs of her old self shining through.

As her small shape disappeared through the door clutching the hand of a Society helper, Sister Bailey waved from the hallway and smiled.

As she returned to the staffroom at St Mary's, she glanced at a Waifs and Strays Society newsletter. The main news concerned the merits of adoption. The society had watched guardedly as the first legislation concerning adoption was brought in a decade earlier. Society matrons were sometimes alarmed at the calibre of parents who came to claim the babies they had nurtured.

Then a figure caught her eye. For the first time in five years the society had taken in 1,000 new children the previous year, and the number was predicted to rise. She shook her head. The society continued to step in when parents struggled and stood like a bulwark between children and destitution, when they were orphaned or unloved. Each one deserved kindness and attention, she thought, especially if they had known hard times already.

Queenie disembarked from the train at Broadstairs

and inhaled the bracing air as deeply as she could. Her chaperone had explained what lay ahead: no more school for the time being, although she had to attend lessons at the convalescence home. There would be new faces – lots of children just like herself who were not in the best of health. Outside there were rolling grounds – but there was to be no running around. This was a quiet home, she was told.

As she approached the building for the first time, she noted how much it looked like St Mary's, the home she had just left. It was of a similar vintage, with both being three stories high, with balconies and tall chimneys. As she scanned the outside of the building, the familiarity of the façade was comforting. Yet when the excitement of her arrival had worn off, Queenie began to feel more guarded. For the first time she felt alone. Her sister Gladys had stayed at St Mary's, of course. And, like the other children at the Broadstairs home, Queenie had been left lethargic and listless by her illness. There was a marked lack of fun among the home's residents, she noticed miserably. But one day soon after her arrival, all that changed.

Her father, sober this time, came to take his youngest daughter out for the day. The details of the outing became etched on her memory as, for the first time, she tasted ice cream. He also bought her a new dress, the only one for the moment that didn't have a number in it, and together they played on the seafront penny arcade. Before he left, he presented her with sweets and for Queenie it was the stuff of dreams. Still delicate from her illness she was nonetheless buoyed by his appearance. Although she doesn't know which childhood illness struck her down in 1936 it seems Hector was told her survival had been touch and go, which is why he didn't pass up the opportunity for the seaside visit.

Back at St Mary's, Sister Bailey was also preparing for a trip, packing her few belongings into a small leather case that lay open on her bed. A new post had been earmarked for her, and she was heading to the Midlands. She knew that by the time Queenie returned she'd be gone. Of course she would miss Queenie, much more than Queenie would her. And that's as it should be, she noted with satisfaction. The year had been fraught from the start, with the death of King George V, a patron of the Waifs and Strays Society. Although she felt rather attached to the girl, it wouldn't do to play on high emotions by telephoning Broadstairs to tell Queenie the news. With the final piece of clothing stowed, she stood erect and gazed around her small empty room. Now it was time to meet the next raft of girls in need that would benefit from her care.

2. New Beginnings

Children are not the people of tomorrow, but are people of today. They have a right to be taken seriously, and to be treated with tenderness and respect. They should be allowed to grow into whoever they were meant to be – the unknown person inside each of them is our hope for the future.
Janusz Korczak, children's author and educator who died in the Treblinka extermination camp in 1942

'Ow,' squealed Sheila, as she wriggled on top of a damp salt-crusted wall facing the sea.

She had been perched there by her grandmother, and the back of Sheila's bare legs scraped along the uncomfortable seat's sharp cement as her feet dangled high above ground level.

'Danma', as Sheila knew her, was now bent over, picking cockles and mussels from the foreshore and didn't immediately pause to acknowledge her. The older woman's clothes were dark in colour and shabby, with the woollen stockings wrinkled round her legs inadequate to keep out the chilly sea breeze. In her wake, she hauled a bucket of briny water to house a growing collection of shellfish plucked from the shallows. Focused on her back-breaking task, which would produce food to sell and some spare for the table, she barely acknowledged the protests of her small charge.

When her squawks of dissatisfaction had no effect, Sheila tried to be still for a few moments. On the air she could smell the pungent detritus of the seabed that had been exposed by an ebbing tide. Her eyes raised to the horizon. Across the water lay golden sands and mysterious grass-topped dunes, a children's paradise. But Sheila lived on the wrong side of the river mouth. Her immediate playground was strewn with barnacled rocks and pebbles slicked by seaweed. As her dress and pinafore began to feel uncomfortably waterlogged, she squinted dolefully out to sea, looking for a shaft of sunlight to brighten her life.

Unknown to her the tide was turning and soon her patience was rewarded as a masted ship crept round the corner of the river, edging determinedly in her direction.

'Danpa!' she shrieked, pointing wildly at the small vessel. As the crew set about offloading baskets of fish on to carts destined for the market in nearby Bideford, she knew she would have to be patient. But finally the men turned their backs to the sea, climbed the gradual incline of the beach and at last the familiar weather-worn face of her grandfather loomed. His muscly tanned arms stretched towards her, swinging her off the wall. Held aloft for a few joyful moments, she basked in the warmth of the man clad in oilskins, who so plainly adored her.

'Bugger,' Sheila cried, as her attempt at a cartwheel, intended to impress her grandfather, dramatically failed. She landed in a heap, revealing that she wore no knickers. Her grandparents were so poor that fundamental garments like this weren't a priority.

Days like these, spent in the face of a brisk onshore wind, had coloured her cheeks a ruddy pink, like those of a child in a picture book. Her hair was soft and bubbly and her eyes were wide. But Sheila's life was about as far from a cosy world of children's fiction as it could be. Although she grew up to become a writer, there were no bookshelves lined with literature at their home.

She was cared for by grandparents who lived in lockstep with the sea in Appledore, north Devon, a village at the mouth of the River Torridge and a stone's throw from the open waters of the Atlantic. Sheila's mother Ethel worked as a maid, but to her daughter she was a mysterious unknown figure. A man she knew as Da occasionally turned up at the doorstep on his bike. After strapping a cushion to his crossbar, she would perch high in the arch of his arms and chest while he pedalled around the neighbourhood. But he wasn't a significant figure in her life either. It was her grandparents who were at the centre of her existence.

At teatimes she was given a bowl of cooked winkles and a pin to spear the chewy morsel and extract it from its shell. While shellfish was the staple diet, it was winkles that delighted the young Sheila the most. And every night of her short life Sheila had curled up in bed with her grandmother. As they slept Sheila's grandfather usually went out night-fishing to keep the family's finances buoyant.

A thriving fifteenth-century port, Appledore had since expanded via a maze of dark streets. The Coxes' home was the last up an alley, in the lee of a steep wall that held back a railway embankment. When she was born in 1928 the railway line was already deserted, closed in 1917 after its locomotives and lines were seized for the war effort. The railway had been operating for less than a decade and didn't link with any other part of Britain's rail network.

With its closure the village once again retreated into isolation. The town's shipbuilding industry enjoyed mixed
fortunes, and some families moved away to find new
opportunities. Once the community was so close-knit it
was said that 'if you kick an Appledore man, they would all
limp'. However, with the town eroded by a slow decay,
those halcyon days had gone.

While Appledore may have been dilapidated in places it
was the only home Sheila had known. Today her grandfather was here after unexpectedly taking a day shift to
spend some hours with her. Otherwise, the day on the
beach, ending in a slow trudge home, seemed like any
other. In fact, for Sheila it would be the last.

The following morning Sheila put on her first pair of
shoes – black patent with a buttoned strap. Danma's fingers, hindered by arthritis, struggled to fasten the stiff
buttons over new hand-knitted pink socks. Wearing a clean
pinafore on top of her dress, Sheila was lost in wonder.
Her first thought was to show off this finery to her beloved
Danpa – but he was nowhere to be found.

Instead, it was a stranger who next appeared, a woman
with unusually smart clothes that made her stand out on
the village streets long before she arrived at the front door.
The woman and her tailored coat leaned forward. 'Would
you like to come for a ride on the train with me?' The
question provoked extraordinary excitement. Sheila had
heard the screech of a steam train whistle during her days
on the quayside and even spotted the distant telltale plume
of smoke at Bideford from time to time. Danma had
explained about trains and promised her a ride one day.
Now the great day had come, just as her grandmother had

pledged. Trustingly Sheila held out a chubby hand to grasp the extended fingers of the stranger. In her rush of excitement she didn't notice her grandmother jerk her head away. Sheila trotted off with her mind focused on the fun in store that day. But for Sheila this would be a one-way ticket, with the train taking her to a Waifs and Strays home in Exeter. The gravity of her situation wasn't immediately apparent.

The journey took several hours but Sheila passed the time gazing out of the train window, seeing more green trees than she had ever seen in her life before. There were thatched houses and the glittering waters of a country stream. It was all very distracting. Before long she had left the train and was being pulled up the drive of a large house.

As she walked inside, past long trestle tables, she noticed the rows of girls there were in identical pinafore dresses and sported the same pudding-basin haircuts.

When it became clear the woman who had accompanied her there was going to leave without her, Sheila clung to her arm until each of her small fingers were peeled back one by one and she was restrained by the Exeter home staff as the woman strode purposefully towards the door. When Sheila saw her last link with home vanishing from sight she sank her teeth into the arm that pinned her back, and received a stinging slap on the legs. As it was delivered her skirts rose and the assembled girls gasped when they realized she wore no underwear.

'Right, young miss,' said one member of staff, hoisting Sheila on to a seat next to one of the trestle tables. 'Try this on for size,' the woman said, tying a regulation pinafore to her small frame. 'And, look, here's your pudding.'

Sheila's gaze locked on to a grey steamed sponge surrounded by watery syrup, before she pushed the plate away. She crossed her arms on the scrubbed table and sank her forehead on to them, to cut from sight the fierce expressions of everyone in view. Sobs ripped out of her as she called hopelessly for Danma and Danpa. There was no one to comfort her, no promises of a swift reunion. Finally taking stock of her position, Sheila decided that would be the last time she ever cried while she was in the care of the Waifs and Strays Society.

Although she was felled by grief at the unexpected parting from her beloved grandparents, she soon learned the disciplines of home life and got used to being called by a number, as well as a name. She stayed at the Exeter home until she was seven. All contact with her family was lost and she didn't even know when her birthday was until the home's matron announced it one morning. It was 6 January, Epiphany in the Christian calendar. Sheila rolled the unfamiliar word around her mouth, then committed it to memory.

The only possession she had in all her years there was a thin copy of *Babes in the Wood*, given to her by a doctor as a reward for not crying after having the smallpox vaccination. She took the worn pages of it with her when she was moved out of the Exeter home to Shrewsbury. Her destination was a home for thirty girls and three staff, run by the Ladies' Association for the Care of Friendless Girls, a name to surely rival the term 'waifs and strays' in its burdensome implications.

The association was a Christian one, although its treatment of its charges wasn't always kind. To keep the girls in line there was corporal punishment, delivered by hand or slipper. Failing that, they were reprimanded by being deprived of food. The matron in charge was seemingly oblivious that the commonest crime, stealing food from the kitchen, was usually perpetrated because the girls were hungry.

Every day – summer and winter – began with an ice-cold bath. Mornings and evenings, girls donned white veils and visited the chapel, accessed through a bead curtain then a baize door. At breakfast time Sheila and other residents had to file into the dining room, present the fronts and backs of their hands for inspection, then kiss the proffered cheek of the matron, saying, 'Good morning, Matey darling.'

It was a ritual that caused unspoken anxiety among the girls, as Matron was not an amiable or motherly figure. But when the chance to kiss that papery cheek was denied by way of punishment, the girls felt worse still. Sheila would often be denied the dubious pleasure of delivering the morning kiss in a hail of sharp words. When the small girl appeared in front of her, the older woman would jerk her head back from Sheila as she leaned in for the kiss, snapping, 'Stand up straight, girl.'

Dejected, Sheila would be sent to eat at 'the piggy table', an upturned tea chest in the far corner of the dining room where girls in disgrace would have to kneel rather than sit.

'Sheila, what are you doing?' The sharpness of tone made Sheila start, and instinctively she bowed her head. Without thinking, she had been energetically scratching the back of her head. Now she looked at her stubby fingernails to find she had traces of blood beneath them.

She looked up, expecting a further rebuke. But Matron's attention was elsewhere now, scanning the roomful of girls who were all distractedly scratching their heads.

'Bathroom, girls, now,' she shouted. 'Sister Jones, bring me the razor.'

Forming an orderly queue at the bathroom door, the girls looked on mournfully as Matron wielded the razor. Piles of hair formed on the floor. Sheila couldn't see them, but she knew lice were clinging to the strands. She exchanged a sorrowful look with the girl behind her. It wasn't the first time their heads had been shaved to counter a nits infestation, and it wouldn't be the last. But tomorrow was the first day at a new school, with all the stresses that ordinarily entailed.

Arriving en masse, Sheila and her housemates caused ripples of merriment from the outset. The girls' recently shaved heads were barely disguised under berets. Happily, a kindly teacher at the school permitted them to keep their hats on during class. But it wasn't long before other children started the break-time game of stealing the home girls' hats. In response, the home girls gave as good as they got.

One day a new member of staff arrived: small, trim and bespectacled. To the nervous eye of some children, Doris Hurford Bailey seemed every bit as starchy as her white collar and cuffs. She knew her neat appearance gave the girls pause. It was a tool she used as she got the measure of the new home. Her mind was buzzing with up-to-date training from the society in childcare and development. But she could see that some of her fellow staff were in the dark about the latest protocols. Granted, there wasn't much that could be done about an outbreak of nits, but she could see plenty of room for improvement, almost from the moment she arrived.

'Here you are,' said Sister Bailey, presenting Sheila with a coat that for once had all its buttons stitched in place.

'Thank you, Sister,' Sheila said politely. But inside she was thrilled that the cold winter air would be more adequately kept at bay. Sheila felt she had noticed Sister's thin-lipped expression when she had first spotted the way the children's coats had gaped and flapped, but thought little about it at the time. And she was sure she'd seen Sister Bailey's eyes narrow slightly when other staff had been careless or even cruel with comments directed at the girls. At any event, Sister Bailey soon began to make small changes that reaped big rewards.

For the first time the girls found a fire lit in the small playroom grate. Swiftly Sister Bailey silenced the coos of excitement and stopped the girls bumping each other as they tried to fit in front of the flames.

'This is a playroom, not a bear pit,' she pronounced, and the girls automatically took one step backwards.

'What's this, Sister?' asked Barbara, running her hands down the length of a toasting fork and putting the pads of her small fingers on the prongs. At thirteen Barbara Phillips was one of the older girls. Taller than most and still speaking with her native Lancashire accent, she was the only one who possessed a wristwatch. She also had a broad knowledge of popular music and could tap dance. As such she had become a natural leader. She had been a recent arrival at the home with her sister, Ida, but was soon motherly towards the younger ones. Sheila, four years her junior, grew especially fond of her.

45

'We are going to make toast,' declared Sister Bailey, and she proceeded to illustrate how to spear without piercing a palm, and where to hold the bread in the fire so the slices wouldn't burn.

Sheila watched with rapt attention as the older girls toasted bread on behalf of the younger ones. The heat of the fire on her face was matched by a rising warmth in her stomach, and it felt good.

'It's your turn,' one of the younger girls said, nudging Sheila out of her daydream. Hurriedly she took the knife. She didn't want to upset this new staff member who seemed different from the rest. Carefully she began smearing the delicious-smelling slices with dripping. It felt like she imagined any loving home would, and there was more excitement to come.

On a spring Saturday afternoon the girls gathered in expectation outside the closed playroom door. 'Stay there until I tell you to come in,' called Sister Bailey.

The girls exchanged glances. What was in store for them now?

When the door finally opened they found the dinner tables covered with clipped piles of soft, silky or exotic scraps of material. Sister Bailey had sought old clothes to cut up, dressmakers' leftovers, lace trimmings, satin ribbons, pearly buttons, rickrack edgings and even beaded borders to make each assortment special.

'Now, eldest first, pick the parcel of material you like best,' she said, knowing that there were enough bundles to afford even the youngest the unusual privilege of choice.

'Thank you, Sister,' the girls chorused.

'I'm chuffed with this,' said Barbara, looking around in wonder. 'It's a proper Aladdin's cave.'

When she had picked her pile, Sheila smoothed each piece of fabric out, enjoying the softness on her fingers. For someone who had no belongings this was a wealth of riches. Instantly she knew where it could be put to best use. The material would be bedding for her beloved paper 'dolls' snipped from magazines and packaging and stored in an old shoebox. Although the manufacture of plastic dolls in the early half of the twentieth century had made the toys much more affordable than ever before, few home girls owned one and they mostly had to make do with cut-out ones. The older, more creative girls had different ideas, covering shoeboxes that held their few but precious personal belongings.

Sister Bailey wasn't the only person to bring them joy. Father Haynes was the home chaplain and he was popular among the girls for knowing the nicknames they gave each other and their individual quirks. If he had a crown, he told them, they would be the jewels in it.

For Sister Bailey there was satisfaction enough in the array of bright faces that now met her daily. Leaving St Mary's Home in Cheam hadn't been entirely easy. She'd grown fond of the children she looked after; girls like Queenie had been flourishing under the warm spotlight of her care. She knew that more than a hundred homes were now being run by the society nationwide and, from the stories she read in society literature, it was clear the crisis in child welfare wasn't abating. Sister Bailey had read that the society had admitted its 40,000th child in 1936, a six-year-old girl whose mother had already died. She was living in a wooden hut with her ageing father, whose health was fading fast.

The girl had been cared for until a cousin could put a roof over her head. Just a year later, the 41,000th child was admitted, a boy this time, one in a family of nine children, whose mother gave him up because she considered him out of control. (Another Society success story, he emerged as a sporty happy lad who eventually joined the Royal Navy, only to be lost at sea in 1943.)

Two other girls also admitted in 1937, aged eight and six, arrived with all their belongings in a string bag. Their stepmother, now a widow, was caring for eight children as best she could. But the society got involved when the girls were reported by their school for being undernourished and neglected. Keeping in touch with family when possible was a key issue and the society kept a copy of one letter the girls wrote home. 'Dear Mum, We like it very much, it is like a holeyday [sic] to us . . .' (When they finally left the society, they were returned home to her.)

Armed with the latest instructions, Doris felt she was ready for anything. However, it turned out that some crises could still catch her off guard.

One day, when a dormitory fight broke out between two girls, Sheila tried to intervene. Unceremoniously shoved aside, she hit her head against a hard bed frame and appeared to be out cold. Not so severely injured as she seemed, Sheila was determined to milk every ounce of drama from the situation and kept her eyes firmly shut during all attempts to rouse her. She felt herself being lifted and heard the carrier being directed to Sister Bailey's room. It wasn't long until she was genuinely unconscious with sleep but woke much later, to hear small sobs nearby. She peeped, to see Sister Bailey keeping a bedside vigil in a chair, visibly distressed. Dim lighting in the room indicated it was night-time. Hair that was normally pinned neatly beneath a white cap was cascading down the older woman's shoulders. And Sheila realized that, having been in charge at the time of the scrap, it would be Sister Bailey carrying a burden of blame and guilt.

Of course, it wasn't the first time Sister Bailey had kept a bedside vigil over a sick child. As she shut her eyes for a long moment, she saw the prone figure of Queenie, swallowed up by the bed as she struggled to throw off a terrible illness. But this was different. There was little she, as a staff member, could have done to prevent Queenie's sickness. But should she have been more aware and alert, to prevent Sheila's heart-stopping injury?

Sheila knew nothing of Sister Bailey's prior experience with poorly children. But she was aware that, although she loved being away from the dormitory, tucked up in the staff bed, she didn't want Sister Bailey to feel responsible when Sheila was, in fact, shamming.

She thought quickly, then staged a recovery. At the sound of a groan, slowly and purposefully made by Sheila, Sister Bailey sprang into action. After mopping the girl's brow, she helped her drink some water before returning to the bedside chair, looking more relieved.

One day Sister Bailey disappeared. As always, no explanation was given, and the girls knew better than to ask questions. They were left to speculate about what had happened, their lives a little duller than before.

In short order, discipline at the home broke down with

a sense of rebelliousness infecting even the mildest-mannered among them. Word whistled around the home that they were all going to be moved. There was barely time to pack their meagre belongings, let alone worry about their destination.

To her joy, ten-year-old Sheila arrived after an uncomfortable trip in a charabanc, an early motor coach with hard bench-style seating, to find a familiar short trim figure waiting for her. Sister Bailey had been elevated to Matron and it was she who oversaw the new home. Not only that, the annual six-week holiday was already approaching fast, to Great Holland on the Essex coast between the resorts of Clacton and Frinton, where the girls and staff camped in the village hall.

The girls paid little attention to the newspaper stands they passed, although the gaze of the staff lingered on them. It was the summer of 1938 and Hitler was muscle-flexing provocatively in Europe. In April that year his troops had marched into Austria, where they were welcomed by cheering crowds. Now he was threatening to invade part of Czechoslovakia, on the pretext of bringing ethnic Germans who lived there behind the frontiers of the Reich. In response there was a flurry of international diplomacy, but Hitler refused to back down.

As tensions escalated, the Waifs and Strays Society decided at-risk homes in London should leave their premises. Still on holiday, Matron received official notification and gathered the staff together. Lucy Briggs, Doris Sheppard and Gertrude Measures, all assistant matrons in their twenties who helped care for the children, were known to the children either as 'Sister' or 'Nurse'.

'We are going to a new home,' Matron informed them. 'We've been given a house in Leighton Buzzard that's been donated to the Waifs and Strays Society by its owner, in memory of his father.'

She glanced at a letter from the society, held in her right hand. 'It used to be called Eversholt House, but from now it will be known as the St Margaret's Home. We will be the first to use it and, as far as I'm aware, there will be no furniture there when we arrive. Of course we will take all our beds, kitchen equipment and lockers from here.'

In an instant she slipped back two decades and experienced the overwhelming anxiety associated with that dark era. The loss of her beloved older brother in the war was, for her, still keenly felt. Few families had emerged from four years of fighting without suffering devastating grief like the one she, her mother and her sister knew, with every fallen soldier sending out a ripple of sorrow that encompassed family, friends and neighbours. The thought of the deaths that any new conflict would bring made her chest feel tight. But just as soon as that thought formed in her head, another rushed in behind. Her responsibility now lay with the girls in her care. If they had to make a transition to a new life, she wanted it to go as smoothly as possible.

Her back straightened and her voice adopted a softer tone. 'We must make sure the girls don't feel unnecessarily anxious. It's their welfare that is at the heart of this operation. We want to keep them feeling safe and secure. Let's not mention it until the day before we leave, and please don't tell them why.'

The three young women needed little further instruction. As the holiday ended, they set about packing up the home's belongings for the journey efficiently and with minimum fuss.

When they were told they were going to Bedfordshire, the girls looked warily at the staff. But the confident smiles they received in return soothed their troubled nerves.

Soon a lorry containing their equipment was heading along narrow, winding country roads. After they had arrived in a coach, ahead of their belongings, the girls wandered around cavernous rooms, with their voices echoing against high ceilings.

Matron gathered them in while they waited for their furniture. 'Now, I want to remind you that war has not yet been declared. Our soldiers are not fighting anyone and we are not at risk for the present. Far from it, in fact.'

The girls struggled to process the notion of war.

'What was it like in the Great War?' Sheila asked, hoping to get a better picture of what was to come.

'Well, I was in London, not in the trenches in France,' said Matron with a thin smile. The trauma of war had been so profound that memories of it remained painfully sharp in her mind.

There followed a chorus of questions from the girls, many of whom originally came from the capital.

'Did you see a Zeppelin?' 'Was you bombed?' 'What 'appened in London?'

Matron thought for a moment, trying to recall the daily journey from her Leyton home into the office at the time. She appeared to be groping for war stories, when, in fact, she was trying to filter some of the upsetting scenes that war brought to the home front.

'Well, you could certainly tell there was a war on,' she

began. 'There were canvas-covered ambulances ferrying the wounded from train stations to the city's hospitals.

'The trains brought injured men straight from the south coast to the hospital. Outside Charing Cross Hospital there was a sign that said QUIET FOR THE WOUNDED and heavy traffic was diverted to minimize noise. That made other roads even more busy with cars and motorized buses. And there were many more horse-drawn carts and bicycles too. Nelson's Column was covered in flags, and most London gardens were dug up to grow vegetables, just like they will be now. In the Mall there were captured German guns on display – and children like you used to climb all over them.'

The girls laughed, imagining the scene, wondering if it had been their relations clambering on the weapons.

'I bet everyone you met was a posho,' said Ida, imagining men in suits and bowler hats.

'Goodness me, no,' said Matron. 'There were people pushing barrows – we used to call them costermongers or hawkers – selling oysters, flowers, roast chestnuts, ice cream, toys and all sorts. Many of them were children too. Often I used to see them with thin clothes and no shoes.'

Matron gave an involuntary shiver and Sheila blushed when she remembered how she had bitterly resented wearing second-hand boots donated to the home by recently bereaved relatives of an elderly woman.

Matron smiled at Ida. 'There were some people who were very smartly dressed. But there were sweeps and boot polishers as well as the street sellers. I can remember the Thames being full of queuing ships because all the dockers had joined the army, so there was no one to unload them. The workhouses were virtually empty then, as there was so much demand for labour.'

'Matron, what's a workhouse?' A few girls chorused the question, too young to have had their lives blighted by fear of workhouse committal.

'Well, it was a place you went if you had no money and no food,' said Matron carefully. 'Nobody wanted to go there but often people had no choice. Thank goodness those places don't exist any more. During the war, when the workhouses were emptied, they were used as hospitals for injured soldiers.'

In her mind's eye Matron also saw the legions of old soldiers on London streets where the human cost of the war was painfully evident. On every pavement there were men bearing physical scars: missing limbs, partial or complete blindness, deafness and varying degrees of burns.

With more than 41,000 British soldiers losing limbs, the science surrounding prosthetics advanced apace and amputees helped to make false legs in a newly booming industry. There were men wearing tailor-made masks – sometimes made of metal – to hide disfigurements caused by blasts.

Then there was the epidemic of shellshock, which affected thousands of British soldiers during the course of the war, who would find there was little by way of comfort or cure. Also called war neurosis or combat stress, it left soldiers with paralysis, palpitations, dizziness and hysteria. Many suffered from perpetual shaking, rendering them unable to carry out the most mundane daily task.

At first the condition was put down to cowardice and those with shellshock found themselves branded shell-shy.

Cruel experimental treatments, including electric shock therapy, were wheeled out as the country's hospital beds filled to overflowing with victims. During the conflict the primary concern for army doctors was to return men to the front. Only a lucky few reaped the benefits of the evolving practice of psychotherapy.

There was scant understanding of mental illness in the community, so it was hardly surprising these men stayed below the radar. Children who had borne the brunt of those conditions were now ranged in front of her, with their eyes locked on to hers. These were stories she would not share. The loud throb of an engine interrupted her musings.

'Here's the lorry, at last,' she said, grateful for the diversion. 'Let's go and help unload.'

It turned out to be a brief stay at Leighton Buzzard, with one memorable highlight. One morning, in the room she used as an office, Matron opened a lined vellum envelope addressed to her with scrolled handwriting, and pulled out a card. 'Heavens, Lucy,' she said, as she spotted Sister Briggs striding past the open door. 'We've all been invited to the big house up the road, to watch their television set.'

With television technology developing in the late 1920s, the BBC began transmitting services in 1930. By 1938 television sets, which cost about thirty-five guineas, were still uncommon, with only an estimated 20,000 across Britain. It was a rare opportunity indeed to see this new technology first-hand.

Visiting the homes of the wealthy was an unusual experience for the girls and the prospect caused considerable excitement. It took Matron and Sister Briggs longer than usual to form the column of girls before heading to the large house nearby.

The outsized front door seemed to get much bigger as they approached, and inside the rich fabrics and highly polished furniture would normally have been enough to fix their wide-eyed attention. But this time it was the wooden box in one of the large downstairs rooms that had them hypnotized. There were six dials on its front, with a meshed speaker and a screen just six inches wide. For now that screen was blank.

Once the girls had squatted in order of size in front of it, with the bigger girls at the back, a butler stepped forward to turn one of the switches. For a while nothing happened. But by slow degrees the image of a woman and the sound of her singing voice brought the convex screen to life. Technology was improving rapidly but a row of vertical lines was still evident on the small screen. Although the girls often went to the cinema – where the quality of picture was far better – the sight of the singer in this domestic setting felt like being in a strange new world.

Matron was watching, as rapt as the girls, until her nose twitched. It was the unmistakable whiff of urine and one glance at the girls in the front row revealed the culprit. Rosalind was not the youngest girl in the home but nor was she one of the 'big girls'. Her cheeks were burning, her eyes were glassy and it looked like she was about to howl.

Quickly stepping up to the side of the wooden box, Matron smiled at everyone and thanked the staff who'd set up the television. She had no option but to dismiss all the girls apart from Rosalind, who crumpled with the indignity of it all.

'There, there, lass,' said Matron. 'Let's get this mess cleared up.' A maid bearing a mop appeared, as if by magic, and Matron slipped a pair of soaked knickers into the side pocket of a bag. Rosalind faced a draughty walk home, without underwear beneath her dress. On the way home Sheila threw Rosalind a sympathetic look but said nothing. Most home girls suffered with accidents from time to time, especially when they were new. And while Matron was quick to chastise poor behaviour, this was different – and she wouldn't have them publicly shamed.

One Wednesday morning at the end of September, Matron and the staff were gathered round the radio to hear what Prime Minister Neville Chamberlain had to say when he got off a plane from Germany, after some whistle-stop diplomacy intended to halt German land grabs.

There was more interference than usual and Sister Briggs struggled to understand what was said. 'Ach, this is impossible,' she muttered. 'What is he saying?'

The voice of the prime minister was suddenly clear, just as his speech on the tarmac at Heston Aerodrome ended. '– and we are determined to continue our efforts to remove possible sources of difference, and thus to contribute to assure the peace of Europe.'

'That's good news, isn't it?' said Matron, looking at the others, and they smiled with relief. They would have to pack up the home's belongings for the third time in a month for the trip back to Ealing, but at least there would be no war.

3. A Momentous Decision

*The greatest legacy one can pass on to one's children and
grandchildren is not money or other material things accumulated
in one's life, but rather a legacy of character and faith.*

Billy Graham, evangelist

Some fifty miles south of Leighton Buzzard, in the impressive drawing room of her secluded home, Dorothy Peyton had also tuned in to hear Chamberlain, who was by now outside 10 Downing Street.

'My good friends, for the second time in our history, a British prime minister has returned from Germany bringing peace with honour. I believe it is peace for our time . . .'

For months she had listened to news reports dominated by the drumbeat of war. Now she heard wild cheers echoing out of the speaker, but she was not convinced by the news. After a snatched telephone conversation with her son John earlier, she was sure that Hitler's galloping ambitions had not been curtailed, despite Chamberlain's promises.

She lived at Englemere Wood, one of many substantial homes built on Crown land in what was once Windsor Forest. The address underlined the royal link. Her home stood in King's Ride, which alluded to the trip made by many monarchs from their home at Windsor Castle to the town's racecourse, established in 1711 by Queen Anne.

From her chair, she could see the high hedges that lined her fifty-yard drive and the towering pines beyond bowing in unison. Although typical of the late-Victorian architecture beloved by England's wealthier classes, hers wasn't the grandest house in the neighbourhood. But its imposing design was eye-catching. With its tall chimneys and prominent angular eaves it was a curious mixture of the austere and the homely. Outside, a vast lawn, fringed by evergreen and deciduous trees, was the perfect setting for a garden party.

But parties were now a thing of the past at Englemere Wood. Inside, Dorothy had discovered the dull echo of cavernous rooms was a sound that deadened the spirits and put lead in the soul. Socially she moved in enviable circles as a lady-in-waiting to two of Queen Victoria's granddaughters. But she was a widow, with her husband Ivor dying in unexplained circumstances just six months before. In her troubled heart, she was still mourning her youngest son, Henry, who had died after contracting diphtheria aged six.

With her elegant room bathed in shafts of late-summer sun, she sounded a bell and summoned butler Jack Chandler.

'Jack, might you get me some tea?'

'Right away, Madam,' Jack replied, moving smoothly out of the room.

Tea – typically taken white and sweet – fuelled the British Empire. But although it was widely considered to be the answer to the nation's ills, tea was unlikely to resolve her dilemma this time.

War was still in prospect, she reasoned, even if the risk

was not immediate. Her thoughts raced ahead. Would she stay in this house to face invasion alone?

She wasn't fearful exactly. A daughter of empire, she had been brought up to display considerable strength of character in times of adversity. But she had two sons who would likely fight in any forthcoming conflict. As her family of five had already been reduced to three, she was desperately concerned for their futures. Both boys were studying away from home and the house was filled with an enveloping silence that was increasingly hard to tolerate.

She had a strong sense of public duty and an unfaltering faith. Instinctively she was aware these twin staves might be her salvation. With the clink of porcelain teacups approaching, Dorothy suddenly knew she didn't want to be defined by events as they developed. She made a momentous decision. Should war break out she would share her home with the 'Waifs and Strays', children looked after by the Church of England children's homes. It was a well-known charity with an impeccable reputation.

Previously she'd heard of wealthy families like her own lending the society grand properties to house unfortunate children. When hostilities loomed with the 1938 crisis that number had risen sharply. And it turned out that the society, with one wary eye on the future, was still keen to enlist potential boltholes for its homes. Englemere Wood was certainly big enough; a playroom-turned-ballroom added to the original building in 1925 would provide a perfect room for a dormitory. The leased house stood on a twenty-two-acre Crown Estates plot, offering plenty of scope for outdoor games.

Still, there was a lot to consider. What would her husband

Ivor have thought of this impulsive gesture? Her stomach tightened with the realization that all the major decision-taking about hearth and home now lay solely in her own hands.

Dorothy had been married in 1917, just prior to her thirtieth birthday. At fifty-four Ivor was twenty-five years older but nonetheless a serving soldier, recovering from illness contracted during the Gallipoli campaign. A traditionalist who observed Victorian conventions, it would be he who made the decisions about matters large and small in their married lives.

No one knows what motivated Dorothy and Ivor into marriage. Ivor was making a slow recovery from physical and mental wounds. Meanwhile, Dorothy had seen many men of her age and class go off to war and never return, with some 17 per cent of officers killed in action. Yet it's unlikely she would have been short on suitors. She was charming, refined, poised and an accomplished amateur artist. Indeed, she possessed all the gifts one might have hoped for in a wife. Yet she saw something in the taciturn Ivor that persuaded her the future lay with him.

As well as being captivated by Dorothy, Ivor may well have finally decided on the merits of having a son and heir. (Still, he wasn't the oldest of the three Peyton brothers to wed. His brother Guy didn't get married until 1947, when he was eighty-five. He died three years later.) At any rate the couple chose not to wait for the end of the conflict. Rather than having banns read they opted for a marriage licence, with Ivor signing a 'bond and allegation' beforehand, to confirm there was no lawful impediment to the union. The ceremony took place at St James's Church in

Piccadilly, designed by Sir Christopher Wren and built in brick and Portland stone. One of Ivor's ancestors, William Pitt the elder, had been baptized in its marble font. The date was 5 November 1917.

Together they had three children: John Wynne William, Thomas Grenville Pitt and Henry Eliot Pitt. Their striking middle names reflected ancestral surnames that recur in the family tree.

When Henry fell ill in 1931, the couple may well have hoped his symptoms of a fever, cough and sore throat meant he was in for a bad cold. Unfortunately he succumbed to diphtheria, the bacterial infection that killed on average 3,500 children each year in the UK until a vaccine was finally introduced in 1942. A jab had been used against the disease in New York during the 1920s but at the time medical officers of health in Britain, responsible for public well-being, were notoriously reluctant to institute vaccination campaigns.

For Dorothy it was painfully distressing to watch helplessly while her young son struggled for breath, as a grey membrane of dead cells crept insidiously round the inside of his throat. As it slowly choked its victims to death, diphtheria also damaged internal organs including the heart. Henry's subsequent death cast a pall over Englemere Wood, where the couple had made their home.

Dorothy was floored by the loss. In her desk drawer she kept a selection of small toys, the last Henry had played with before his death. Often, when Ivor was distracted, she would open the drawer and turn them over in her palm. The items would continue to hold enormous sentimental value until her death decades later.

For Ivor too, then in his late sixties, the emotional toll must have been great. It was an era in which men typically chose not to express high emotion. Instead, he turned his attention to the education of his two elder sons. They had to excel as scholars, he felt, to secure their own financial futures, as Ivor had been financially squeezed by the effects of the Wall Street Crash. But his expectations were not met by the youngsters despite their enrolment at Eton, the country's most prestigious school, which was just a few miles from Ascot.

John was part of the Officer Training Corps and formed part of the guard of honour inside Windsor Castle at the funeral of King George V in 1936, which must have been the source of some pride. But years later John recalled being told that average was not good enough. As a result, he grew to loathe and fear academic work. Anxiously Dorothy looked on from the sidelines as she saw a chasm widening between father and sons.

She knew that though Ivor's approach was clumsy, his concern for his sons and their prospects was without doubt genuine. The key, she felt, lay in his early life. Ivor's mother Emily had died when he was young, soon after giving birth to his younger brother William. And their father had been found wanting. Keen on hunting game, shooting birds, betting and horse racing, Lieutenant Colonel John Peyton – a veteran of the Indian Mutiny – told his three sons there was only enough money in the family for one to wear patent leather boots – and it was going to be him.

At eighteen, Ivor and his older brother Guy, twenty, were on the SS *Orient* when it sailed for Australia from Britain in the spring of 1886. There he spent nearly a quarter of a century managing sheep stations in Queensland, an existence characterized by solitude, shortages of supplies and unrelenting sunshine.

When the First World War erupted, Ivor was back from Australia and living at the Albany in Piccadilly, one of London's most exclusive addresses. Previous tenants in the Georgian flats included poet Lord Byron and former Liberal prime minister William Gladstone. Still, Ivor's advancing years did not stop him joining the army at the start of the First World War – nor was he the most senior in years to head for the front line. The oldest man to enlist was William John Paxton, a London bricklayer, at the age of sixty-eight. Having lied about his age, he was discharged for health reasons in 1916.

The most senior serviceman to die is thought to be sixty-seven-year-old Henry Webber, who was commissioned in 1915, having already retired from the Stock Exchange. He was a pillar of the community in Surrey, sitting on the county council, parish council and magistrate's bench. Still, had he met three of his four sons, who were serving at the time, he would have had to salute as they were all senior in rank. He perished in one of the Somme offensives.

However, it seems the rules may have been bent to accommodate Ivor, so he could rally to the flag. He opted for the Territorial Force Reserve, entering as a captain, and probably passed the compulsory fitness examination without difficulty, given the active outdoor life he had led. The rules clearly stated that forty-five was the upper age limit for joining as a captain. In 1914 Ivor was fifty years old.

It can only have assisted his ambitions to have his

younger brother in the higher echelons of the military. William Peyton began his distinguished army career in the 7th Dragoon Guards in 1885, aged eighteen when their father John had been Colonel.

In 1909, when John Peyton died, aged eighty-two, he left his estate to William alone, ignoring Ivor and his eldest son Guy, who were both in Australia at the time. Perhaps surprisingly the sum involved was under £300. By way of comparison, a Hampshire labourer who died around the same time left £211 in his will.

In the First World War William – who stood six feet six in height, and was known as 'General Bill' – found himself at Gallipoli, trying to execute an ill-conceived plan to undermine the Ottoman Empire, and Ivor ended up on his staff.

Life in Gallipoli was tough, even for officers. Men were felled by enemy bullets and disease, leading to casualties of more than 160,000 for the British Empire in a ten-month campaign. Ivor was among them, suffering diarrhoea before contracting jaundice. When he was admitted to hospital he was, according to reports, 'in a weak and mentally depressed condition' and his inevitable departure was not a matter for regret, as it had been for his younger brother.

On 10 December Ivor was dispatched to Malta and from there travelled to England. It would be a long road to recovery. A medical report filed after he had returned to the UK said: 'The jaundice is not perceptible and the general health rapidly improving.' However, the medic noted that: 'He feels a good deal run-down and at his age recovery is not rapid.'

By April 1916 he was judged ready to return to light duty.

Letters he wrote at the time acknowledge that joining the army had been a mistake and he asked to be transferred to the Territorial Force Reserve, given, he wrote, 'my age, 52, my entire lack of any military training and the general state of my health . . . it would be difficult to find employment for me which would be useful to the state'.

The switch was duly made, but by December 1917 he was newly married, without a job and still struggling with his health. It was the same year his brother William was knighted.

If anything, the illness that afflicted him in the war made his behaviour more prickly than ever. He was such a stickler for rules that when dinner guests arrived even fractionally late at Englemere Wood he would curtly send them away, disinterested in excuses. Dorothy was left numb with horror. But to share her concerns about an increasingly irascible husband would have been tantamount to betrayal, Dorothy felt. To talk to her sons about their father behind his back simply would not do, even if it lightened their own loads. She tried as best she could to smooth everyone's ruffled feathers, without provoking the ire of her husband.

At the start of his seventies Ivor bore all the outward symbols of success, being a Berkshire county councillor, a Windsor rural parish councillor and on the board that ran Holloway Sanatorium, an asylum in nearby Virginia Water. Yet inwardly he was a man irreparably marked by an emotionally isolated childhood, the horrors of the First World War, the loss of a child and fiscal anxiety. Less than twenty years earlier fighting men like himself had been promised that 'the war to end all wars' was over, yet now there was jarring uncertainty in world politics once more, and it seemed that his and Dorothy's sons were destined to fight in Europe once more. The sum of his worries proved a greater burden than anyone might have predicted.

On 11 April 1938 he died after falling twenty feet from Swinley Bridge, a mile outside Ascot, in front of the Waterloo to Reading train.

An official at Ascot station was quoted in one newspaper report at the time. 'The driver saw his body in mid-air and applied his brakes but was unable to pull up until the train wheels had passed over him.'

His two terrier dogs were left on the bridge when he fell, and a coroner later recorded a verdict of death by misadventure. In his will he left more than £22,000 to his wife, something in the order of £1.5 million by today's standards.

It would be she who missed him most, rather than his boys. Despite Dorothy's efforts to bridge the emotional and generational gap between father and sons, Ivor had remained a remote figure. Had she been too tolerant of his unbending ways?

Absent-mindedly, Dorothy fingered the prominent gem in her necklace. The high-value stone had long since been filleted and sold to resolve a now-forgotten financial difficulty. Stealthy substitutions of this ilk were common among wealthy families buffeted by financial woes. Likely it was done without her say-so, probably without her knowledge. Now it was for her to take control and start determining life's course.

Dorothy had grown up in a man's world. Her older brother Montague had even bizarrely tried to part a son from his mother from beyond the grave . . .

Montague was one of a number of servicemen who saw action in two wars – the Boer War and the First World War. Nine years Dorothy's senior and grey-eyed, he had joined the newly constituted Imperial Yeomanry at the turn of the century, a cavalry regiment that attracted large numbers of middle- or upper-class volunteers. Afterwards he became an actor and, with dashing good looks and charisma in his peacetime armoury, found some success in the West End and the provinces during the Edwardian era, as an 'actor, manager and director'.

Although newly married and the father of a baby, he enlisted for a second time at the outbreak of hostilities in 1914, aged thirty-four but still a trim nine and a half stones. He opted for the Army Service Corps, finally becoming a major. But a new age of military hardware had caught his imagination. Early in 1916 he won his pilot's licence and joined the Royal Flying Corps, the predecessor of the Royal Air Force.

It was a novel breed of men who climbed into the exposed cockpits and took to the skies in notoriously flimsy machines less than a dozen years after the first-ever powered flight. But death rates soared as technology ramped up, until British and Commonwealth pilots on the Western Front became accustomed to an average survival rate of eleven days.

Montague lived long enough to witness a see-saw in fortunes between the British and German air forces before his two-seater Morane-Saulnier parasol plane crashed in the Somme region on 22 March 1917, his thirty-seventh birthday, almost certainly due to an accident rather than enemy action. His death was caused by multiple fractures, according to a note sent by the military secretary to his widow. He was buried in Heilly Station Cemetery, Méricourt, in a grave bearing a durable wooden cross that would ultimately be replaced by a stone.

The inscription read: 'He has cast off the armour of darkness and put on the armour of light. Your wife Norah.'

The couple, married for barely four years, had wed within weeks of her divorce from a first union. Norah received Montague's personal effects including a silver watch, cigarette holder, photos and insurance certificates. She also got a letter begging her to give up their son to Dorothy and Montague's sister Ethel. In it was a sobering assessment of their married life, and the revelation of how he wanted to steer his son's destiny even beyond death.

It seems that, above all, Montague was fearful of three-year-old Derek being spoiled. He told Norah that Ethel and her husband had the home, the will and 'the severity' to 'make a man of him'.

'Oh my dear I know you are thinking me cruel & unfeeling for you in asking you to let him live with them. Whatever I was, I am none of those things now, & from beyond the grave I implore you, by your love for me & the tears you have shed . . . leave him to those who can discipline him.'

Before he closes the letter, he writes in disturbing terms: 'My voice from the grave will be with you in the night, it will be with you always.'

As the war ended Dorothy's father Henry went to the High Court to become young Derek's legal guardian, serving papers on Norah, who had married for a third time, four months after Montague's death. The 1921 census reveals young Derek was living with his grandmother, Dorothy's mother Harriet, in Kent. The youngest of eight children, and with four older brothers, including the forceful Montague, Dorothy learned early in life to acquiesce. She had witnessed how men exerted all kinds of constraints on family life. They could even ensure children were parted from their mothers, with access to the legal system and a few well-chosen words. Now times had changed. War was surely approaching and her sons would be in the thick of any fighting. At fifty years old she felt ready to make some decisions of her own.

Dorothy sat down at a stout wooden bureau to write to the society, offering to shelter some of its children in graciously looping lettering. She'd considered her options carefully before committing her kind gesture to paper, hoping for the best while fearing the worst.

Still, even after the letter was in the post, small doubts crept into her mind. If war broke out, as she feared, would the children she was now beckoning into her home be like her own? She'd heard stories about London children trapped in grinding poverty – and not just in the notorious East End but in pockets across the capital, particularly in the vicinity of major railway stations. At times London children were portrayed as almost feral in newspaper reports she'd seen.

She put aside her concerns for the moment, to deal with the necessary paperwork.

4. London Life

'Argh,' Sheila cried, as she instinctively ducked her head.
An apple core had whistled past her head, narrowly missing her black velour hat with its green band.

She was part of a line of children heading to Christ
Church School on New Broadway, Ealing, from the Maurice Home in the spring of 1939. At the sound, Sister
Briggs turned sharply and threw a ferocious glance in her
direction. Although Sheila had been a target rather than
the antagonist, she knew that retaliation was out of the
question. Sister Briggs would brook no nonsense from
any of them, no matter the cause. Sheila had enough time
to send a stony look towards her tormentors before getting back in step with the rest of the girls.

Early-morning pavement footfall was typically heavy
in this leafy London suburb, not only with school pupils
but also the students of Clark's Business College. The
fee-paying college was a reputable institution founded in
Victorian times to help ambitious young people pass

demanding civil service exams. If they were successful, those students would soon be instrumental in running the country. The public perception of the middle-class men and women drawn to its courses was of keen, driven young people. Expectations of the scholars by college staff were high.

Clark's Business College was next door to the Maurice Home on Mattock Lane and its students arrived for lessons as the girls left for school. And it was then that those living at the Maurice Home saw a different side to the aspirational college students in which the country was investing its hopes. When it came to the Maurice Home and its residents, smartly dressed students wearing comfortable loafers and scented hair oil quickly became tormenters who threw assorted missiles and hurled abuse on a daily basis. Even the relatively benign terms 'waifs and strays' or 'home girls' were spat out as insults.

Despite the hurt and humiliation caused, especially among older girls, any form of reprisal was forbidden. They had to bite their tongues and turn their gaze away, with incidents like these only serving to reinforce a view that was widely held in society, and sometimes even among the residents of the Maurice Home themselves, that these girls were at the bottom of the pile, the downtrodden dregs of society, the no-hopers, going nowhere.

It wasn't always Sheila who was the target. Nansi Finch breezed past the tormentors. Any finer feelings she had were blunted after being the sole child in a family of five sent to a home by a recently widowed mother, having been dubbed 'a handful'. Later, her sister Connie would say Nansi was the lucky one. Their mother, a committed Salvationist, was always swift to raise a hand to her brood. More often unwelcome attention was directed at young Jenny Logan, a new girl who was struggling to settle at the home. She had knock knees, weak ankles and flat feet, and her awkward gait marked her out. If abuse was hurled, she kept her eyes facing downwards while fighting back tears.

When she arrived at the Maurice Home at the start of 1939, Jenny became the twenty-sixth and youngest resident, although she was allocated the number fifteen for the purposes of identifying beds, clothing and a place at the table. For a while being the youngest equated to acting like a baby, whining for attention and crying easily. At any moment, when things did not go her way, she would instantly dissolve in whimpers.

'Oh, do be quiet and stop grizzling,' rebuked Barbara, as Jenny howled while she waited for a turn at the sink.

'You really are the baby of the family,' remarked Ida, when Jenny cried as she didn't get the slice of bread she'd hoped for.

If Matron overheard the harsh comments, she said little. The Maurice Home was a family, she often told the girls, and every family had to put up with some bickering. It was unfortunate, though, that Jenny, more than most, seemed to be on the receiving end of any barbed comments being thrown around, not least for her slight frame.

She had spent her childhood in the Hampshire countryside and, when she had arrived, she was dangerously undernourished after apparent neglect, something that would impact on her childhood health for years to come.

From the window Matron had witnessed the throwing of missiles and winced. With some satisfaction she saw

Sheila pull her chin up and set off with the rest. Although she had spent most of her life in care, Sheila was a bookworm and something of a star pupil at school by all accounts. Sheila was irrepressible. But poor Jenny trudged along looking like she had the weight of the world on her shoulders. *Probably daydreaming about having a visit from her dad. In her eyes, he can do no wrong,* thought Matron impatiently, her mouth set in a firm line.

At times it seemed to Matron like everything was up against the girls in her charge: their ill-fitting clothes; a telltale haircut; an assortment of sad family backgrounds and a society all too willing to consign them to a scrapheap. Inwardly she vowed once again to renew her efforts to raise their rock-bottom sense of worth.

She called to the staff member usually responsible for cooking. 'Nurse Measures, if you wouldn't mind, I think we might have cake for tea tonight.'

The Maurice Home had existed since 1865, a pet project of Rev. Frederick Denison Maurice, who was a founder of Christian Socialism and much admired by authors Charles Kingsley, who wrote *The Water-Babies*, and Lewis Carroll, creator of *Alice's Adventures in Wonderland*. Initially it was as an industrial school – a term used in education for vagrant or destitute youngsters – and was based in Portland Place, central London. After it opened a dozen girls were placed there by magistrates. In 1912 the Maurice Home for Girls moved to Ealing, and the Waifs and Strays Society took over its administration. The building in Mattock Lane was refurbished before opening its doors to twenty-nine youngsters aged between seven and sixteen, and now it was busier than ever. The Waifs and

Strays Society received 450 new children in the wake of the 1938 crisis. More than 1,600 children joined the ranks of the society that year.

Clark's Business College and the Maurice Home were both housed in towering stoutly built villas that were by now thickly layered with city soot. Across the road, behind a 10-foot wall, lay Pitzhanger Manor, a stately home turned public library, surrounded by glorious parkland, where Sheila was often found choosing her next book. Ealing, branded the 'queen of the suburbs', was also famous for its film studios where talking pictures were made, lending it a glamour that dazzled.

But despite the natural elegance of their home, pity left a bitter taste, just as much as disdain, and nowhere was this more apparent than when they were penned in pews at Christ Church during Sunday services.

Before heading to church the girls lined up at the door of their Mattock Lane premises. Jenny tugged Sheila's coat sleeve. After being ignored, she pulled at the fabric again.

'What is it, Jenny?' Aged eleven, Sheila couldn't mask her irritation with Jenny, who was three years her junior.

'Why are we lining up like this? I thought we were going to church,' said Jenny meekly. 'Why don't we just get going?'

'We have to collect a penny, for the church collection,' Sheila explained quickly. 'Quick, you go next.' She pushed Jenny forward in Matron's direction.

'Ah, Jenny,' said Matron. 'Here's a penny from your savings, put it in your pocket and keep it safe. Today's collection will be for the Waifs and Strays Society.'

Collectively all the older girls groaned.

'Now, now,' said Matron reprovingly. 'We all have good reason to be grateful to the society.'

But the girls were more uncomfortable than ungrateful.

When the service was followed by a collection earmarked for the Waifs and Strays Society, the heads of other people in the congregation inevitably swivelled in their direction, with expressions that ranged from open curiosity to lofty disparagement. Self-conscious, they grimaced in shame as they dug into their own pockets to find that coin extracted from their pocket money. Afterwards they filed out with bowed heads, so as not to meet anyone's gaze, and the trip back to the home was usually made in reflective silence.

At the home there was solace to be found for some in the certainties of a strict timetable. Every morning, without fail, beds were straightened, floors were swept, breakfast was served and cleared – all with an overarching no-talking rule. There was no question of shirking. The home's staff were on hand to ensure everything was done to their satisfaction before anyone headed off to school. Matron's homilies were ringing in all their ears: 'Don't ignore the corners just because you can't see them. The corners matter just as much as the places you can see.' And 'If you are going to do a job, do it properly.' Most fell into the routine as if it were second nature. However, it wasn't the same for all the girls.

'Jenny,' hissed one of the bigger girls, 'get a move on, will you?'

The sickly seven-year-old with posture problems was struggling to sweep the dormitory floor, awkwardly manipulating the long handle of the broom. Her bottom lip began to quiver. Other girls scurried around her: tidying, dusting and making beds. Jenny shut her eyes to stop her tears escaping, knowing that her bed-making skills were not up to standard just as her sweeping had been found wanting. She would get another mark against her today as her hands and nails were dirty; she hadn't had enough time to wash them properly. The aching silence of the hour – which included breakfast – seemed to sap the strength out of her, although the no-talking rule was designed to help the youngsters speed through their chores.

She had been the apple of her father's eye. But the chequered pattern of her childhood meant she had emotional as well as physical issues to contend with and, as she struggled with the unspoken knowledge that she had been rejected by a busy mother who appeared to favour the brothers who'd remained at home, she cried at every opportunity.

Jenny was as confused and weary of this characteristic response as the rest of the girls. At home she had stood up to five brothers – three of them considerably older than herself – without difficulty, to defend her domestic rights. Now she seemed incapable of rational behaviour. But she couldn't articulate her feelings, still less rein in these fits of abject misery.

Soon after she arrived the Maurice Home celebrated Mother's Day, with a visit from Matron's own mother Emily, known to the girls as Nanna Bailey.

Nanna sat on a small stone veranda outside the building to receive posies made by the girls from the meagre selection of flowers growing in their townhouse garden.

With her beaming face framed by white hair, Nanna Bailey, a widow for many years now, could not have been more delighted with the procession of offerings. She gave effusive thanks to each child in turn, passed observations about the flowers in the posy or the way it was held together. When the presentations were over, all of them felt tingly and warm, as if they'd been bathed in stardust. For Jenny it was an unaccustomed feeling. She'd had a mother, certainly, but not one who'd ever made her feel so special with thoughtful words and a kindly expression. Not for the last time she took a sideways glance at her own childhood, pondered the meaning of motherhood and reflected on the flaws in her own mother's behaviour. Even at this young age she began to see the tremendous advantages of living at a children's home. But she found the perpetual change in personnel disconcerting. The oldest girls would leave, usually heading for domestic positions in larger London houses, making way for new arrivals. And some of those struggled with the transition from a home life to an institutional home. If they were too shy to speak much during the day, the other girls often became aware of them at night as they sobbed quietly into their pillows.

One night Sheila was fighting a wave of irritation at the choked sniffles from the neighbouring bed. But a fleeting memory of how she had felt long ago at the Exeter home stopped her shouting aloud. That and the fear of being hauled out of bed for punishment by one of the home's sisters.

The next morning she vowed to make an extra effort and began a short whispered exchange with a girl who looked the same age as herself, as they busied themselves with chores.

'It's Monica, isn't it?'

'Yes,' said Monica, her eyes raw from lack of sleep.

'Sssh,' said Sheila urgently. If Monica didn't yet know how those who broke the rule of silence were loudly and roundly ticked off, Sheila was all too aware. Both girls looked around nervously. No one was on hand to hear Monica's plaintive response made in her usual voice.

Sheila turned back and started talking in a well-practised whisper. 'Look, there's nothing to worry about. You'll soon get used to all this.' Sheila motioned to the busy figures of the other girls, silently setting about tasks like sweeping and cobweb clearance. 'Let's get together at break time in school.'

A flare of hope filled Monica's eyes. She had been feeling the burning pain of an outsider at a home in which everything appeared to run contentedly and like clockwork. She'd cried herself to sleep at night and had even half-heartedly planned to run away. But she knew 'home' was miles away and, without any money to her name, she had no means of getting there.

Monica was used to big households and doing chores. She'd lived most of her life with her father in a house that also contained her grandmother, two aunts and their respective children. Despite the size of the family, it was only a three-bedroomed home, with the lounge converted to a further bedroom. There was an upstairs bathroom, although it only had cold running water. In the kitchen there was a built-in copper to boil hot water. Consequently baths were a relatively rare event because it meant hauling hot water up the stairs.

Her dad, a hotel porter from Eastbourne, Sussex, and her mum had separated acrimoniously. Monica's father, Percy, served in the Royal Field Artillery from the outbreak of war, riding horses that pulled gun carriages into position, sometimes during a barrage of enemy shells. At one point he was hospitalized after being gassed. When Percy left the army in 1920, he was, like Hector Clapton, given a Silver War Badge signifying his exemplary conduct. It wasn't all bad. When she visited the hotel where her father worked, she was given treats by other staff, who knew she was 'a motherless child' because of her parents' separation. And there were other attractions in Eastbourne, including a lake where men and boys played with model yachts. From this she was banned by her grandmother, who was fearful she would get into trouble. So it was with some surprise that the older woman surveyed a dripping-wet Monica on the doorstep one day.

'What's happened to you?' she asked the shivering child.

'I went to the lake,' admitted Monica with some trepidation. 'Someone's boat sank, and I went to get it. But I fell in. Jane went to get a man who was there, and he pulled me out with his boat hook.'

Hot tears started to fall as she remembered the fear of slipping beneath the murky water, becoming embroiled in sticky mud, followed by the indignity of being hauled out.

As her grandmother's spine straightened with fury, the playmates that had accompanied Monica home vanished from her side.

'It's bed for you, my girl,' said her grandmother. 'And no

supper either.' But no punishment could be worse than the dunking she had experienced that day, which instilled in her a fear and loathing of water.

Although she was chastised by her grandmother, Monica idolized the older woman. She was mostly parented by her grandmother and Dorothy Hobday, her aunt and a mother of two who was also separated from her husband. Sometimes her ex, a ploughman, couldn't find enough money to send home to pay for food and Dorothy, who had a goitre – a large lump on her throat – was given a chit worth seven shillings and six pence by the local court. Together with Monica, she went shopping to exchange the voucher for groceries. For Monica the crowded house was home and the people within it were cherished family. But the welfare authorities had different ideas.

After it was discovered she was sleeping in the same bedroom as her father and his new partner – called 'this woman' in official reports – it was made clear Monica could no longer stay there. The authorities contended that the good influences of her grandmother and aunt were cancelled out by the apparently dubious presence of her father's girlfriend.

Initially Monica was sent to her mother who was in service in Tunbridge Wells, Kent. It wasn't a move she relished because of her fondness of her Eastbourne grandmother. Moreover, her mother had two fingers missing from one hand, the result of splinters turning septic in an age before antibiotics could be administered to control infection. The stumps were perpetually swathed in bandages but were nonetheless an alarming sight for a child.

With her mother at work, Monica once again lived with a

grandmother, this time one who was frequently ill. When it became clear the older woman could not cope, Monica was sent to the Waifs and Strays Society and landed up at Ealing. Until then she'd been known by her first name, Phyllis. But as there was already a girl at the Maurice Home with that name she became known by her middle name, Monica, a name that's stuck ever since. At first she resented the name change, which seemed to underline how she was being reluctantly crammed into a new life. But the structured routines of life at the home helped the days pass quickly.

Sheila was as good as her word, seeking Monica out at school and afterwards back at the home. She took pains to introduce her to all the other girls; Barbara, Phyllis, Joan, Kathleen, Mary and Penny were bigger girls, while June, Nansi and Florence were about the same age as Monica and Sheila. Ida, Peggy, Marguerite and Jenny were younger.

At first the fast-paced conversations between them all at teatime had made her head hurt.

'Barbara, pass the bread.'

'Don't be greedy, Peggy. There's plenty to go around.'

'You've spilled your drink, you donkey.'

Gradually the homesickness ebbed away and Monica's cautious guard began to fall away. She had no idea that Matron and her attentive staff were keeping a careful eye on her, monitoring her levels of distress.

With one grandmother a strict Baptist, Monica – who remained terrified of drowning – would have been immersed in water to enter the faith. As it was, she was christened with just a few drops of water when she arrived at the Maurice Home. Dependable Sister Lucy Briggs, with her Scottish brogue, was godmother.

If life at the home was routine, to the point of being humdrum, the politics of the outside world continued to spiral haphazardly. The promise of 'peace for our time' was now a memory, with the British government distributing free air-raid shelters in February 1939. Two months later, far-reaching evacuation plans were drawn up, with the proviso of 'women and children first'. In Ascot, Dorothy Peyton had the grim satisfaction of knowing her fears for the future had been well-founded, and she was quietly pleased to have been one of the first to put her home at the nation's disposal.

All premises offered for evacuation purposes had to be inspected for suitability, a job for the Air Raid Precautions (ARP) warden. After tensions in Europe began to rise, it was a service established by the government in 1937 when it was advertised as 'a responsible job for responsible men'. After Dorothy Peyton's letter was received an ARP warden sent by London County Council appeared at the door of Englemere Wood.

Wearing blue overalls, he removed a steel helmet marked with a letter W as he was shown inside the house, where he cast an admiring glance around at the hall.

'Nice place you've got here,' he said unnecessarily. Dorothy, walking towards him, dismissed Jack and looked at the warden levelly.

'I understand you have come to inspect the house on behalf of the Waifs and Strays Society,' she said without shifting her gaze.

'Yes, well, there's a few things I have to ask,' he said, shuffling from one foot to another as he finally focused on a form he'd produced from one of his many pockets. He cleared his throat. 'Mrs Peyton, do you have a gas-proof room in which the little children can be kept safe if there's a gas attack?'

His pen was poised to take down the answer. He'd been to inspect some of the other public services where gas masks had been distributed, along with gas-proof clothing and a decontamination room had been installed. It was these high standards to which he aspired.

'A gas-proof room?' she asked a little incredulously. 'Pray, tell me what would a gas-proof room look like?'

He floundered for a moment. 'You know,' he said, 'one that would keep the little children safe from poisonous gas, if there was a gas attack.'

'Well, I certainly have a number of rooms, all with doors and windows, much like everybody else. However, would not gas escape into it under the doors or through gaps in the window?'

Warming to the subject, she asked, 'How many people do you know who have rooms that are proven to be safe from gas? Is this not an impossible request? Or do you mean a cellar?'

Feeling somewhat flustered, he chose not to tackle the series of quick-fire questions. Instead, he scribbled something illegible on a printed form and continued, unabashed.

'Mrs Peyton, do you have anywhere that you can use for a food store?'

'Certainly,' said Dorothy. 'I have plenty of spare rooms, including a few with large cupboards that could be used as larders.'

There was a momentary silence.

'Listen here,' said the warden conspiratorially, belatedly

trying to break the ice. 'No one even thinks there will be another war. If there is, it won't be a long one. But it's like the Board of Education says, we can't make these arrangements on the spur of the moment. If they are going to work, we must make them in times of peace, and not on the hop. It's my job to fill in the forms, that's all.'

'Quite so,' said Dorothy, her irritation at what she considered to be silly questioning beginning to evaporate. Her mind moved on from the frustrations of apparently aimless paperwork for a moment. 'What kind of children would be coming to my house?'

'Oh, I don't know that information, Mrs Peyton, really I don't. You'll have to wait and see what you're given. I've heard some of them can be quite all right, you know, on a good day. That's me done anyhow. I wish you all the best with it,' he said, throwing what she felt was a sympathetic look in her direction.

As Jack was showing him out again, Dorothy was thoughtful. The pressing weight of bureaucracy had given her pause. Of course she wanted to help out, but no one would tell her what calibre of child would be crossing her threshold.

Queenie attended a school a short distance from her home in Garratt Lane before being taken into the Waifs and Strays Society. She is pictured grasping a maypole ribbon, second from the left.

Before the outbreak of war, when they lived in Ealing, Maurice girls enjoyed annual holidays at Great Holland in Essex.

Queenie and Matron met for the first time at St Mary's Home in Cheam, Surrey, built by the Waifs and Strays Society to accommodate fifty girls and opened in 1914.

Princess Marie Louise was a staunch ally of the Maurice Home, both at Englemere Wood and here, at Grenville House.

Precious recollections of Englemere Wood during the Second World War were treasured in an album that today has found its way to The Children's Society Archive. These two snaps show one aspect of the house and the visit by Queen Elizabeth and her daughters, Princess Elizabeth and Princess Margaret.

A Royal knitting circle: every week, girls from Englemere Wood joined two princesses at the house across the road to turn out knitted garments for servicemen.

Maurice girls and the staff who looked after them were thrilled when the Queen and her daughters, Elizabeth and Margaret, paid a visit.

The opening of Grenville House in 1946 was a proud day.

Jenny and Jacky, two donkeys kept at Englemere Wood by Mrs Peyton, were cared for by the evacuated girls.

Maurice girls were proud to wear guiding uniforms as they scoured the grounds of Englemere Wood for firewood.

Maurice Home girls enjoying Christmas games.

Sisters Gladys and Vera Raffell arrived at Grenville House in the spring of 1947, after persistently truanting from school.

Commando Tommy Peyton stands with his mother, Dorothy, outside Englemere Wood, for a photo that became a treasured memento.

Before facing action, Lt Tommy Peyton wrote letters home, confiding his hopes for the future.

Grenville House girls on holiday at Cromer after the Second World War.

Close friends Dorothy Peyton and Irene Borthwick, who both championed the girls, pictured at Foxhills, with one of Mrs Borthwick's Dalmatians.

After the conflict, Mrs Peyton sometimes joined the Grenville House girls on holiday on the east coast.

5. Going Away

A person's a person, no matter how small.
Dr. Seuss, Horton Hears a Who!

Blissfully unaware of the immense issues unfolding on the international stage, Sheila was growing in confidence. She was progressing so well that she had been invited by the school to sit for a scholarship that would take her to the Central School for Girls, sited in one of Ealing's parks, which offered a higher standard of education and better prospects. She hadn't expected the laurels. When she trooped into a school assembly that morning, there seemed nothing to indicate the day would be extraordinary. However, when the names of the successful candidates were read out by headmaster Mr Chandler, Sheila's was on the list.

Instantly her face coloured and she mutely received the grins and nudges from her fellow home pupils, with a smile pulling at her lips. Her thoughts turned to a bright future: one with more books, expanded subjects and a uniform of beige and blue rather than bottle green. Excitedly she danced back to Mattock Lane at lunchtime to share her good news.

When she walked in she found Matron Bailey in the middle of ironing, and approached her with the necessary paperwork in hand, a gang of girls close behind her, pleased to share the sunlight of the moment. Matron glanced up, before turning her attention back to the laundry.

'Put it down there, lass,' she said, nodding towards a tabletop. 'What is it?'

'It's the scholarship, Matron,' said Sheila. 'I've got it. And Mr Chandler says if you'll sign it, I should take it back to him this afternoon.'

Although she tried to keep the unbridled excitement out of her voice, Sheila failed miserably.

'I shall not sign it,' said Matron, meeting the young girl's eyes for the first time.

'But I've won the scholarship, Matron. I'm going to the Central School,' Sheila replied, unsure why Matron wasn't sharing her own boundless joy.

'You may have won the scholarship, but you are not going to the Central School. Now go and wash your hands, all of you, your food is ready.'

The girls who had been poised to watch Sheila being lauded for her achievement had already melted away, having heard the tone of Matron's voice. Dumbstruck, Sheila went off to the sink. She knew better than to question any decision handed down from the home's hierarchy, but she couldn't understand why she was being denied such an opportunity.

Matron had chosen her words carefully. Her core philosophy was that all the girls in the home should be treated as equals. That meant the same clothes, the same haircut and the same education. She didn't dish out cuddles or hugs either. A needy child might try to monopolize her

attention, she reasoned, when it was fairness not favouritism that counted. The consequent lack of physical
contact affected some girls more than others. But for
Sheila, it was being deprived of an educational opportunity like this one that had a catastrophic effect.

Afterwards Matron would no longer find Sheila on Saturdays pestering to visit the library or curled up in a chair,
browsing through the well-thumbed pages of the ten volumes of Arthur Mee's children's encyclopaedias that lined
the bookshelves in the playroom. For half an hour after
midday meals at weekends and in the holidays there was a
rule of silence. All the girls who weren't washing up were
expected to spend it reading. Until then Sheila had needed
no encouragement.

In her place, though, was Jenny, who quickly became
lost in the world of exotic animals and far-off places illuminated on the page. On the first Sunday of the month
the girls were encouraged to write to their families. For
Jenny that meant Mother and Father, although she didn't
understand why they weren't living together or why her
mother now had a different surname from her dad. She
had no comprehension of the phrase 'stepfather' used by
her mum in letters.

Her father wrote regularly with news from her village
and the surrounding areas. Sometimes there was word of
her brothers. In letters from her mother she became inured
to barbed insults directed at her father and focused on the
more benign bits of the bulletin. Even at a young age,
Jenny enjoyed writing back.

'Do you need help, Jenny?' Sister Briggs asked, as the
household settled down to the task of letter-writing. Brisk,

she may have been, but Sister Briggs knew that contact with her parents was important to Jenny and needed to be accommodated at all costs.

'No, thank you,' she said. 'I'm fine.' And with her tongue poking out of the corner of her mouth in concentration, she set about her correspondence, detailing her news.

Monitoring of the letters by Matron and other members of staff was intended to help identify the onset of any emotional crises linked to home. But as they inspected the sentiments set down by the girls, they were always impressed with seven-year-old Jenny's spelling and sentence structure.

While Sheila and Jenny were both keen on reading and writing, they parted company when it came to sports. When she lived at home Jenny's mother had taken her to clinics in Hampshire for treatment of her physical difficulties and that continued in Ealing at Mattock Lane hospital, with a series of exercises and electrical stimuli. For her there could only be limited participation in the regular Women's League of Health and Beauty sessions at the Maurice Home, although she longed to get into the uniform of white blouses and black sateen shorts, hand-stitched by the staff. Sheila, meanwhile, would learn the routines so proficiently she could eventually teach keep-fit classes herself. The league – motto: movement is life – was started by Mary Bagot Stack in 1930 and centred on mass synchronized keep-fit routines. By 1938 it boasted a worldwide membership of 170,000.

One of Jenny's golden memories was the relationship forged with Mrs Stone and her daughter Phillipa, both recruited as supporters of the home. Matron Bailey sourced families willing to act as 'aunts' and 'uncles' to the girls, providing some of the comforts that were acknowledged to be missing in their lives. Sometimes Jenny, paired with an older girl, Joan, went to the Stones' house. At other times, the Stones came to the Maurice Home, with all three girls playing with a doll's house kept in the staffroom, to which access was permitted on special occasions like these. At Easter Jenny and Joan were given a hand-crafted chocolate egg and both received a hand-knitted blue sweater from Mrs Stone just before she took a family holiday in Switzerland. Then there were other treats from wholly unexpected quarters.

'Girls, please file in and sit down.' Matron's voice was firm but not unkind. Yet the men that stood in one corner of the room grasping clipboards weren't smiling.

After the girls had assembled, one of the men stepped forward, cleared his throat and explained why they were there.

'We are from Mars – the confectionary company, not the planet.' He paused to allow a ripple of nervous laughter to go around the room. 'We are here because we want you to try our latest products and tell us which you like best.'

Solemn faces erupted into grins and the sound of excited chatter filled the room.

Matron stepped forward and quietened them with a meaningful 'hush'. 'This is not a monkey cage, and you will do as you are asked in silence,' she said sternly. Immediately the room was quiet again.

Packets marked with an 'A' were swiftly distributed among the girls, who were told to eat it slowly. When the last crumbs of chocolate had disappeared, a package marked with a 'B' was sent around.

Afterwards girls were beckoned into the next room, one at a time, to describe to one of the men which chocolate bar she had preferred and why. Mars was a US confectionary company that had expanded into Britain in 1932, basing itself in Slough, Berkshire. Adaptations inspired by Swiss chocolatiers marked a departure from the original US recipes and it was this new flavour being put to the test.

As the girls gathered afterwards, Monica asked tentatively, 'Could you tell the difference?'

'Not really.'

'I thought they tasted the same.'

'I think they were the same.'

'B was definitely better, I'm sure.'

The volley of replies confirmed that no one had come away from the trial with firm opinions about the effect the chocolate had on their palates, not least because they had no great experience of eating quantities of it.

'They were both scrumptious,' said Sheila firmly, summing up the views they all held.

In June that year a strawberry tea party was held in the garden of one Miss Findlay, where there were not only succulent fruits to enjoy but also games. Using only newspaper older girls had to fashion a costume of a nursery rhyme character for the younger girls. Barbara took Jenny away and returned her as Little Bo Peep.

When Jenny was permitted to choose the lunch to mark her birthday in July 1939 she decided on macaroni cheese – a meal she'd never had before coming to the home – to be followed by jam tart and custard. The Stones had given her a doll with bright blue eyes that closed when it was laid down. The doll's outfit was a stylish scarlet and white polka dot and Jenny named her 'Margaret' for the youngest royal princess, the same age as she was and the subject of much conversation and speculation among the girls at the home. Dolls were still rare among home children and at last she became the object of some envy.

For Jenny this was a joyful time, with most of her painful childhood memories starting to blur. Although she was still subject to bouts of illness her recoveries came more quickly with Matron monitoring her progress.

'Come on, lassie,' said Matron encouragingly. 'Mind over matter. You'll soon feel better.'

Through it all Jenny badly missed her father, whose visits to the home were infrequent.

For Sheila the acid sting of losing the scholarship remained. Her behaviour deteriorated and she was often chastised at night for talking, storytelling or even singing in the dormitory after lights out. That meant dragging her eiderdown and pillow from the bed under the stern eye of the duty sister and sleeping on the landing by way of punishment. Morosely, from her isolated spot, she watched night life unfold outside through a portion of an uncurtained landing window. In the distance she could see the bright signs of the Forum Cinema, a grand building with eight high pillars on its façade, which had been opened five years earlier by actor Jack Buchanan amid a blaze of publicity. Some nights she could even hear the organ accompaniment to the film. What would life hold for her now her greatest chance in life had been snatched away? she wondered. Sheila had yet to discover that sometimes opportunity knocks twice or even three times.

Summer soon unfolded and it was time to embark on the home's annual holiday. In 1939 the destination was once again Great Holland, with each girl permitted to take one toy and one book. During the five-week holiday the girls moved into the village hall. Once again, a lorry took kit from Ealing on a hundred-mile trip so the girls enjoyed some home comforts, including mattresses.

Each day a picnic was put together in the hall's small kitchen. The girls all played their part in transporting it to the beach, crossing a golf course in the process, always alert in case a player shouted 'Fore'. Although they were ready to duck at a moment's notice they could still find plenty to talk about en route. Staff had deckchairs while the girls each had a waterproof square cut from an old raincoat to sit on. Matron Bailey carried with her a small suitcase filled with mending, so she could darn socks and stockings while supervising games on the shingle beach. There was, she reasoned, no point in doing just one job when you could do two just as well.

She knew she wouldn't be able to open the suitcase until all the girls were beach-ready, though, and it took some time for them to change from clothes into bathers. Matron and other staff were on hand to help – and they all stopped to admire Jenny in her new costume, which had been knitted by one of the friends of the home.

'That's a very good fit, Jenny,' said Matron. 'Now, don't wear that one into the water. You will have to change into your old costume before you go swimming.'

The continuing efforts to help other girls into costumes

and pack away clothes so they stayed dry for the return journey, were suddenly and unceremoniously interrupted by Jenny's wails. Proud of her new knitted bathing suit, she had ventured into the water even though she knew she shouldn't. The woollen garment had immediately soaked up water and was now hanging almost round her ankles.

'Come here, Jenny, and stop crying,' said Matron firmly. 'You were told not to go into the water, not least because there was no one to keep an eye on you. Let's get you out of this wet costume and into your other one.'

The moment may have been delayed, but soon everyone was ready to head for the sea. When it came to swimming, Matron would be on her feet at the water's edge.

'In you go, girls. Yes, I know it's cold.' Suddenly she became aware of a figure standing behind her, with arms folded and pink skin turning grey in a chill sea breeze.

'I don't want to go in,' said Monica stoutly. Her memories of a dunking in Eastbourne's boating lake had not left her. If anything, her fear of water had increased.

Matron took in the scene, wondering how best to tempt Monica into the lapping waves. 'But look at all the fun everyone is having. Can you give it a try? I know. Let's go in ankle-deep together and see how it feels. You see, it's not so bad.'

They held hands, with Matron careful not to pull Monica in the direction of the sea. Gradually, with gentle encouragement, Matron persuaded her it was safe to join the other girls in the shallows. After her feet were covered, Monica became more distracted by the antics of the rest than by the incoming ripples. Although she actively avoided the splashing, it was clear to Matron that Monica would submerge herself into the sea to swim before the holiday ended.

Then a sudden shout drew her attention further out to sea. Jenny had been floating as far out to sea as she dared, showing off to the older girls to get their attention. Now she had found herself out of her depth and drifting away from the group.

'Penny,' called Matron calmly. 'Please fetch Jenny back to the shore.'

Penny was one of the oldest girls and a strong swimmer. She duly returned Jenny to Matron's side, shivering as much from foolishness as the cold.

'Never mind, Jenny. You were doing very well and now you are safely back on shore,' said Matron. Jenny clutched Matron's forearm and tried her pull her back to the beach camp. 'Don't swing on me,' she said, removing her arm from Jenny's grasp before once more scanning the sea swimmers. 'I am not a garden gate.'

Monica had glanced back, momentarily uncertain. Matron gave her a smile and a wave before leading Jenny back to the beach camp, leaving the other staff in charge. Monica was quickly distracted as Sheila called her name.

After lunch the girls rested for half an hour before resuming beach activities like making sandcastles and collecting shells. Together they worked out the very best way to make a human pyramid before practising handstands and organizing races.

There were two cinema outings, and two church services to attend every Sunday they were away. On the last Sunday of their stay the church celebrated the harvest festival, decorating the windows and pew ends with foliage and vegetables.

After walking to Frinton, the girls spent their limited pocket money in Woolworths, the mass market retailer with an upper price limit of sixpence, which by then had more than 600 stores in the UK. Focused on their new prized possessions, the girls with heads together didn't see the posters on the town's walls, urging men to join the armed forces. Nor did they particularly notice messages emblazoned on news stands, revealing that major European countries were once again dividing into two camps. The calls of the newspaper sellers that warned of the developing crisis were carried away by the brisk sea breeze.

At night the children slept soundly after the exertions of the day. Only if they had lain awake might they have made out some of the words repeatedly used in the radio broadcasts straining from Matron's wireless: Danzig, Chamberlain, evacuation, war. And they might have even heard tense low voices among the staff.

'I've had a letter from the society,' Matron said solemnly. 'The Maurice Home is being evacuated from Ealing.'

Gertrude Measures and Doris Sheppard gave small gasps while Lucy Briggs remained grimly silent. Once again the future seemed perilously uncertain.

'The society wants us to keep all the children together, so I'm relieved about that,' Matron continued. 'Really, the thought of splitting everybody up would be too much. This time we are going to Ascot, in Berkshire. The name of the house is Englemere Wood.'

'Is it an empty house, like last time?' Sister Briggs asked.

'No,' said Matron, rereading a line of the letter that had

been marked 'confidential'. 'It belongs to a Mrs Peyton. And she will live there still, alongside us. She's one of nine people to have already offered their homes to the society, whose places have been checked. So that's very kind indeed of her. But I don't know much more than that. There's a list of equipment that we must take to Englemere Wood. I must get in touch with the traffic commissioner in Ealing to arrange transport.'

There were murmurs from the home sisters, all trying to place Ascot geographically.

'It's near Windsor, near the royal castle,' said Matron. 'I don't know it well, but I believe there is a great deal of parkland nearby. Given the news bulletins we've heard this week I think we might be away for much longer than last time.'

The next morning Matron kept a smile fixed on her face when she watched the girls running carefree into an incoming tide. It seemed to her that no amount of parkland in Ascot would save them from the bomber's aim. And what about her staff? If conscription was widened to include young women, as it surely would be, they would disappear to serve the nation in a different way. How would she find anyone to care for the children in the home? But she didn't want to broadcast her fears; she knew from experience that, like chickenpox, they would spread swiftly among children.

The last few days of the holiday slipped away dreamlike. Soon the hall was cleansed of the last vestiges of beach grit, and the children were seated in the charabanc taking them back, chatting idly among themselves.

Matron dwelled for a sombre moment on the prospect

in store. The move to Leighton Buzzard had been a dress rehearsal. Now it was time for the real thing and, with it, the challenge of facing up to the unknown. All the girls would cope with the upheaval, she felt, except for Jenny. But for once that wasn't what worried her most.

As the shadow of war had loomed larger and darker than ever before, how, she wondered, would she keep the girls safe?

6. Home From Home

Children are likely to live up to what you believe of them.
Lady Bird Johnson, former First Lady of the USA

Shortly before the journey back from the Essex coast, Matron announced to the children that the Maurice Home was to be evacuated. Sheila was immediately perplexed. If the term 'evacuation' had been used the year previously when they went to Leighton Buzzard, it hadn't registered with her. To her, the word meant 'to empty'. *All children will be emptied?* It didn't sound feasible. In fact, it was the address at Mattock Lane that was emptied, or, rather, the holiday items were never unpacked. After one uncomfortable night spent on the floor of the Maurice Home, it soon became clear that evacuation involved heading to an unknown destination, somewhere Matron called Ascot, although it wasn't somewhere Sheila had heard of previously. For the girls it meant a fretful uncertainty, coupled with no small degree of excitement.

The girls themselves didn't have much to take, with only the luckiest owning a doll, teddy or book. Then they themselves were counted on to a coach that would take them to their new home. Ealing was geographically the most convenient side of London for the trip. But although it's only fifteen miles from Ealing to Ascot, it proved quite a trek on narrow roads clogged with traffic.

Sheila and Monica sat together, watching in silence the scenes unfolding in London's suburbia outside the slow-moving coach. Cars were being piled high with cases, queues were forming outside railway stations and shops, and there seemed to be sandbags everywhere. Only after terraced houses gave way to the greenery of open countryside did they settle back in their seats. They didn't chat much as they thought apprehensively about their destination.

For Jenny it was a different experience. She felt queasy almost as soon as the vehicle pulled on to the main road. Swiftly she was whisked up to a front seat, next to Sister Briggs, who held a washing-up bowl at the ready. Although there were twenty-five girls on board the coach, with Matron and her three assistants, there was a muted anxious atmosphere, in place of the sing-song that usually happened when they went on holidays.

At Englemere Wood Dorothy Peyton was preparing for what she felt would be a momentous day. It was Friday, 1 September 1939, and her new house guests were due to arrive.

Cupboards had already been emptied and furniture moved. Earlier she'd seen her butler, Jack, ensuring some of the doors between her side of the house and theirs were locked. Unobtrusive and efficient, she'd had high hopes for Jack – but she knew that he would not stay part of the household for much longer now war was almost upon them. Although he'd narrowly missed being called up in a recruitment drive for the military six months previously, conscription was imminent. The anticipation was almost palpable, and they were both taut with expectation.

Even with Jack gone, Mrs Peyton knew she would still have two housemaids: Margaret Osborn, the same age as Mrs Peyton, and fifteen-year-old Doreen Dorgan, as well as Ellen Bartlett, the cook. Then there was the gardener and the chauffeur. She was lucky, she knew, but she couldn't help but think wistfully of previous years, when there had been even more staff on hand. But back then there had been her husband and grown-up sons living in the house, all leading busy lives. She shook herself. Those years were gone and, with both boys already in uniform, it was time for new thinking.

From communications sent by the Waifs and Strays Society, she knew she would be receiving the residents of a London girls' home. That made her feel a little ill at ease. As a mother she'd known only boys. But it was too late to worry, she realized, as a crunch of tyres on gravel told her they had arrived.

There were gasps from its goggle-eyed passengers when the coach carrying the Maurice girls to their new wartime home turned off a major road and pulled into the splayed drive. The ivy-clad house ahead was ample and the grounds beyond were sprawling. Immediately they caught sight of a harassed-looking man, vigorously motioning for the vehicle to keep driving towards the back of the grand property.

When the vehicle finally came to a halt, there was a series of instructions issued before the girls could disembark.

'Now, girls, remember. We don't shout,' Sister Briggs almost bellowed to counter the throb of the engine. 'Mind your manners. First impressions count. The woman who lives here has been most kind in agreeing to share her house with us. She doesn't want to be disturbed dawn until dusk by you now, does she?'

The question was rhetorical and there was no doubt in their minds that the debt of gratitude could best be repaid by flawless behaviour. But for the girls evacuation was proving to be an extended adventure that made it difficult not to either shriek, or at least squeak, in anticipation. The house ahead of them had a lead spire, broad porches and shadowed entrances, its fine brickwork a warmer colour than the Victorians traditionally favoured. Taking in the huge house, just how grand could their new living quarters be? The volume of their incessant chatter rose by notches.

After shooing everyone off the coach, Matron and Sister Briggs stood back for a moment and took in the house as well. They exchanged a glance. It was far grander than they had imagined. Matron had braced herself to meet the woman who owned this impressive pile but thought it more likely she would be greeted by staff instead. And indeed it was a uniformed chauffeur who stood to attention, while keeping a wary eye on the progress of the girls.

Chauffeur George Moore had a daughter of his own but had no idea that a group of girls together could be so noisy. The serenity of Englemere Wood was about to change; he could see that. Having ushered the coach out of the eyeline of the house's front windows he swiftly beckoned the phalanx of guests along a privet-lined path away from his employer. By then the girls could see they were heading towards enormous windows on one side of a generously proportioned wing. Once inside they were breathless with excitement.

'It's simply huge!' cried Sheila, as she took in the dimensions of the former ballroom that was going to be their bedroom.

'Look, there's a stage for the band,' said Monica, her gaze drawn towards a raised area at one end of the room. Meanwhile, Jenny was crouching down to run a hand over a richly varnished and silky-smooth parquet floor. To her the word 'evacuation' had seemed linked to cowardice and implied running away. It was, she now realized, nothing of the sort, and seemed, on the face of it, to be a very positive thing indeed.

The ballroom would be a dormitory once their metal-framed beds arrived. Until then the mattresses they had taken on holiday would be on the same floor that had once carried the light footsteps of exquisitely dressed dancers. The room's large windows, already encased in black-out curtains, looked out on to a terrace, a lawn and into the sloping pastures beyond. If that wasn't enough, there were woods and a shimmering lake.

There were two other rooms earmarked for use by the girls. One was a garden room, where Mrs Peyton previously arranged flowers. In it was a floor-to-ceiling cupboard containing the household's best china. This room would now be used to dish up food and wash up plates. Then there was a dining room next to the ballroom. Laundry facilities – two big tubs and a large mangle with wooden rollers – were installed on the hard-standing outside, sheltered by an overhanging roof. Monday wash days would be a considerable undertaking for small-framed girls.

Although there may have been only one bathroom and a single toilet the girls were too thrilled by their new environment to be in the least bit concerned. In short order a piece of plywood was fitted across the bath, big enough to hold six wash bowls, so all the girls had the opportunity to wash before dressing in the morning.

For the Maurice girls some aspects of life at Ealing were replicated in Ascot, including the staff. With them went the familiar copper tea urn that had brass handles and a brass tap. A brew was made with a single reusable tea bag made of calico and containing a heaped spoonful of loose tea along with two spoonfuls of sugar. The bag was attached to the handle of the urn, which was filled with water and milk. After the bag was swished through the steaming liquid the resulting infusion was poured into enamel mugs. Whatever the merits of the tea it produced, more memorable was the task of heaving the hefty unit into its new home.

Mattresses were quickly offloaded after the lorry arrived to line the ballroom, and on top of them went the blankets. Tucked into the windows were small lockers for the few personal items retained by the girls.

Dog-eared cardboard cartons containing food supplies and clothing were also deposited at Ascot. Included in the supplies were the green tunics, green blouses and green blazers with the Maurice Home moniker on the pocket. Precious Brownie and Guide uniforms were also among the items. The tradition of guiding would be maintained even during the war.

Matron supervised the unpacking process, hoping that

by keeping the girls busy the wave of excitement could be tamed. 'Clothes in the dormitory, books in the dining room for now. Yes, I can see Jenny has gone into the garden but please speak more quietly. I'm not deaf or in Timbuktu.'

While each girl retained their identifying number, previously sewn into clothing and marked on personal belongings, some facets of life at Englemere Wood were entirely new, like identity cards and the wearing of gas masks.

During the First World War the most feared weapon had been gas, and forty-four million masks had been distributed prior to the outbreak of war. Gas-mask bags were duly marked with individual identity card numbers and had to be carried at all times. Everyone was directed to go to the kitchen area in the event of an air raid or gas attack, judged by the ARP warden who had visited the year before to be the safest bolthole in the house. The girls were also issued with kit bags – known to them as bundle bags – and at night they packed clothes and their gas masks into the bags, ready for a quick exit with all their necessary items if there was a bombing raid.

In fact, it wasn't the advent of enemy bombs that brought the first screams from the Maurice girls, but the appearance of a small and vigorous puppy that came tearing into the dining room just before they had dinner.

A combined scream came from girls who'd rarely encountered animals before, let alone barking, jumping, yipping bundles of white fur like this one, the clack of his teeth enamel coming dangerously close to the hems of their dresses.

Behind him came Mrs Osborn who darted about between the girls, trying to grab the puppy.

'Come here, Jimmy, you devil,' she threatened, as he once again evaded her lunge.

Only when he was safely tucked under her arm did she stop to explain.

'Jimmy is Mr John's dog,' she said. Greeted with a sea of blank faces, she went on, 'Mr John is Mrs Peyton's oldest son. He's in the army now, and so is his brother Tommy. Of course John couldn't take him into the army with him, so Jimmy lives with us now. There are two other dogs as well, Judy and Tony,' said Mrs Osborn.

A few of the girls looked like they might faint.

Mrs Osborn grinned. 'Don't worry. They aren't like this one. Terriers, yes, but much older. You'll end up loving them. And you'll probably end up loving this one as well.' She gave the dog a gentle squeeze and took him back to the other side of the house.

Not long after that, it was the girls' turn to explore the garden and the woodland area beyond. Some looked up to watch the tops of the pines tremble in the breeze, others stooped down to run inquisitive fingers across soft mosses, while a few kept a wary eye out for rampaging dogs.

When Sheila called out, they gathered in a tighter bunch once more. 'This area is like an open-air theatre!' she exclaimed. 'We can use it for plays and pageants, or just for singing.' An open crescent was bordered by rhododendrons that could be used as wings and even offer a 'backstage' area screened from any audience.

Fears about the perils of a major conflict had already eased among the girls, who were far more focused on finding new and exciting trails. Soon, during walks around the garden, they would strike up in song – 'Jerusalem' was a favourite. It meant girls who were vocally less gifted could join in with gusto, without fear of causing a disturbance in the house.

Dorothy was looking out of one of her windows when an unnatural movement among low-hanging branches caught her eye. Almost immediately a procession of young girls came into view, with bobbed hair, grazed knees and well-worn clothes. They were chatting animatedly, although Dorothy couldn't hear what was being said.

At first sight the girls seemed charming enough. They didn't look particularly noisy or destructive, which was a relief. She had already observed that Matron was disciplined and efficient, as were the rest of the home staff. But there remained a bubble of anxiety inside. Apart from one girl, they seemed to walk – or run – with ease. That meant they didn't suffer from rickets, which hobbled numerous metropolitan children. But was there more to discover?

The girls looked clean but would she find out they were, in fact, riddled with unspecified diseases, the kind that haunted the poor? Was their hair kept uniformly short because of infestation? She took a deep breath and rang for Jack. 'I want to meet the girls as soon as possible,' she instructed.

As for the girls, the identity of their host had been the subject of much whispered debate.

'I'll bet she's beautiful, like a princess,' said Jenny, still beguiled by fairy tales. Some of the others had their doubts but kept silent on the issue. Together they concluded that none of them had seen a rich person before so would have no idea what they looked like.

The mystery that swirled around her came to an end

that first evening when Dorothy Peyton appeared in the ballroom on a small platform at one end of the room flanked by Matron Bailey. Whatever the girls had imagined, it wasn't this. She was a silver-haired vision of poise and refinement, standing tall in a long black evening dress and exuding a quiet dignity.

Silently the girls stood in awe as the introductions were made. Mrs Peyton was almost regal in her bearing and possessed the kind of elegance that they had previously only witnessed in films.

'Girls, I'd like to introduce you to Mrs Peyton, who has so kindly offered part of her lovely house to us,' said Matron. 'You may call her "madam".'

Mrs Peyton smiled serenely at the girls, her manner effortlessly unflappable. 'I'm delighted to welcome you to Englemere Wood,' she said. Then she turned towards Matron to affirm her hospitality. 'Please do mention if there's anything else we can do to help you while you are here.'

'You've provided us with so much already,' responded Matron, her heart lifting. 'So kind of you to come and say hello to the girls.' A momentary flash of alarm had passed through Matron when Jack had come to arrange the meeting. Would this woman be a harridan, reeling off a list of rules that would suffocate them all? The challenge of having the girls creeping around the place to prevent any undue noise would be exhausting. But those fears vanished in an instant.

After Mrs Peyton left, the girls huddled together, agreeing that without doubt she was the perfect host. Immediately a deep attachment for her was inspired among the girls.

Jenny, who was by now harbouring secret and ultimately unfulfilled ambitions to become a nun, adopted a virtuous expression. And she won some rare validation from the rest when she said, 'She has opened wide her heart and home, just for us.'

The same day the girls arrived at Englemere Wood, German troops began pouring into Poland. Now it wasn't a case of 'if' war was declared, but 'when'. The Maurice Home had become part of a huge exodus from the capital. Out of a hundred Waifs and Strays homes nationwide, thirty were evacuated, with the girls in the first wave out of London.

St Mary's in Cheam was among them. Queenie was still at the home where, three years earlier, she had been poorly and was tended by Matron Bailey. Like her compatriots at the Maurice Home, her destination was a magnificent country house. Shernfold Park was a three-storey mansion set in 182 acres of grounds at Frant in East Sussex. It was a Regency building with a circular carriage drive, fish ponds, tennis courts and a heated winter garden. It seemed Queenie too had landed on her feet.

Long after the Maurice girls were installed at Englemere Wood and Queenie was bedding down at Shernfold Park, teachers, railway staff, local-authority officials and 17,000 members of the Women's Voluntary Service up and down the country remained hard at work, organizing the departure of 1.5 million children from cities to the countryside, where it was thought they would be safe from bombs. Planning had started many months beforehand. The three-day operation was the biggest mass migration in British history and barely a family was left untouched by it.

Rural Ascot was chosen as a safe haven, separated as it was from the outskirts of London by miles of open landscape. It had a buzzing town centre with a butcher, fishmonger, pub, coal merchants and hairdressers among many other businesses on its high street.

As evacuees, the girls were not alone in the town. Although the number in Ascot fluctuated, it peaked at 1,891 in January 1940 and still stood at more than 1,300 in 1944, increasing the population by about 50 per cent. Those evacuated to Ascot came with institutions like the Maurice Home or were directed there by the government. Then there were private evacuees, who had organized their own living arrangements. It was the same picture across the nation.

Perhaps the most famous evacuees in the Ascot area were the Royal Family – King George VI, Queen Elizabeth and their daughters Elizabeth and Margaret – who chose to spend the conflict at Windsor Castle. Initially the government had urged the Windsors to make for the safety of Canada. At the time Queen Elizabeth – Queen Elizabeth II's mother – declared, 'The children won't go without me. I won't leave the king. And the king will never leave.' This open defiance of Hitler's threats earned her the undying affection of the people.

For the moment the Maurice girls had an advantage over many other young evacuees that had flocked to Ascot. Any pangs they felt at being separated from their parents were already long forgotten. For them evacuation became nothing short of a great escapade filled with possibilities. It wasn't the same for everyone. Many evacuated children were so homesick they took the first opportunity to return to their parents. Despite a government information campaign pleading with them not to, a few mothers who couldn't abide the separation soon came to fetch their children. More parents arrived when they had a first letter home from their offspring, pleading to be saved from dire domestic situations. Not everyone had parents to liberate them from evacuation homes that didn't suit and Queenie Clapton was among them.

For reasons quickly forgotten Queenie and several friends disliked their new living arrangements so much that they plotted to run away. They hadn't got far before they were returned to Waifs and Strays Society staff but Queenie was branded a ringleader and was swiftly dispatched to Leamington Church House outside the society, a former reformatory school with a notoriously inflexible regime.

Gladys Raffell was another girl who, like Queenie, would one day mean the world to Matron and her staff. For now she was just a tot. And from the family home in London she went to Marlow, Buckinghamshire, but was among those who didn't linger long before heading back to the capital when the anticipated attack by Hitler did not materialize.

At the end of the day, evacuation was voluntary, but billeting was, when necessary, compulsory. Anyone with a spare room was supposed to register with the authorities and could find themselves hosting children, teachers or mothers. Host families received a billeting allowance of ten shillings and six pence for the first child they took and eight shillings and six pence for subsequent ones. Parents of evacuees were means-tested and expected to contribute to costs if they could.

For now Ascot was changed beyond recognition. Other institutions, like the Robert Spurrier Home for the Blind, the Barclay School for Partially Sighted Girls and Stepney's open-air Geere School, for children with tuberculosis, moved to Ascot. At the opposite end of the social scale wealthy exiles from Czechoslovakia and Austria arrived at the Berystede Hotel as those countries were taken over by Hitler's forces. King Zog of Albania with his wife, Queen Geraldine, and son Leka, were also guests there for a short spell. Later the hotel would become the temporary home of the Courts of Justice. During the Second World War 180 cases were heard there, with prisoners being ferried from London for trials.

Other new arrivals to the town were forced to stay in far less salubrious circumstances after an area previously used as the winter quarters for the Bertram Mills Circus was turned into a camp for internees. These included German and later Italian nationals and their British-born families living in the UK after war was declared, some of them refugees from the Nazis. They were detained without trial alongside many members of the British Union of Fascists, who had supported Hitler, as well as Irish Republican Army sympathizers, who had been waging a bombing campaign in England. The winter months were the hardest for those interned at Ascot as they had one blanket and a straw-filled sack for bedding and endured a shortage of food. Accommodation was mostly huts but included former elephant houses. And there was a substantial army presence beyond that needed to guard the prisoners held there. The army commandeered the grandstand on the town's famous racecourse and racing thoroughbreds were replaced with horses from the Royal Horse Artillery, formerly housed in the barracks at Woolwich Arsenal.

Fussy-minded Windsor councillors, responsible for Ascot, had their concerns from the get-go, believing the sanitary infrastructure of the neighbourhood would not withstand such an influx. Hardly in a position to deny new homes to vulnerable children in times of national crisis, a letter was promptly dispatched to the army, asking for assurances that no more soldiers would be billeted in the district. And there was antagonism between the council and the Women's Voluntary Service that resulted in resignations, petitions and hotly disputed debates.

The day after the Maurice Home arrived was a Saturday and, after the usual chores had been completed, there was an opportunity to further explore the extensive gardens. For children who had grown up in the heart of London the rolling green hills alongside fresh air and a chorus of birdsong was a revelation. For Jenny it was a welcome return to the countryside.

'Lucy,' Matron called, 'can you get the other sisters here immediately? We are being shown around the grounds. And we need to know if there are any dangers out there for the girls so it's important we go. I'll pick up a notebook.'

Matron busied herself, thinking of questions for a tour she assumed would be given by the butler. When she saw Mrs Peyton hove into view, she straightened up and smiled tentatively.

'This is really very kind of you to take the time,' said Matron, almost perplexed that her host had stepped forward for this task. 'I'm sure you have many, many things to do in the day, other than see to us.'

For a moment Mrs Peyton looked askance. 'I couldn't possibly leave you to wander around on your own; what would you think of me? And no one knows this garden better than I do. It will be my pleasure to guide you.'

Matron's face relaxed into a broad smile. So her host prized good manners, just as she did herself. When she told the girls that good manners cost nothing – as she frequently did – Matron meant it wholeheartedly. It was just one of the values she and Mrs Peyton would soon discover they had in common.

As they set off, Mrs Peyton pointed out the nooks and crannies of the garden, some already discovered by the girls, as well as the broad sweep of pastureland.

'I do hope the girls make the most of the parklands. There is so much that might amuse them out here. This is a place we call the dell,' she told them, as they came across an area with one end marked by a granite slab, and the other a flower bed.

'Well,' said Matron, thrilled with the site, 'this will be perfect as an outdoor chapel. We can come here for prayers before we go to school.'

'Our church is very close,' said Mrs Peyton, gesturing with her hand. 'It's through that gate, beyond the Lodge. But how lovely to worship in the open air.' Staunch faith was something else they shared, and by degrees both women began to feel a little more relaxed around the other.

Mrs Peyton herself soon had good reason to feel fortunate. Issues with evacuees swiftly became local talking points, with rumours running around the town like wildfire. Some homesick children were openly hostile, she was told, while others were crawling with lice and other diseases. When conversations of this tenor reached Dorothy Peyton she merely raised her eyebrows, always sceptical about gossip or hearsay. It wasn't in her nature to be swept along by other people's opinions, or in turn stoke any fires through idle chatter. More likely the stories were inflated nonsense, she decided.

Perhaps there was trouble with some of the new arrivals in the village, but she wasn't persuaded any of those complaints would apply to her girls. Undeniably they were bright and curious about their surroundings. Dorothy was finally convinced her first intuition, to welcome the Maurice Home into her own home, had been the right one.

In fact, all the evacuees that descended on the Windsor area at the beginning of September mostly enjoyed good health. Admittedly there were cases of lice as well as five cases of impetigo and three of scabies, both notoriously infectious conditions.

Lice were easily dealt with using a razor or paraffin. At the time most people had paraffin in their sheds as it was widely used for heating and even lighting. A far greater challenge were the emotional difficulties that came with the trauma of separation. It was these emotional difficulties that often caused both heartaches and headaches.

Bed-wetting was a common symptom long encountered in children's homes. It's thought as many as a third of evacuated children suffered with this, causing a practical problem for host housewives who had to hand-wash bedding and brave the elements to dry it outside. Government ministers, who mostly still had servants at home to deal with laundry, were slow to pick up on how detrimental bed-wetting – enuresis – could be for an evacuee and host family relationship. Finally, in June 1940, an allowance of three shillings and six pence a week was approved for households affected.

With the evacuation of the Maurice Home going like clockwork, the Waifs and Strays Society turned its attentions to other pressing issues, including the refugee crisis. It was caring for almost 5,000 children at the outbreak of the war, faced a substantial shortfall in donations and it was continuing to take in children on the home front. In 1939 it welcomed its 44,000th child. The nine-year-old girl and her brother had been sold by their mother to a travelling hawker for a pound. It seemed they were destined for a life of professional begging until the National Society for the Prevention of Cruelty to Children became involved. From there the boy was adopted and the girl taken into a Waifs and Strays home while their callous parents were duly prosecuted. Still, a few years later, the girl resumed contact with her mother, building the necessary bridges with the help of home staff.

Two days after the girls from the Maurice Home arrived at Englemere Wood it was Sunday and, for the first time, the girls filed into All Saints Church, Ascot. Initially they felt conspicuous as they came through the door of the red-brick building standing just across the road from Englemere Wood, not least because they were wearing the green blouses and blazers initialled with 'MH', indicating they were Maurice Home children. However, as they were being herded into their seats, they noticed they weren't the only evacuees to turn up in church that day. The place was bursting at the seams.

Any residual self-consciousness quickly gave way when they sensed the weight of solemnity in the near silence of the congregation. All the pews were packed and the rows of upturned faces were lined with grim expectation. Just a few moments late, with cassock billowing, Rev. Herbert Walton arrived for the 11 a.m. service. Now the vicar of All Saints Church, he was a former archdeacon of Grenada. Today he had to draw on all his years of experience as he surveyed the church and those inside it. Standing tall in the pulpit, he struggled for words. Finally, as he twisted a sheet of paper in his hands, he repeated the announcement he had just heard on the wireless from Neville Chamberlain. Britain and Germany were at war.

Although he focused on the flock in front of him his thoughts were with his son Jack, who was in the Royal Navy. Jack's wife Margaret and their three-year-old son lived at the Rectory with Rev. Walton and his wife Gladys. Finally he abandoned his now crumpled sermon and instead asked everyone to pray. It was a little over twenty years since the end of the First World War and many people remained haunted by it. Their thoughts lay not with new arrivals but with those already missing from the pews.

Serving soldiers, including John and Tommy Peyton, had been called away to their regiments. Now all men aged between eighteen and forty-one would be compelled to join the services, in a general mobilization being orchestrated to meet the German forces head on. Dorothy Peyton's butler Jack was also required to register for active service by midnight to get the luxury of choice about which branch of the armed forces he would serve in, or no later than October if he didn't. In fact, Jack didn't travel far. When he got married, two years later aged twenty-seven, he was a soldier based at the nearby Cavalry Barracks in Windsor.

Everyone took to their feet for the national anthem, which was followed by a stirring rendition of 'Eternal Father', a hymn typically associated with seafarers. It became the norm every Sunday-morning service at All Saints until the war years ended.

Afterwards the girls were quiet, absorbing the news. The outbreak of war was expected but nonetheless sobering. The Sunday-school class held that afternoon bore a similarly sombre tone and the joy of the move from Ealing was, for the moment, put aside.

7. Sunday Treats

It takes a village to raise a child.

African proverb

'Blessed are the poor in spirit, for theirs is the kingdom of heaven.

'Blessed are those that mourn, for they shall be comforted.

'Blessed are the meek, for they shall inherit the earth.

'Blessed are those who hunger and thirst after righteousness, for they shall be satisfied . . .'

Rev. Walton was closing his eyes as he recited the Beatitudes to an attentive congregation. His face was serene while he related Jesus's teachings in the Sermon on the Mount, wisdom shared centuries before that still held good today in his view, especially in uncertain times such as these.

Sunday services during the early weeks of the war continued much as they had in peacetime, even if the congregation was expanded with evacuees. But today a small squeak in the front row interrupted his thoughts. When his eyes flew open he saw the girls from Englemere Wood smiling and, yes, nudging one another. Whatever effect he might have hoped his carefully chosen words might have, the cheeky grins he was witnessing directly ahead of him wasn't among them.

He drew to an abrupt halt midway through the biblical verse. For a few moments the girls, as always dressed in their

123

green Maurice Home uniforms, were blissfully unaware of this sudden silence. Elbowing one another in the ribs, their faces continued to twitch with barely suppressed mirth. They were fully focused on the choirboys standing behind Rev. Walton, who had risked a wink to the girls.

But the beams froze on all their faces when they finally realized the rector's booming voice was quiet. As his eyes stared out from under bushy eyebrows, the girls adjusted themselves uncomfortably, their shame-faced demeanour now far more suited to worship. No words were necessary as the lingering silence and exacting gaze of the rector spoke volumes. As they trooped out of All Saints Church, a red-brick building consecrated in 1864, their shoulders slumped as they knew Matron would get to hear of their behaviour and that they would be duly punished.

Most misdemeanours were dealt with by Matron with a fixed glare. Girls froze when their name was called in a particular tone of voice. They would glance up to see Matron's normally warm brown eyes looking stony. This offence, however, was more serious.

As expected, Matron was furious and, after she had forcefully outlined how their behaviour was particularly disappointing as it came at a time when they were trying to make a good impression in a new home and neighbourhood, they were punished by not being allowed jam that week. It was a much more significant sanction than at first it sounds.

Each girl was entitled to one teaspoon of jam for tea on Sunday. Being hungry most of the time, they craved the sweetness that was sadly lacking elsewhere in their diet at that time. Without the fruit spread Sundays seemed a lot less special. But they knew better than to object to their punishment. 'Ours is not to reason why, ours is not to even sigh,' became something of a mantra among them.

Jam wasn't the only indulgence they had to relish during Sunday teatimes on days when they weren't being punished. In its absence there was 'stringy' cake, the recipe for which the girls never learned. However, the dry crumb in their mouths left them in no doubt that it was the product of wartime privations in the kitchen.

On the second Sunday they had been installed at Englemere Wood, there was a knock on the door that linked the Maurice Home accommodation with the main house.

'Come in,' called Matron, as the girls gathered in the room looked up enquiringly.

To their surprise Mrs Peyton entered with a gentle smile on her face. 'I was wondering, might I join you?'

'Of course,' said Matron. 'Barbara, fetch a chair for Madam. How lovely to see you.'

At the sight of her the girls felt awkward and tongue-tied. But soon all the tensions ebbed away, as they all became absorbed in conversation. From then on Mrs Peyton joined them every Sunday evening. She discussed with them the topics that had emerged from that day's sermon, or the activities they had enjoyed at Sunday school. When some of the younger girls stumbled as they expressed their thoughts, she waited patiently and helpfully interjected as they groped for words. But their greatest joy was when she went on to describe an event in her own life, transporting the girls back in time, which often involved her sons.

'You've met George Moore, the chauffeur?' Mrs Peyton asked the girls. She waited until she could see an array of nodding heads. 'Well, he used to pick up Mr John when he arrived back from university for the holidays. You'll meet Mr John soon enough. Every time he used to beg George to be allowed to take the wheel. George would always say no, of course. Mr John hadn't passed his driving test and George knew I would never have allowed it.

'Just once, he said yes. Then the poor man had to sit in terror as Mr John tried to race the train along a road that ran parallel with the track.'

Mrs Peyton chuckled indulgently. Although it seems strange that George would agree even once to the younger man's request, driving tests were only introduced in 1935, just two years before John had started at Oxford University. Until then people learned informally and took to the roads without scrutiny. And with the advent of the Second World War, driving tests were abandoned for the duration.

'Do you like living here?' Mrs Peyton asked the girls one Sunday soon after they had moved in.

'Yes, Madam.'

''Course we do.'

'We love it 'ere, Madam.'

When she heard the chorus of approval for her home and garden, she smiled before questioning a few of the girls individually.

'Jenny, what do you like best about Englemere Wood?'

'I like the trees and the fields; it reminds me of home,' said Jenny, briefly recalling in her mind's eye the rolling Hampshire countryside where she'd grown up.

'And, Monica, what about you?'

'It's the animals and the birds. I never knew there were so many different birds until I came here,' replied Monica.

It wasn't long after Mrs Peyton had identified this curiosity about animals and nature among her new tenants that she began to orchestrate Sunday treats for the girls among her friends. One Monday afternoon, not long after, she once again appeared in the Maurice Home wing, asking if Matron would accompany her on a short walk around the grounds.

Keen to oblige her host, Matron put on a stout pair of shoes and the two women set off around the generously sized lawn. The girls watched the backs of the women, and saw Matron stop and look at Mrs Peyton, as if she was astonished by all she was hearing. Almost immediately the pair began to walk in step again, perhaps a little faster now. When the girls were called back to teatime duties by other staff members they forgot to question each other on what the interlude might mean.

'Get into line, please. Stop messing about.'

Sister Briggs's words had the desired effect. After a few moments of mayhem the following Sunday, the girls were formed into such a close queue that their noses were almost touching the short bobbed hair of the girl in front, although speculation about what was going to happen next continued.

The buzz of excitement was silenced by Matron.

'Girls, best behaviour now. We are all hoping for great things from you,' she said, her voice firm but also sunny with expectation.

Mrs Peyton was taking them to meet one of her close friends. At first, when the suggestion was made as she walked around the Englemere Wood grounds with Mrs Peyton, Matron wasn't sure. The gesture was simply too kind. If the girls got overexcited, she feared they might forget their manners, although their conduct had been exemplary so far, within the boundaries of Englemere Wood anyway. But, she reasoned with the other staff, it was a wonderful opportunity.

Two large cars purred into the Englemere Wood drive, one belonging to Mrs Peyton and the second one, much larger than the first, to Australian-born Irene Borthwick. More people than ever before owned cars, with some two million on British roads by the start of the war. But these two cars were more grand than any the girls had seen before, let alone travelled in. When the doors were opened by each chauffeur the girls stood back and watched as Mrs Peyton got into one vehicle, with the home staff and a few of the girls. Then the rest of the girls squeezed into the next. Slowly the cars continued their turning circle in the drive and embarked on a ten-mile trip to Ottershaw. They were heading for Foxhills, a grand pile owned by the Borthwick family. Irene's husband James was the second son of a baronet.

Once the home of political radical Charles James Fox, Foxhills had served as a convalescent home for wounded officers in the First World War before being purchased by the Borthwick family. Now the estate and farm, with its fifteen staff, including two chauffeurs, was turned over entirely to the Dig for Victory campaign, producing food to stop the nation from starving as supplies from overseas were being sunk by U-boats.

Mrs Borthwick was relaxed and welcoming as they tumbled out of her smart vehicle on to a vast drive. On their first visit the children were transfixed by her perfectly coiffured white hair and charming brogue. But soon they discovered there was much more to Irene Borthwick than met the eye. It all started with a song . . .

'Come this way, girls,' she called, heading off through the heavy skirts of a horse chestnut tree. Emerging the other side, they joined a path to the farm and went towards one of the field gates to survey the dipping agricultural landscape beyond. Quizzically the girls looked in. The field appeared to be empty.

Mrs Borthwick looked from their confused faces into the field and back. 'Do you think I've brought you to see an empty field?' she asked with a broad smile. 'Listen, gals, you need to start singing softly, and then we'll find out if it's empty or not.'

Choosing one song to which everyone was guaranteed to know the words, Mrs Borthwick began with the first line of 'Londonderry Air'. The girls were always happy to break into song, although they had no idea on this occasion why they were doing so.

'But come ye back when summer's in the meadow . . .'

As they reached the third verse, it all became clear, as the ears, eyes and finally the noses of a herd of inquisitive cows came into view, drawn from a valley hideaway by the sound of their voices.

'Oh, Danny boy, Oh, Danny boy, I love you so.'

By the time they were singing the last verse, the cows had sashayed to the gate and had the girls squealing with excitement as they stroked rough bovine noses, before feeling the coarse lick of a cow's tongue on their hands. With the end of the rendition Mrs Borthwick put a finger in front of her lips to maintain the silence. Sure enough, the cows ruminated for a moment before turning and plodding back down the field, unruffled by the encounter and with curiosity satisfied. Eventually they disappeared, and the field seemed as empty as it had before.

Mrs Borthwick continued leading the girls on a tour of her model farm. When it came to the hens she let rip with a 'cock-a-doodle-doo'. Beside the turkey she made a gobbling sound, immediately repeated back by the bird. The girls were in fits of laughter. Putting two fingers into her mouth, Mrs Borthwick issued a piercing whistle and she tried to teach the girls to do the same. Then she led them to another special tree, this one split almost from ground level so it resembled a wishbone.

'When you step through the gap in the trunk, you must make a wish,' Mrs Borthwick advised, and she watched in evident delight as they took turns to take a giant step between twin trunks, each closing their eyes for a moment as they did so.

Walking behind the group, at a distance, was Matron. It was clear Mrs Borthwick had the girls under her spell and her supervision wasn't needed. Still, Matron wanted to be sure there were no overexcited outbursts from the girls that might ruin the outing.

From the farmyard they all headed for Mrs Borthwick's walled garden, home to trees drawn from across the world. With autumn already advancing fast, the trees were shedding their leaves.

'Gals, pick up the best leaves you can find and take them back to press them. I'll teach you the names and you can label them.'

There was a pond buzzing with insect life and, at the

right time of year, tadpoles. Yet perhaps the greatest excitement came when tea was served.

Dainty sandwiches were served alongside a range of cakes by an army of white-gloved servants. Some of the cakes were iced and had a cherry on the top, some had chocolate sprinkles and still more were coated with a generous dollop of melted chocolate. This was in stark contrast to the three squares of bread served with two cups of tea to the children every evening.

Still, despite their excitement at the sumptuous fare, they knew not to be greedy. 'Don't take more than you can eat,' Matron often chided at mealtimes. Each girl was quietly confident she could clear a plateload of cakes on her own. But with Matron's warnings about gluttony ringing in their ears – and the sight of her, sitting alert, at the other end of the table with a flinty gaze being thrown in their direction – they turned down the offer of a second cake, despite continual efforts across the Borthwick household to make them have more.

It was not the kind of food many of the girls had seen in their own homes, or in the Maurice Home. The invitation was a supremely generous gesture and one that the girls would never forget. But sitting in the lush garden in weakening sunshine, appetites partially satisfied at least with delicate and delectable cakes, no one in the group had properly considered how food – supplied in large quantities by the countries of the empire – would reach their plates as the war continued. Those at the Foxhills feast that day weren't aware that at the start of the war two thirds of Britain's food was imported, nor did they spare a thought for how Britain might fare in its new geographical isolation.

None guessed that basic foodstuffs would be threatened as Hitler's war machine began to choke British supply routes, or that later girls would try to steal food from under the very noses of Matron Bailey and her staff to assuage their hunger.

The outing to the Borthwicks came before rationing was introduced. Minister of Food William Morrison didn't forewarn the nation about rationing until 1 November 1939. Three months later coupons were needed to access supplies of sugar, meat and cheese, among other food items. During the war more items were added to the list of rationed food, along with clothing. With the era of coupons came shortages and queues.

For now the girls of the Maurice Home were bathed in happiness. As they made their way back to Englemere Wood that night, the chauffeur-driven vehicle was loud with conversation.

'What did you wish for at the tree?' asked Jenny. She had hoped fervently for a visit from her beloved father.

'If you tell anyone, it won't come true.' Mr Moore's voice attracted all their attentions, although his eyes didn't leave the road. The chauffeur still had reservations about great flocks of children like this one but had been swept up by the excitement of the day, joining the conversation without a second thought.

'Then I won't say,' said Jenny with determination, filling a short silence. 'Thank you, Mr Moore.' In response his nod was almost imperceptible, and for a moment his face formed a half-smile as the conversation bubbled on.

'I loved the animal sounds Mrs Borthwick made,' said Nansi. 'The best, I think, was her rooster. I have never since heard anyone as good as she was, not even Percy Edwards.'

At the time Percy Edwards was a radio star famous for his bird impersonations, allegedly able to replicate the chirp of 600 species.

That certainly wasn't the last they saw of Mrs Borthwick. It wasn't unknown for her to poke her head round the dormitory door after 'lights out' and reduce the girls to helpless giggles by once more making the sound of a turkey gobbling. She would then turkey-strut across the dormitory, with the girls wilfully forgetting Matron's well-worn instructions to ignore Mrs Borthwick should she appear after dark. As the youngsters sat up on their beds, clutching their blankets, she would begin a rambling tale that was interrupted only by the timely appearance of Matron Bailey, insisting the girls lay down once more. Mrs Borthwick would return to her friend Dorothy's side of the house with a grin planted across her face, one that would instantly infect her host.

Yet Irene Borthwick's life would not perpetually be filled with laughter. She had two sons serving in the army, with the eldest, John, becoming a major and, in 1945, an MBE. However, her youngest son Peter, a captain in the Rifle Brigade of the Middlesex Regiment, died on 15 November 1944 aged twenty-two as the Allies struggled to free the Netherlands from Hitler's grip. Afterwards the animal imitations, uproarious storytelling and easy laughter disappeared from her repertoire. His gravestone in a distant Dutch cemetery reads: 'Dear Peter, he died as he had lived, helping others'.

Still, Mrs Borthwick remained a friend of the Maurice

Home and an ally of the girls throughout the war, often bringing spare produce grown in her capacious garden to the kitchen at Englemere Wood to help supplement meals.

In addition, the shelves were sometimes replenished by wooden chests sent by the Canadian Red Cross, which were packed with large tins of jam, marmalade or fruit. Providing food remained a problem for staff. Before the war the Maurice Home and others took advantage of a bulk-buying scheme through the Waifs and Strays Society. That had come to an end and now food had to be purchased on the open market, where it was pricey.

There was no question of leaving anything on the plate. 'A clean plate means a clear conscience,' Matron often said, underlining the government campaign against food waste. To enforce the message, a cartoon character known as the Squander Bug, dubbed 'Hitler's pal', appeared on posters and he was often mentioned at mealtimes at Englemere Wood, as staff tried to make a virtue out of the meagreness of their meals. But often the girls left the dinner table with still grumbling stomachs.

Hungry the girls may have been at times, but they were better dressed than they had ever been before. The Canadian Red Cross and other North American groups also sent generous quantities of clothes and shoes for the girls at the home. The transatlantic styles made of good quality cotton were instantly popular. Now their clothes had flattering darts, diamanté flourishes and pretty motifs. One large package included dressing gowns and hand-quilted bedspreads, with enough for one each for the girls. Known as Bundles for Britain, they included medical supplies, field kitchens and even ambulances, and were delivered before America's entry into the war, which came in December 1941.

Mrs Peyton also asked her friends to donate their old clothes to the home and, while they might have been cast-offs, it meant that some of the girls got to wear some high-class labels like Hartnell, Harrods and Molyneaux, which any British teenager would have coveted.

'Look at me,' said Kathleen as she paraded in a new drop-waisted dress, twirling so the pleats of the skirt flared.

'Mink coat and no manners,' piped up Peggy, spouting a phrase she remembered from the family home.

The donations were fortuitous as the supply of clothes became a headache in Waifs and Strays homes everywhere. With a quarter of the population now in uniform, garment factories had been diverted from peacetime work by the government. Moreover, the society headquarters in Kennington took a direct hit in 1940, destroying a large store of children's clothes kept there. The girls at Englemere Wood knew nothing of these issues, even after clothes were rationed from the middle of 1941. While each child was weighed and measured to get supplementary clothing coupons at the end of that year, their wardrobes were already enviable. And with better clothes came improved self-confidence.

With some satisfaction, Sheila added a flannel shirt to her 'wardrobe'; it was crimson in colour with a white collar. Only later, when she wore it to Ascot to post a letter for Matron and encountered a gang of boys from the local preparatory school in the middle of a games lesson, did she realize it was, in fact, part of a school's PE kit.

Looking left and right, Sheila sought a way of escape. As

a 'home girl' there was no way of hiding she was wearing a hand-me-down from one of the wealthier local families.

But before she could vanish the games master caught sight of her and made the assembled boys part like the Red Sea on the pavement, to create a strawberry-coloured avenue. Instinctively Sheila knew she had no choice but to walk through it with her head held high. And as she strode ahead, she surprised herself by being flushed with new pride. This was the era of make do and mend so wearing something second-hand meant she was being as patriotic as she could be. And she thought her original response to the school top was a solid one; it was soft, colourful and, well, it was the way she wore it that counted.

Still, the girls were not always 'angels'. There were misdemeanours for which girls were duly punished. The sanction of having carbolic soap smeared on a toothbrush and then being made to clean one's teeth wasn't considered the most severe by the girls. At a time when most were hungry most of the time, worse still was being sent to bed without any supper.

But Matron had structured a scheme that helped nip bad behaviour in the bud. The points system she coordinated even had girls policing each other. Each girl was assigned to a team, which had a points tally on which to build. Deductions were made for lost handkerchiefs, lying, backchat or bullying. If six points were lost during a single week, the offender missed Sunday tea with Madam and its attendant privileges of jam and cake. There was also the question of spoiling the chances of teammates to win the points challenge that week. There might have been no prizes to reward the best behaved, but nonetheless every girl hoped for the accolade.

Shrewdly Matron also knew that great adventures and physical exhaustion helped to keep bad behaviour at bay. Although the home could no longer enjoy an annual holiday as it had done previously, Matron and Sister Briggs led mighty treks into Windsor Great Park. Armed with packed lunches and bottled drinks, they embarked on day-long walks, with the 'Copper Horse' as a familiar and much-loved destination. The statue depicting a man on horseback stood proudly on Snow Hill, marking one end of the Long Walk, which leads arrow-straight to Windsor Castle.

At the time the girls had no idea the man on the horse in Roman garb, now made green by the elements, was George III, and far less that the Latin inscription on it ordered by his son George IV in 1831, meaning 'the best of fathers', was an ironic one. The men were known to loathe one another. Now it simply served as a landmark for the day's ramble, with glorious views that made all the effort worthwhile. In the distance, some two and a half miles away, lay Windsor Castle in all its splendour, surrounded by lush countryside.

For the girls the walk from Ascot was lengthy but un-hurried. After crossing the road outside Englemere Wood they were soon on Ascot Heath, skirting the areas used by the army. Beyond that lay Windsor Great Park.

'Look, there's the picnic area!' the youngest in the front shouted. It meant the first part of the walk was out of the way and they could look forward to their meagre bread allocation sitting on tree stumps or their mackintosh squares.

After eating there was time for games. Sardines was a favourite. The girls hunkered down in high bracken, squeezed together so they wouldn't be seen. Then they had to race 'home' before a catcher spotted them. With stealth they cautiously stalked one another in the undergrowth, trying to still the shaking grasses. But usually it wasn't disturbed vegetation that gave away their position, more the helpless giggles of girls who met unexpectedly as they tried to make their way to safety.

When they finally reached the Copper Horse, the view never failed to inspire. They clambered on the rocks that surrounded the statue base and explored nearby fields and walkways.

During these first weeks at Englemere Wood, Matron surveyed the situation with something approaching rapturous joy. Instantly she could see that, despite the war, this was an ideal platform from which to offer her girls an uplifting childhood experience, one they would recall forever. It felt like she had a platoon of Cinderellas in her care, who finally had the opportunity to go to a ball in an actual ballroom. And already she judged Mrs Peyton to be someone who was not only kind but, like herself, ambitious that the girls should also get the best out of life.

As far as the girls were concerned, no ballroom would be complete without a prince – and they had the choice of two. The biggest events in the girls' lives occurred when John and Tommy Peyton came to see their mother. For the moment both were based in the UK and could sporadically get home leave. If the girls missed their arrival at Madam's front door, they might have known from the perpetual smile on her face that one or another of her sons was back in the embrace of Englemere Wood.

One Saturday afternoon John popped his head round the door of the dormitory and said, 'Hello, girls, anyone up for cricket?' In one hand he waved a wooden cricket bat and he held a tennis ball in the other. John had arrived at Englemere Wood for the weekend dressed in his army uniform. Now he wore casual clothing for what he anticipated would be a hard game. Never fond of organized games at school, he had grown used to the army's exercise regime and was ready for some sport.

Sheila was the first of an excited bunch to respond. 'Yes, but I don't know how to play cricket. We've never been taught how,' she told him.

'Nothing to it,' he said with a grin. 'Easy as pie.'

Sister Briggs threw him a quizzical look. Cricket was not, in her opinion, at all easy for anyone to understand, let alone girls whose experience of team games was limited.

John caught sight of the look and his smile got wider still. 'Come on, Sister Briggs, come and show us how it's done.'

The girls were thrilled at the offer and soon lined up in front of him, the excitement palpable. While they had grown used to conversations with Mrs Peyton, they didn't think for a moment that her handsome son would be interested in them.

'This way,' he said, motioning, as he led the column of girls outside.

Instead of heading to the area that had been earmarked for the Maurice Home outside, he took them to the front lawn, which was usually forbidden territory, to school them in the art of bowling and batting. He was smiley and gave a light-hearted commentary throughout the game that ensued. Even Sister Briggs was bowled over by his easy charm.

Just a few weeks after that, Tommy appeared at the door. He was taller than his brother but every inch as sophisticated and charismatic, with a broad smile that lit up his face.

'I say, Matron. I thought we could have a bit of a party this afternoon,' he said, and stood back to reveal his mother's gramophone that he had wheeled along the corridor, with a pile of records balanced on top.

Matron's face had already broken out into a beam. 'Well, I think the girls would love that, wouldn't you, girls?'

There was a chorus of approval and the rest of the afternoon was spent jigging and jiving, with Tommy dancing with them all before returning to his mother's side of the house for dinner. By contrast the meal seemed a quiet formal affair. Yet conversation between mother and son flowed easily and centred on the extended Englemere Wood family.

'They seem a lively bunch. Are you coping with them all?' Tommy wasn't entirely sure his mother was cut out for housing gangs of girls.

'My dear, they are simply *lovely*,' said Dorothy. 'Of course I was worried before they arrived. I had no idea who might be coming over the threshold. But, really, they are delightful, all of them.'

'And good company for you?' It wasn't so much a question as a statement.

'They are indeed,' said Dorothy. 'With you and John away the house felt so empty. Now there's plenty going on – although I miss you both very much.'

Her hand closed over his as she spoke. After the agony of losing a child, the time she spent with her handsome soldier sons was highly prized.

Mrs Peyton had made her way through to watch the impromptu party, just as she had previously watched the cricket unobserved from a window. Whenever her sons visited, she monitored their every move. As the feared aerial bombardment had not materialized, the threat that Hitler posed to the welfare of her family seemed to have receded somewhat and she took pleasure in the way the boys interacted with her new house guests.

Afterwards the girls would huddle together in quiet moments, debating the merits of both young men, about who was kindest and who the more handsome. It seemed to the girls that life couldn't get much better than this. There may have been a war in progress, but it seemed distant, inconsequential even. Evacuation, as it had unfolded, was just fine, as far as the girls were concerned. But another major challenge was waiting in the wings. School in Ealing seemed so long ago now, followed as it had been by the long summer holiday and an eventful evacuation. But a new term was starting – and at least some of the girls at Englemere Wood were filled with a sense of foreboding.

8. Schooldays

Children need models rather than critics.
Joseph Joubert, French moralist

Just two weeks after moving to Englemere Wood, girls aged twelve and under had woken up with butterflies in their stomachs. It was the day they would be starting at Ascot Heath School.

They still had to begin the day with chores, like every other. But then they put on their Maurice Home uniforms in preparation for lessons and steeled themselves not only for educational challenges but social ones as well. A classroom where pupils from a children's home were not teased or bullied was rare indeed.

At least some of the first-day nerves evaporated during the walk to school. It was nearly two miles away from Englemere Wood, along one of the main roads, then a good distance down Fernbank Road. Staff members that accompanied them pushed a bike so they could cycle back. Some girls settled more quickly than others and it wasn't long before both Sheila and Monica were identified as being the most academically talented of the new batch of Maurice girls to join Ascot Heath School.

'Stop jogging me,' said Monica tersely, as she hunched crossly over an exercise book.

'It wasn't me,' responded Sheila, but only half-heartedly. She was concentrating on the task in hand.

'Well, someone knocked me,' Monica fired back. 'Look, you've made a fine mess on my work.' Droplets of ink had sprayed across the exercise books.

'Shut up, both of you,' hissed someone from across the room.

Both girls exhaled loudly as they got back to work. The best of friends when they were playing together in the grounds of their new home, there was an element of competition between them after they walked through the school gate.

'Sheila, can you clean out the stationery cupboard?' The teacher, Miss Rigby, chose to diplomatically diffuse an escalating row, at the same time creating more room at the crowded workspace. On another day she would ask Monica to fill the inkwells. It left the rest of the girls to catch up with work that Sheila and Monica found easy and finished quickly.

After Ascot Heath School had reopened, nine days after the outbreak of war, twenty of the girls from Englemere Wood attended as 'private evacuees'. Of course they were not the only new arrivals. Among other new attendees were Jewish children from London's East End. These were the grandchildren or even great-grandchildren of Jews who'd fled violent persecution throughout the sprawling Russian Empire in the last two decades of the nineteenth century. Woodcote House, a grand country pile opposite Ascot Racecourse, was turned into a Jewish community hostel for thirty-one boys and eleven girls. As well as lessons during the day at school, children studied Hebrew there in the evenings. Then there were other evacuees drawn from different areas of London who flocked into the school.

Desks that were designed for two now had to accommodate at least four. A classroom split by a curtain rather than a wall helped to define academic ability as the numbers rose from 110 in July 1939 to a challenging 182 by September.

More floor space still was devoted to buckets of sand and water, strategically positioned in case of fire caused by falling incendiaries. And classrooms were made gloomy by the tape fixed to the windows to stop the glass shattering if bombs exploded nearby. Still, no enemy planes had yet ventured in numbers into the skies over the Home Counties. Pupil numbers began to fall away as evacuees filtered home when the anticipated air raids didn't happen. But the lack of school accommodation continued to present a serious problem.

One of the most essential lessons of the curriculum now was how to wear gas masks. They had been distributed during the Munich crisis the year before, but there had never been a need to wear them. When it was time for tuition, a groan arose around the classroom. The smell of the rubber, the misted visor and the shortage of oxygen once masks were clamped round small faces often induced panic in the wearer and ensured they were hated by the pupils. But anyone seen removing their mask to gulp fresh air was roundly lambasted by the adults in charge.

Into the room came Miss Mabel Cory, the experienced no-nonsense school head, followed by Rev. Walton, a significant figure on the school's management board. He made it his business to visit the school several times each week, visits that surely must have exasperated Miss Cory, forty-one, who had many pressing issues to deal with, not least the non-arrival of some promised extra desks and what she viewed as the inadequacies of the stirrup pumps left at the school to be used by older girls for firefighting.

Despite increased pupil numbers, there were no air-raid shelters at the school. The provision of these fell to the local education authority who deemed rural schools like this one were likely to escape the worst effects of any bombing. It left Miss Cory in charge of keeping the girls safe and in the first months of the conflict gas-mask drills were central to everyone's thinking.

'Now, girls,' announced Miss Cory, 'you know what to do. Put your gas masks in front of you.'

Cardboard boxes containing the 'life-saving' kit were swiftly produced and placed on the desktops, each marked with official identification numbers.

'Hitler will send no warning,' announced Rev. Walton unnecessarily, 'so always carry your gas mask.' He was parroting the government message, doing his bit, as he saw it, to drum the importance of this idea into the girls.

Miss Cory cast him a surprised glare before returning to the matter in hand. 'Right, imagine you have just heard the gas rattle, sounded by the ARP wardens, so you know there has been a gas attack.' Miss Cory's voice was clear and calm. 'Hold your breath; now, get out the gas mask and hold it in front of your face, with your thumbs inside the straps. Poke your chin into the mask – that's right – and pull the straps over your head. Make sure the straps aren't twisted.'

Rev. Walton chimed in, taking the opportunity to repeat another government slogan. 'Take care of your gas mask and your gas mask will take care of you.'

Behind the visor Jenny smiled to herself, thinking – not for the first time – how like Friar Tuck he seemed, a character from the Robin Hood tales she'd read.

Sheila's earnest expression was largely obscured by the black-rubber mask and the cylinder attached to it to filter out poisonous gases. But Monica, who could hold her breath no longer, suddenly exhaled. With the rush of breath came the sound of a raspberry being blown as the air forced an escape between skin and mask.

She glanced over at Sheila and, when their eyes met, they giggled – but not for long. It was a struggle to breathe in again, with inadequate air making its way through the filter. The smell of rubber soon started to make the girls nauseous and the visors rapidly began fogging up. One by one they began fighting a rising sense of panic. The sound of raspberries across the room no longer reduced the girls to laughter. They were too busy trying to catch their breath.

'That's very good,' said Miss Cory, deciding to momentarily ignore their evident discomfort. 'Now take cover at the foot of a wall.'

Rev. Walton interrupted. 'No, take cover under a desk.'

'The lee of a stout wall is far safer,' insisted Miss Cory.

'My dear woman, it's clearly better to get under these robust desks.'

'Not at all. In the last war it was chimney stacks of bombed houses that stayed upright when the rest of the building collapsed,' Miss Cory responded shortly.

'These desks are stout enough to protect them from debris.' Rev. Walton was insistent.

Still struggling for breath, the girls turned their heads from one to the other, although they were barely able to see anything at all now as condensation trickled down the inside of the gas-mask glass.

Thump. A small masked form hit the deck. The adults' argument was now abruptly ended after one of the girls fainted.

'Right, off with the masks now,' barked Miss Cory, adopting a tone that simultaneously implied concern for her pupils and fury at the visiting reverend, as she made her way to the collapsed pupil.

'Well, really I must protest,' Rev. Walton said. 'They are supposed to wear a gas mask for at least fifteen minutes a day. And please do try to have them stop fiddling with the gas-mask straps. It will damage the masks – and we can't afford replacements.'

As Miss Cory turned away from him, he continued, 'I'd also like to see the girls carry iron rations in their gas-mask cases. Invaluable in times like these. And they should be checked every day, of course . . .'

On 23 October 1939 the county surveyor came to inspect how the drills were carried out at the school, presumably laying to rest this argument between Miss Cory and Rev. Walton. There's no evidence that the surveyor was dissatisfied with what he found.

While Britain was largely underprepared for war in 1939 the country had been stockpiling gas masks, mostly made at a former mill in Blackburn. There was widespread conviction that the Germans would resort to gas attacks against

British civilians as it had been used by both sides in the First World War against soldiers. Masks seemed the best way to counter the threat. What no one knew then was that the gas-mask filter contained chrysotile or crocidolite, types of asbestos later proved to have devastating consequences to human health. So it was fortunate that no one in Britain heard the sound of the gas rattle or the handbell that would have sounded the all-clear. In the absence of a gas attack by the Germans, focus on the gas mask would ultimately diminish.

Given the overcrowding it perhaps wasn't surprising that an epidemic of scarlet fever soon raced around the school, with Englemere Wood girls being kept at home for its duration, doing chores rather than academic study. By the time they rejoined the school population, everyone felt more settled.

Ascot Heath School was two single-sex units under one umbrella, but boys and girls were kept strictly apart, with all communication officially barred. The girls' classroom was long and thin, while the boys' room was at right angles to it. Both had separate entrances and playgrounds. Any boy who was found in the girls' playground could expect swift punishment, and vice versa. Only the bravest would dive round a corner at break time to conduct illicit meetings. That didn't necessarily mean communication couldn't take place, though, as twelve-year-old Sheila discovered.

The Maurice girls walked to school in what they called a crocodile formation (although sometimes the line of paired girls was a snake) with Sheila and Monica partnered somewhere near the back. It was led by Nurse Sheppard, who was frequently distracted by the demands of the younger children at the front. Maurice girls had something of an advantage here. As they went home at lunchtimes or after school, they were permitted to take a shortcut across the boys' playground.

At first it was a case of exchanging glances with the boys who lined up in the playground to scrutinize the new arrivals. After a few weeks, comments from the boys about the physical assets or deficiencies of the Maurice girls were left hanging in the air.

Inevitably the older girls snatched opportunities to communicate when they could. Gestured conversations were begun, then the idea of passing notes was quickly accepted. Sheila, trusted by the teachers for various extra-curricular duties, was soon called on by older girls in the home to secrete notes around the school for their admirers.

'Sheila, come here,' called Violet one morning. Although newly arrived at the school, Violet had quickly made her mark. 'I want you to deliver a note for me.'

Violet was older, more developed and considerably more self-assured than Sheila. It proved difficult to say no when she pressed a note into Sheila's hand, destined for a local boy called Ronnie. Habitually Ronnie was one of the lads parked on bicycles who watched the girls go by.

Later Sheila confided in Enid. 'I have no idea how to deliver this note.'

'It's easy,' replied Enid. 'When you go past Ronnie, dip down and pretend to tie your shoelace, then quickly tuck it under his bicycle tyre.'

The system worked and Sheila eventually graduated to delivering notes when she took out the milk crates from the classroom, after the pupils had drunk the contents of the small bottles provided. She was picked because she was ahead of schedule with her schoolwork. With luck she would bump into her opposite number from the boys' school and thus the note would be passed on.

One day she found herself alone in the playground after stacking the milk crates during lesson time. When there was no sign of her opposite number she kicked her heels for a bit before reluctantly returning to the door of the girls' school. Suddenly she heard the door open and dashed back, note in hand. To her horror it wasn't a pupil but the boys' school head teacher who greeted her. Sheila was duly summoned to his office, along with Miss Cory, and a single stinging stroke of the cane was administered across her hand and registered in the punishment book.

Meanwhile, the tension between Miss Cory and Rev. Walton continued. Friction became evident after Miss Cory aired what the school managers' committee noted as 'certain grievances' about Rev. Walton. The root of the issue seems to have been the marital status of one of the teachers. While single she was a valued member of staff. As soon as she married, the school committee led by Rev. Walton expected her to leave her post and she was given two months' notice. Miss Cory, head of the girls' school since 1936, made plain her outrage.

Still, given the era, it was likely this was the first time anyone had publicly challenged the reverend, let alone a woman, and it sent shock waves around the school community. The response of the school committee, which included Mrs Peyton, was blunt. One of its meetings, held in autumn 1939 at Englemere Wood, concluded that: 'It would be in the best interests of the school if Miss Cory sought work elsewhere.'

The school committee members hoped this would happen speedily, so much so they would be willing to forego the customary three months' notice period. They also felt it only right to warn Miss Cory that any other acts of insubordination would lead to her immediate suspension.

Nevertheless, the minutes of meetings, which were written by Rev. Walton, continued to be peppered with grim warnings about Miss Cory. Owing to her lack of experience and the difficulty she found in cooperating with others she was unlikely ever to be successful as a teacher, he wrote. She resented any suggestions made and 'there had been a marked decline in the manners and behaviour of the girls within and outside the school,' he insisted. It was specifically apparent with senior girls. (This coincided, of course, with the arrival of the girls from the Maurice Home – and the outbreak of war – and it's not known if note-passing between the girls and boys was a factor.) Rev. Walton had hoped that by 'guiding and advising' Miss Cory that might have been avoided, but it hadn't turned out that way. Miss Cory was not willing to walk in his shadow. Another set of minutes, taken by the reverend, calls for her to be severely censured for her conduct.

In the middle of October Miss Cory wrote to Rev. Walton, saying that for some time she had been applying for posts elsewhere and intended to keep doing so. She wanted this passed back to the management committee to prove she was concurring with their wishes.

In a terse reply Rev. Walton wrote: 'I cannot of course

say until your letter has been considered at a meeting of the managers whether it will meet with their wishes or not.'

It seems unlikely that he presented her plight to the meetings, all being held at Englemere Wood, in a sympathetic light. Miss Cory was asked to write a report of where she had applied for jobs and when she had been granted interviews. However, the reverend's enduring sense of victimhood was clearly starting to grate with at least one member of his committee. While the minutes reveal that school managers felt she'd received ample time to find a new job, for the first time there's a note in the minutes of an interjection by Mrs Peyton. She spoke out in favour of the teacher that had been forced to leave and gave support to Miss Cory, before asking to be excused from the meeting. She'd heard from the Maurice girls how much they liked Miss Cory and thought the school couldn't risk losing a teacher of her calibre.

It stands out as the first time one of the committee members had interrupted the invective levelled at Miss Cory, principally by Rev. Walton. It must have been with immense reluctance that he included Mrs Peyton's dissenting words in the handwritten minutes at all. Previously Dorothy Peyton might have been persuaded by any man in her immediate company, but these days she made her own decisions. Now Mrs Peyton wasn't afraid to stand out against the tide – and Rev. Walton felt he had no option but to respect her view, although it was contrary to his own. Mrs Peyton was fond of Rev. Walton, of that there was no doubt. But there was a war on and personal connections couldn't stand in the way of her girls' education. Afterwards meetings of the managers' committee were held at the Rectory rather than Englemere Wood, presumably at Mrs Peyton's request.

The girls knew nothing of the ongoing enmity between the two significant figures in their school life and held both adults in genuine affection. Nothing could disguise the singular care Miss Cory took with the pupils, treating all evacuees the same as those pupils born and bred in Ascot. Yet Rev. Walton too would earn their undying affection, by ending the use of the hated phrase 'home girls' among pupils and his congregation. He made it known they should be called 'Maurice girls', which, they felt, was far more dignified.

Still the feud rumbled on. In visits that sometimes occurred twice daily Rev. Walton questioned why lessons overran and quizzed Miss Cory about the symptoms of scarlet fever to look out for once a case was identified in the school. She had spotted the last outbreak without any help from him whatsoever, she reflected sourly.

Through gritted teeth Rev. Walton finally reported to the committee that an education official from the county council said it was in the interests of the school that Miss Cory should continue as head teacher indefinitely.

When Miss Cory wasn't dealing with his queries she was struggling to find appropriate accommodation for her growing classes. Desks for the first raft of evacuated children didn't arrive until January 1940. Six months later, a school from Croydon arrived, adding twenty-six children to the infants' class and thirty-three girls aged between eight and fourteen. That made the school roll shoot up to 229, and by October 1940 there were 250 pupils.

When the children returned to the school after the

summer holidays in 1940 the Battle of Britain was dominating everyone's thoughts. Although they were removed from the primary target of enemy bombers, the number of air-raid warnings increased in September and October, and pupils often hunkered down by classroom walls for a couple of hours until the all-clear.

By the end of the year the air-raid siren had sounded with monotonous regularity, but no damage had been done to the school or Ascot itself – although an unexploded bomb in the vicinity had caused the school to be shut for a day that November. Indeed, enemy aircraft were by now barely sighted. Accordingly teachers decided to continue in the classroom regardless.

In 1941 there was proof of Miss Cory's abilities as a teacher. A diocesan report on her teaching was laden with praise. 'Miss Cory gave an exemplary lesson on the opening chapter of the Acts,' the report said, and 'the whole class was eager to respond. Such an inspection lasting fully three hours is exacting but the pupils were so keen that it might well have lasted longer. It seemed to me the complete justification of a church school.' In August that year all fifty girls at the school gained good marks in a religious knowledge test.

For pupils there was more to look forward to than merely lessons. The work-a-day life of the school included milk and a Horlicks tablet, widely seen as a sweet but charged with all the nutrients of a malted drink. Horlicks tablets were so nutritionally valuable they were included in the escape kits issued to airmen in the Second World War.

For the children there were celebrations that underscored their role in the war. They took part in school events to mark Empire Day (11 March, now known as Commonwealth Day). The government sought to raise money through national savings during various specially designated weeks, like 'Wings for Victory Week', 'Spitfire Week', 'War Weapons Week' and 'Tanks for Attack'. Before the girls left for school, they filed past Matron to receive a coin taken from their savings that they donated to these numerous good causes.

It was an equally busy time for the Waifs and Strays Society nationally, which received its 46,000th child in 1940, who had been ill-treated by her parents and so neglected that she arrived at school with her feet tied in sacking rather than shoes. And for the society numbers were set to rise.

Many more children faced uncertainty during the war as their fathers joined the services. Any illness in the mothers that were left behind put the welfare of the children in immediate jeopardy, and some children would be left orphaned after devastating air raids, desperately needing the food and shelter that a Waifs and Strays home could provide. Settled into their new home and relishing every moment, the Maurice girls remained singularly unaware of their good fortune.

9. Knitting Circle

The soul is healed by being with children.
Fyodor Dostoevsky, Russian novelist and philosopher

Wide-eyed and wearing their best clothes, the girls stood obediently in front of Matron and Mrs Peyton. It was Friday night – and life was about to catapult them into a new social norm.

'Girls, you are going to join a knitting circle,' Matron explained. There was nothing unusual in that during the war. 'If you can knit you can do your bit', the government's propaganda unit declared to the population at large via billboards and newspapers.

But when Mrs Peyton stepped forward to address them, the girls knew it would be no ordinary outing.

'We are going to see Princess Marie Louise and her sister, Princess Helena Victoria,' Mrs Peyton began.

There were gasps and gulps from the girls, who had no idea that two of Queen Victoria's granddaughters lived close by.

'You must address each as "Your Highness",' Mrs Peyton continued. Language that came naturally to someone who regularly socialized with royalty sounded strange to the ears of girls who'd mostly grown up in slums. They mouthed the words tentatively, and a knot of excitement formed inside them as the necessary etiquette was explained. 'And when you meet princesses like these, you must curtsy,' she said.

Matron waited for a moment for the words to sink in before interjecting. 'Now, girls, before we go, I'd like you to practise a curtsy. Put your right foot behind your left foot, with the ball of your right foot on the floor and bend your knees – and now bow your head and look at the floor. No, you don't need to hold the skirts of your dresses out to the side; they simply aren't wide enough.'

Girls bobbed and dipped in response to Matron's instructions. Some girls moved much too fast, some wobbled and some dropped too low, risking an outright collapse. Matron and Mrs Peyton fought to maintain their composure as an orderly line became a jumble of angled legs and nodding heads. As a buzz of conversation started to rise, Mrs Peyton took the floor again.

'I'm sure they will want to make conversation. Have something interesting to say about yourself at the ready. Don't stand there tongue-tied.'

A look of alarm flashed across the faces of the youngest girls and it didn't go unnoticed.

'Try not to worry,' said Mrs Peyton more softly this time. 'After all, they are evacuees, just like you.'

Indeed, the princesses had come to Ascot to escape the worst of the London bombings and sought refuge with Lord and Lady Weigall, who lived just across the road from Mrs Peyton. She knew them all well.

It was another of Mrs Peyton's ideas, a knitting circle that blended girls from a children's home with royalty. Matron didn't need much persuasion this time. She knew that most of the girls were capable knitters and felt they should together make a tangible contribution to the war effort.

Mrs Peyton slipped away and, without much ado, the girls sorted themselves into the familiar crocodile formation. They left the ballroom and, using the main drive, stopped by the front door for Mrs Peyton, who had gone to fetch a coat. Usually the girls chatted animatedly with their walking partner when they left Englemere Wood. This time, though, there was silence. Each girl felt the weight of expectation, a responsibility for keeping the good name of the Maurice family unblemished by a clumsy verbal slip or an ungainly physical trip. They gripped their knitting bags tightly in their hands and their faces furrowed in concentration as they tried to recall everything they had just been taught. Almost as soon as they set off, they came to a halt. These days the road that separated Mrs Peyton's home from the Weigalls' was always busy with military traffic, with the strategic army base of Aldershot less than fifteen miles distant.

After they were safely shepherded across their feet soon started crunching on a pea-shingle drive and they approached the Italianate mansion for the first time, now silenced by its imposing grandeur. Built in 1815 and named Englemere House, it made the substantial mansion they presently called home look almost pedestrian. The girls came to know it as 'the white house' for its painted walls. Outside were extensive lawns fringed by mature trees and punctuated with fountains. The sweeping drive was lined with tall poplars. Inside, opulent fabrics adorned floor-to-ceiling windows. There were ornate fireplaces, oil paintings, graceful sweeping staircases, antique French furniture and crystal chandeliers.

At the main door they were greeted by a butler and a maid who showed them where to leave their coats, then ushered them into the vast downstairs billiard room. Soon the girls were sitting cross-legged on the floor while Mrs Peyton, Matron and Sister Briggs sat in richly upholstered chairs.

A few moments later, the girls scrambled to their feet again as the princesses arrived – two elegantly dressed women in their late sixties but not yet stooped by age. They shared the same heavy jawline and both grey heads of hair were crimped into submission. Princess Helena leaned on a stout walking cane. But the first impressions perpetuated by their noble bearing – that the women were austere and stand-offish – soon gave way when their eyes began to sparkle as they surveyed the group.

A third woman soon joined them, gliding into the hall in a wheelchair. It was Lady Weigall's house and she seemed equally delighted to welcome the girls.

Jenny was contorted with nerves. She felt it was only a matter of time before somebody said something wrong, and she thought it was most likely going to be her. Yet she also became mesmerized by the older women and their exquisitely good manners.

With every introduction and curtsy the princesses and their companion exclaimed with delight. Now it was their turn to memorize names and faces. They all asked questions of the girls, who summoned up individual responses when required then withdrew, all relieved they hadn't blundered.

When the formalities were completed, Princess Marie Louise asked the group of awed girls surrounding her,

'What do you make of this evacuation business? You are evacuees, and so are we. And we are having a fine time.'

Without expecting an answer the princess turned to lead the girls into an adjoining room where they would squat down and start knitting. To Jenny's guarded gaze, the two princesses appeared to float across the parquet floor rather than walk.

Wielding their knitting needles at Englemere House, the girls joined a vast army of volunteers drawn from across the nation. Knitting offered those at home a way to help frontline soldiers, sailors and airmen, and it also passed as a vital distraction in tense times. Knitting items, including socks, balaclavas, hats, scarves and sweaters, became a universal gesture of loyalty and support, with far greater value attached to hand-knits than any equivalent machine-produced garments. Despite a shortage of wool, the clicking of needles became a soothing soundtrack in homes across the country during the years when the enforced blackout cast living rooms everywhere into perpetual gloom. Practised knitters who worked by instinct and touch didn't need the glare of electric light. The clickety-click sound was heard in factories and offices during lunch hours, among male and female patients in hospitals and in bomb shelters during raids.

Many women knitters had already done the same service for soldiers and sailors twenty years previously, initially turning out garments in numerous, sometimes garish, hues. This time firms like the Sirdar Wool Company began producing wool dyed in service colours. Until this was widely available jumpers liberated from bedroom drawers everywhere were unravelled and the wool was reused.

The Women's Institute and the Women's Voluntary Service were just two of the national organizations that orchestrated knitting circles. Many more were established among neighbours and friends, but few were as special as the one hosted at Englemere House.

Largely the girls were respectfully silent, speaking only when spoken to. In turn the trio of women made nothing of the deprived backgrounds that each of the girls had known prior to arriving at Ascot. All were united in one aim, to bring warmth and comfort to the men charged with defending Britain from an enemy pushing at the door. The knitting bag was a great leveller and everyone in the circle carried their own. Soon it would take priority over gas masks, being carried wherever they went. For now it was time for everyone to get settled.

The four older women sat down and began exchanging news about society figures they used to socialize with regularly. Matron and Sister Briggs listened deferentially, although their focus was mostly on the girls.

Princess Marie Louise lit a cigarette held in a long ebony holder as the girls squatted on cushions and began tackling patterns with varying degrees of success. Setting about their tasks, they quickly forgot to tune into the adult conversation. As some of the youngsters began to struggle, it became clear there should be two groups. Lady Weigall took the six youngest to a side room where they would remove woody residue from the material used to pad splints and roll up bandages.

Jenny was instantly resentful. Certainly she was the youngest in the Maurice Home, which is why she was whisked away by Lady Weigall, but she knew her knitting skills far exceeded those of some of the older girls. Her bottom lip jutted forward. However, on this occasion she didn't dissolve into tears. Instinctively she knew it wasn't the time or the place. Jean Moore, the chauffeur's daughter, was also part of the knitting group and, although younger even than Jenny, was also an accomplished knitter. Her face bore no sign of resentment, Jenny noticed.

As the older girls sat cross-legged on the floor at Englemere House they strived to produce the neatest stitches, not least because their work was closely inspected by Sister Briggs.

'Mittens must have their tops grafted together properly and the thumbs smartly finished,' she reminded them. And each week came the warning: 'No knots or ends are allowed. We don't want these gloves to start unravelling on the high seas. I want to see neat grafting of one piece of wool to the next – and there's no excuse to waste wool.

'Take special care when joining the ends of socks. No soldier or fighting man will want sore toes from lumps at the ends of their boots.'

Once sock heels were completed staff inspected the girls' handiwork to be sure it would reach the exacting standards required. It was down to the staff to press the work and sew together the sleeves of pullovers to the breast and back-plates, and everything was added to rising piles on the billiard table before being taken to distribution centres.

The girls were given patterns produced by the government and aimed at grown-up experienced knitters. Wool was also dispatched by the government to knitting circles like the one at 'the white house'. At first it was a struggle to concentrate on the exacting demands listed on the paper in front of them as they were being scrutinized by the adults. But week by week, as they became more adept at the demanding knitting patterns, the attention of the girls wandered to the content of the adult conversation and, in turn, the grown-ups paid greater attention to the girls. The uniform movement of forearms working rhythmically backwards and forwards helped everyone feel at ease and it wasn't long before Princess Marie Louise took a lead.

There were anecdotes from the princesses about Queen Victoria, or 'Grandmama', as the princesses termed her.

'Do you know, my dears, when I was young I stayed with all my siblings with Queen Victoria and she sent a telegram to my mother, who was recuperating from ill health in the sun, in the south of France. The telegram read: "Children very well, but poor little Louise very ugly." Just imagine that!'

There was instant concern among her young audience for her hurt feelings. But Princess Marie Louise beamed, revealing the robustness that advancing years can bring. 'Well, I think she must have been right. Years later, I took it up with Grandmama. But she said, "My dear child, it was only the truth."'

There were many other tales that were less distressing for the girls. The princesses often talked about King George VI – 'dear Bertie', as the girls began to know him. They learned that when the national anthem was played for him he hummed it quietly to himself because he thought it 'a rattling good tune'. Rather than Princess Elizabeth, they began to think of the future queen as Lilibet, as that's how the princesses referred to her.

And all the girls were delighted to hear about Princess

Margaret. A doll given to Jenny at Ealing had been named for the younger princess, who had star status among the Maurice girls.

Princess Marie Louise endeared herself to the girls not only by her wealth of anecdotes but also by never forgetting their names. She had come to Ascot at about the same time as them. She and her sister had visited their old friend Grace Weigall at Englemere, having been told they could no longer live in London for fear of falling bombs. As it happened the top of the Weigall home had been divided to provide two additional flats, one of which seemed perfect for the sisters. The other flat was occupied by the former Polish ambassador Count Raczynski and his family.

Lady Weigall was ultimately rewarded for her kindness in allowing the princesses to stay. Englemere House had been earmarked by the government for use during the Second World War but because it became the home of two princesses it was declared a royal residence.

The move to Ascot was fortunate for the princesses too. Between the wars they lived at 82 Pall Mall, also known as Schomberg House, a grand building previously used by artists. Together the women transformed their drawing room into a musical salon where famous singers and musicians of the day played to selected audiences. However, it was wrecked by a bomb during the Blitz.

When the girls first arrived at Englemere House the princesses welcomed them as fellow evacuees. But that's where the similarities ended . . .

Matron Bailey's charges had by and large spent a haphazard childhood dressed in scruffs and marked by hunger.

For the princesses it had been a heady blend of tutors, dance classes, picnics, piano lessons, boating – and tea with Queen Victoria, their beloved grandmother. When they were older there were balls to enjoy, alongside riding, weekends at country estates and international receptions.

Princess Marie Louise lived through six reigns and sixteen prime ministers. She was christened Franziska Josepha Louise Augusta Marie Christina Helena – but was better known as Louie. Her sister, Victoria Louise Sophia Augusta Amelia Helena, who was two years her senior, was commonly called Thora. Their mother was Princess Helena, third daughter and fifth child of Queen Victoria, who married Prince Christian of Schleswig Holstein, a Danish-born member of the German royal family. Both Louie and Thora were born princesses through their father's German heritage and in the twentieth century the family had conflicted loyalties. Eldest brother Prince Christian Victor died in 1900 during the Boer War after a bout of malaria. A British army officer for a dozen years before his death, he had previously fought alongside Lord Kitchener in Sudan. Another brother, Albert, was also a military man but served with the Prussian army. Later he was in the German military in the First World War, although he was excused from frontline duties by Kaiser Wilhelm II, who was a cousin. (King George V was another cousin of Louie, Thora and Albert's, along with the king of Sweden and, by marriage, the tsar of Russia, the king of Spain and the king of Romania.) Both princesses remained close to King George VI and his family. However, Louie found plenty to talk about regardless, for she did not live a cloistered life despite her privileged background.

Following the shining example set by their mother, both sisters shouldered charity work in an era before this became protocol and Princess Marie Louise told the girls about the Church Army's 'Friends of the Poor', started in 1911 to provide support for the homeless.

'That's where I met a reformed burglar, "Smith", and his wife,' she explained.

The girls stopped knitting for a moment, imagining a man in a striped shirt and a black mask. Some began to think of him visiting the neighbourhood to rekindle this association.

'His wife wore a low fringe and that's because he bashed her head, leaving a scar,' the princess said seriously. 'In the end he and his whole family emigrated. I hope he is enjoying his new life.'

The girls were reassured but the princess fell silent. Privately she had her doubts about the promised 'new leaf'.

Matron and Mrs Peyton exchanged relieved glances, having feared the princess was about to delve into some unsavoury tales, less suited to young ears.

Some stories the princess did keep to herself, like the young mum she encountered who used a drawer as a cot for her newly born twins, as many people did at the time. However, the woman pushed the drawer into its housing before going off for a drink and couldn't recall the whereabouts of the babies when she returned, until it was too late to save them.

As the weeks went by, the Maurice girls became comfortable in the presence of royalty. The more experienced knitters were soon making thigh-length 'seaboot stockings' for trawlermen, made from oiled yarn that was particularly difficult for small hands to manipulate. And the piles of garments on the covered billiard table got ever higher.

A former president of the Forum Club, located in London's Grosvenor Square and expressly for Women's Institute members, Princess Marie Louise was not only dispatching this group's knitted garments to the services but was also helping coordinate collections across the capital. An estimated twenty-two million knitted garments were produced via the Women's Institute in the war, which were parcelled up and sent to prisoners of war as well as servicemen.

Every week Princess Marie Louise surveyed the girls in her group with growing affection. Once she had set up a girls' club in Bermondsey, east London, where she'd had to stand on a table with a railway whistle in her mouth and a dinner bell in her hand, just to catch the attention of the riverfront factory girls who went there. At least the girls sitting before her were not cut from this cloth, she mused.

Among all the stories she regaled, the one the girls loved the best was about Queen Mary's Dolls' House, which was made in the early twenties to illustrate a royal household in miniature. At Ealing there had been a doll's house in the office and the girls were allowed to play with it on special occasions. As much as they loved it, the Ealing model sounded like a pale imitation of this one.

The idea had been conceived by Louie as a gift from the British people for Queen Mary and everything in it was a perfect replica, only a twelfth of the size of the original items.

'My dears, it has everything,' she told them. 'There's full running water and electric lights. There are tiny books in the library, written by people like J. M. Barrie, A. A. Milne and Sir Arthur Conan Doyle. In the royal beds there are tiny hot-water bottles. And a marble staircase connects the King's bedroom and the Queen's. There's a jar of boiled sweets in the day nursery, real ones. And in the garage there are five cars, all different. There's a Daimler, a Rolls-Royce, a Lanchester, a Sunbeam and a Vauxhall.'

The girls were listening with rapt attention.

'When she saw it Queen Mary said it was "the most perfect present anyone could receive". So many people saw it fifteen years ago when they visited the British Empire Exhibition. Now it's just down the road at Windsor Castle. It's been built to outlast us all.'

When the doll's house had been fully described, the girls lowered their gazes to their knitting once more. But they were imagining the grand doll's house that had earned the admiration of royalty.

From her chair Matron looked across the tops of their heads and smiled to herself. Her girls, in the company of princesses . . . She would never have thought it possible. Mrs Peyton was also surveying the room, with something approaching satisfaction imprinted on her face. She caught Matron's eye. This time they exchanged a smile, knowing that everything was progressing as well as it possibly might when a global conflict was raging.

10. Family Life

For children, childhood is timeless. It is always the present. Everything is in the present tense. Of course, they have memories. Of course, time shifts a little for them and Christmas comes round in the end. But they don't feel it. Today is what they feel, and when they say 'When I grow up,' there is always an edge of disbelief – how could they ever be other than what they are?

Ian McEwan, The Child in Time

The uniformed figures of Matron Bailey and Sister Briggs stood together at the furthest reaches of the garden. Not only had Mrs Peyton opened her house as part of the war effort, but she had also permitted the government to raid her woods as well. Wood was a valuable commodity in wartime, necessary for ships, troop huts and service vehicle interiors among other things. As a result, the two women were running their gazes over an untidy tangle of branches, shredded bark, pine cones and twigs.

'This could be a fire hazard if bombs start to fall,' said Matron Bailey as she surveyed the thick carpet of woody debris.

'Yes, absolutely,' agreed Sister Briggs. 'And there's far too much work here for Mrs Peyton's staff to do. Her butler will be going any day now.'

'Could the girls set about this area, clean it up? Would it be too much for them?' pondered Matron. 'It would be a wonderful way to show our gratitude to Mrs Peyton.'

'Well, they're a very determined bunch,' said Sister Briggs, smiling. 'And wouldn't it fit with some of the work they need to do as Brownies and Guides? I think they will make a fine job of it – and it will keep them out of mischief.'

So from the earliest days of their time at Ascot the girls took part in what they knew as 'wooding', clearing swathes of fallen tree limbs and leaves.

The girls rested branches on their shoulders that measured at least their own height, sometimes more. With larger branches two or more girls took the weight to transport them to the area designated for sawing, a task done either by the home staff or under their instruction. Logs – known as bunker fuel – were then hauled to the store on a cart, destined for the woodshed, to be used throughout the winter either in fireplaces or for the notoriously stubborn hot-water furnace installed in a bygone age in the house, which provided water for the girls' twice-weekly bath night. Wooding proved especially useful during the cold winters, like the first they experienced at Englemere Wood, when the weather was so harsh the mere froze over – offering a new and different set of delights. But wooding was a year-round activity for the girls and became a significant part of their recollections.

To their enormous joy they weren't always alone as they sorted branches and twigs.

'Una,' called Sheila. 'Come here, sit down.'

Agreeably Una bounded over to Sheila's feet and

plonked herself down, panting. Here was another 'waif and stray', a black-and-white terrier that had been found in a nearby army camp.

When she'd heard the dog was unwanted, Matron had decided she would offer it a home – although not before getting permission from Mrs Peyton.

'Of course you must have the dog,' said Mrs Peyton instantly. 'It will become great friends with mine and the girls will adore having a pet of their own.'

For reasons unknown the girls picked Una for a name and found they had a loyal and appreciative companion during wooding, sports and walks.

And in the near distance stood two donkeys, Jacky and Jenny, both belonging to Mrs Peyton and usually to be found surveying the girls as they worked. Girls that had once shrieked at the sight of a puppy were now often to be found hugging the donkeys or racing the dog. On special occasions Mrs Peyton permitted them to ride Jenny, the larger of the pair, with an accompanying staff member on hand.

When the burden of paperwork allowed, Matron herself went to observe, although there were usually other staff on hand to supervise. It was the autumn of 1939 and, with the unrestrained laughter of the girls echoing around and the mere sparkling nearby, life in Ealing seemed a distant memory. As she approached, she heard the girls singing 'Heigh-Ho', a song made famous in Walt Disney's *Snow White* film, released in 1937.

'Matron, look at this huge branch!' Jenny called over, as she heaved one up into the crooks of her arms.

Smiling and nodding, Matron then caught sight of Monica attempting to haul a mightier log still by herself.

'Monica,' she called. 'Wait until someone else is free to help. It's too big for you all by yourself.'

Mr Moore, the chauffeur, strode up to Monica, with a grin on his face.

'Here, give me that, mind,' he said. At first he had been sceptical about having a gang of girls around the place. Now he had thawed so completely that he helped to haul and saw the biggest logs. His daughter Jean was among the girls dashing around Englemere Wood's grounds.

Their clothes were getting muddy, Matron observed, but that didn't matter. Today was Saturday, and Monday, laundry day, would soon be here. And the sight of the girls outside and at one with nature warmed her heart. Her girls were happier and healthier than ever before. Wooding became a memorable part of life at Englemere Wood.

Sometimes Phillipa Stone – Jenny's friend from Ealing – visited Englemere Wood on Sundays, when she taught the girls basic leathercraft. As a result, the girls combined their talents to make Matron Bailey a leather blotter engraved with scenes inspired by 'wooding' in the gardens of the house.

In the sweltering days of summer they would go up to the woods in swimming costumes once reserved for holidays on the east coast. In the winter they were snug in hand-knitted hats, scarves and gloves, and ended the day with a fire that cooked potatoes in their jackets. Before the bonfire was even lit the girls had wheeled buckets of water into position, to be sure they didn't start a blaze that would attract the attention of any stray enemy aircraft.

There was always an underlying fear of fire in their daily lives now, linked to the threatened Luftwaffe raids. It was enough to provoke the girls into action in the dead of night. However, some – exhausted by the day's activities – slept more deeply than others.

'Wake up, WAKE UP!' Sheila cried. Her voice raised suddenly to compete with a jangling bell that sounded the alarm. But Jenny, always subject to deep dreamless sleeps, remained difficult to rouse.

'Come on, Jenny,' pleaded Sheila. Initial prodding at Jenny's shoulder was now replaced with a series of energetic shakes. Eventually Jenny began to stir, and Sheila could detect small movement in the previously prone shape. It was pitch black in the dormitory, but Sheila's eyes had by now grown used to the darkness. It wasn't the first time they had been woken like this, in the middle of the night, and it wouldn't be the last. This time the moan of the air-raid siren could also be heard behind the clang of the bell.

Was it an air raid? Was it a drill? It didn't much matter to the girls now residing at Englemere Wood. Whatever the cause they had to evacuate the ballroom where they slept and assemble in the garden room next door.

Every night they went to bed with their clothing and gas mask wrapped in a bundle that they used as a pillow. At the foot of their mattresses lay their dressing gowns, with slippers side by side on the floor, ready for small feet to move fast. Older girls had been put in charge of a young partner and Sheila was responsible for Jenny.

When Matron Bailey began ringing the brass handbell the aim was to line up, ready to shout their identifying number as quickly as possible. Only after Matron was sure they were all accounted for could they return to the warm mattresses they had so reluctantly left, if no threat from the Luftwaffe transpired. If a raid was unleashed, they headed for a different location. Also, before bed every night a stout table was put on its side in the garden room, next to another upright one, to provide protection for curled-up girls when bombing raids occurred. It seemed like this would be where the girls would spend an uncomfortable few hours.

It took a lot of chivvying to get Jenny to her feet. Aware that nearly all the other girls in the dormitory had departed, Sheila grew increasingly anxious. 'That's right, we're on our way. NO, not that way.'

Sheila's voice veered between softly encouraging – and barkingly harsh. The only thought in her mind was to have them lined up alongside the other girls, as swiftly as possible, because she knew speed was deemed essential. It wasn't just Jenny that impeded her progress, though. She had to haul the younger girl's bundle as well as her own, and both their blankets, while manoeuvring the sleepy Jenny. Matron's flickering torch in the next room was the sole source of light. Sheila pointed Jenny towards it and shuffled her along, fighting more rising irritation as she did so. Despite the darkness, she couldn't help but notice they were the last to reach the line.

Sheila's number was twenty-one while Jenny had been given the number fifteen. Sheila thrust Jenny into the line and dashed behind the backs of five girls to her own appointed place.

'Well done, girls,' Matron's voice rang out.

'Elsie, are you here?' Matron was asking if the chauffeur's wife, Mrs Moore had turned up. She and her six-year-old daughter Jean preferred to take shelter with the Maurice Home staff and girls when her husband George was on duty as an ARP warden, and they had dashed from the nearby lodge where they lived when they heard the warning.

'Yes, Matron, Jean and I are both here,' Elsie called.

At first glance it seemed all the girls were in line as well.

No matter how many times they practised, there was always palpable relief when the operation was successful. Then came the roll call, starting with number one. After each number came an instant reply, even if that voice sounded befuddled with sleep.

'Thirteen?'

'Yes.'

'Fourteen?'

'Here.'

'Fifteen . . . Fifteen?'

With the silence a wave of tension washed over the small room.

'Speak up, number fifteen. Will you call your number, please?'

Once again, silence. Number fifteen simply wasn't there.

'Jenny, where are you?' called Matron, the apprehension in her voice now more evident.

Sheila's heart was sinking with every sentence. She turned on her heels and returned to the dormitory, where she found Jenny sinking back on to her mattress. Nobody had spotted the thin small child drifting away from the line, responding to her bed's siren call. Sheila grasped her once more and steered her back to the others, this time at some considerable pace.

Now Jenny was sufficiently conscious to answer Matron's

177

call. But the darkness was hiding Sheila's face, fiery red in failure, and Matron's sternly troubled expression.

When the calling of the register was finished, all the girls melted away – all except for one.

'Sheila, can you stay behind?' Matron's voice was tense. Tired and stung by a sense of unfairness, Sheila had remained in her place, aware that a telling-off was afoot. She already knew there would be little opportunity to present her case.

'Jenny was your responsibility,' chided Matron. 'If a bomb had dropped, that poor child would have been all alone among the wreckage.'

'But I did –'

'No, you didn't. I trusted you and you have let me down. But we don't have time to discuss this now . . .'

Matron turned her head to acknowledge the importance of speed, even if there seemed little danger of a raid taking place on this occasion. Together they made their way to the garden room and hunkered down to await the all-clear, which would surely be sounded soon.

The echoing siren was the most sinister of the noises that plagued the household – but it wasn't the only unwelcome noise to disturb Englemere Wood during the war years.

Although they felt 'at home' the staff were still keen to keep any commotion at a minimum. And noise often reached a crescendo after meals, when cutlery, mugs and plates being washed and dried as fast as possible, crash-landed on to tin trays, making a din. Jenny was one of the worst offenders as she dried up the cutlery in a daze.

Jenny was already tired at teatime, Sheila noticed grumpily, even though she had slept most of the night before, while everyone else had been disturbed.

'Lockharts,' Matron called with meaning. She often told the girls about a cafe she knew in London in her youth, in which the cutlery was chained to the table to stop it being stolen. Staff lugged a washing-up bowl full of murky water between tables to clean used implements, causing a huge commotion. At the sound of the word the girls would instantly know to quieten down.

Every day the distribution of bread was a major operation. But despite the vast number of slices being produced a close count was kept by staff. In the morning one of the older girls was responsible for slicing the leathery bread, if staff couldn't coax an ancient bread-slicing machine into life. Each slice was quartered. The maths were inflexible, with three pieces of bread for each girl at tea that day, and three being prepared for breakfast the following morning. For thirty girls that meant 180 pieces of bread. A pound of fat was used to scrape on top. Given the tiny amount allocated per head it was often easier to melt the butter or margarine and apply it with a pastry brush. Then the bread allocated for tea that day was put into one tin, with the rest put in the breakfast tin for the following day. But sometimes squares of bread went missing.

Girls responsible for cutting up bread or spreading it with margarine or, on Sundays, jam, used to stash a square of bread up their sleeves and rush to the toilet to eat it behind closed doors. Or opportunists would happen on the tins during the day and dip a hand in.

Of course, at mealtimes the theft became quickly apparent – and the punishment was always the same. Home life came to an abrupt halt as the girls were made to sit in silence at their places in the dining room, without food, until the culprit owned up. It was a process that could last for hours. Matron sat with them throughout.

'We have now wasted three whole hours sitting here,' she rebuked. 'The girl who took that piece of bread knows she took it. Now come along. Own up then we can return to normal.'

In the icy silence that followed innocent girls reddened under the hard glances of the staff.

'It was somebody in this room,' she reminded them.

Only the bravest threw angry stares at the girl they thought was responsible.

Finally, reluctantly and sorrowfully, a girl owned up to the misdemeanour with the words 'Please, Matron, I took it', and faced a punishment much harsher than she would have received if only she had owned up promptly.

Ironically bread wasn't rationed. However, white flour imported from Canada and America occupied valuable cargo space on convoys or was being regularly sunk by U-boats. The ensuing shortages meant flour became highly valued and government posters urged people to 'eat less bread'. Eventually the National Loaf was derived, mostly from whole grains, which was smaller and saltier than normal bread and notoriously dry.

There were agreeable distractions, though. Nurse Measures left and Miss Hutchings, a personal friend of Matron's, joined the staff. She had long been a friend of the Maurice Home, both in Ealing and at Ascot. A small woman with grey wavy hair, she had a brilliant soprano voice and was a skilled pianist. Even before joining the staff, she led the girls in singing sessions, which now increased in number. After her arrival, the singing voices of the girls sounded altogether better.

'Come on, girls, let's try that again,' said Miss Hutchings, after she distinguished a duff note. 'We are so very close to being perfect.'

The girls always wanted to do their best for Miss Hutchings, and all their eyes were locked on to her.

Matron lent an ear from the next room, appreciating the improvements. *Good old Hutch*, she thought.

By now Mrs Peyton had orchestrated still more of her friends in a supportive committee for the Maurice Home and ensured all the girls received presents on their birthdays, regardless of their circumstances. Mrs Elliot, who lived over the road at Sandridge, was part of the committee, and so was Mrs Borthwick, of course. Retired bank manager Cyril Fyson and his family joined, along with many more, as Mrs Peyton found she could capitalize on the goodwill the girls had inspired. Those in Ascot who met the girls were impressed by their cheerfulness and good manners. Without realizing it the girls were breaking down long-held prejudice among those who were stand-offish or even fearful of anyone from a children's home. Still on the school committee, Mrs Peyton was chair of this new support group so had plenty of paperwork to keep her busy.

If a girl was fortunate enough to receive a gift, one strict rule kicked in, to which all the girls adhered. Matron had them sit down and write a thank-you letter on the same day, telling them that the sender had probably worked very hard to get the money for that item.

For gifts that were sent to the home there was a 'correspondents pool', comprising Sheila, Monica and two other girls, Ida and Phyllis. Gifts ranged from two new bicycles, giant dolls and floppy teddies to hand-knitted tea cosies and cotton dishcloths or home-made jam and home-grown marrows. But each was treated in the same respectful manner, and every letter ended with the phrase 'yours gratefully'.

In November the pool was expanded to include all the girls as the annual Christmas appeal cranked up. A printed appeal together with a gift envelope was carefully folded into addressed envelopes that were then taken to a different table to be stamped. It was a process universally loathed by the girls who always felt awkward about asking for money.

But hot on its heels came December and the creation of Christmas cards for friends of the Maurice Family. The plywood used across the bath to hold enamel bowls was removed to become a drawing board. Working in shifts, girls drew or copied festive designs hoping to win Matron's approval.

She would scrutinize each one carefully, praising neat writing and tidy colouring. A fresh idea on the Christmas theme would be heaped with praise.

'Is that Father Christmas?' Matron asked with a quizzical expression.

'No,' said Peggy, frowning and looking again at her handiwork. 'It's a Christmas elf.'

'Well, I like it very much anyway,' said Matron, moving on. 'Those baubles are super, Ida. If that's a robin, Nansi, it's upside down, surely.'

'No, Matron,' Nansi said, hiding her indignation. 'It's Father Christmas, with his sack.'

'I'm sorry, dear,' said Matron. 'I think there must be something wrong with my glasses tonight.'

Once again, the greeting was couched 'with gratitude' from the girls, who then tramped around the village to hand-deliver as many as possible to save on postage costs. Some had to be posted, of course, including to all the old girls that Matron remembered at Christmas.

Thanks to the generous donors recruited by Mrs Peyton, Christmases would be more memorable than ever before. As the festive season approached the girls were invited to write a short list of the presents they hoped for, ostensibly to send to Father Christmas. In fact, the list was distributed among Maurice Home committee members and each girl would get four presents, mirroring those on the list she'd written weeks before.

Festive excitement began in earnest on Christmas Eve, when the tree in the dining room was decorated. As always, the girls had hung a sock at the end of their beds. That night the patience of staff was sorely tried as they attempted to get small heads laid on pillows.

'I think I can hear him now!' cried one voice in the darkness of the ballroom dormitory.

'Nonsense,' said Sister Briggs firmly. 'Now go to sleep.'

'What if he forgets us?'

'I can hear the reindeer.'

'Do you think it will snow?'

'Is that your voice I can hear, Monica?' Sister Briggs's voice notched up in volume. She and Monica shared a close relationship – she was, after all, her godmother – but she was always at pains not to show favouritism.

Hearing the briskness in her voice, there was no reply from the figures hidden by mounds of eiderdowns along the rows of beds.

'That's better. Now, for the very final time, go to sleep. Or none of you will get a visit from Father Christmas.'

Satisfied the girls were finally either asleep or dozing, she withdrew to the room being used by staff, where Matron and the other sisters were seated, enjoying the final cup of tea of the day and wrapped up in blankets, even though the room's open fire was lit. Una was sleeping in her customary spot in front of the hearth.

'I think they are settled at last,' she said, surveying a table covered with oranges, apples, nuts and small bars of chocolate. These were soon to be distributed among the socks. In the corner was a pile of presents that would be given to their recipients over the next few days. Not all at one time, though, as staff sought to prolong the thrill of the season.

'What time will they receive their first gift, Matron?' Miss Sheppard was herself looking forward to the following day when they would witness the unfettered joy of all the girls in an atmosphere charged with excitement. She was also excited at the prospect of presenting Matron with a new pair of gloves that she had knitted secretly in the best wool she could find.

'There's church in the morning, of course,' Matron said. 'I think they will be ready for one gift when they return. Then one in the afternoon and a third before bed. We will keep the last for Boxing Day, like we normally do.

'Mr Moore is going to dress up as Father Christmas and give out the last one that morning. Mrs Peyton has found a costume for him to wear. I wonder if his daughter will recognize him.'

'Perfect,' said Miss Sheppard, clapping her hands together. The transformation in Mr Moore, so gruff as they arrived that first morning at Englemere Wood, was complete. Now there was nothing he wouldn't do for the Maurice girls.

'It will be a busy day. Mrs Peyton has a large chicken for us at lunchtime with all the trimmings. And some Christmas crackers, which the girls will love. She will be joining us.

'Then at three p.m. we must all be sitting by the radio because the king is going to address us.'

His father George V had begun giving Christmas broadcasts in 1932. After his accession to the throne in 1936, George VI had opted not to continue the tradition, not least because he suffered from a stammer, but with the advent of war he recognized there was a need for him to speak to the nation.

'Are the king and queen at Windsor?' Sister Briggs asked.

'No, Mrs Peyton told me they have gone to Sandringham for the season. Lucy, how are the Boxing Day games coming on?'

'Almost finished,' Sister Briggs replied. 'We have pin the tail on the donkey as usual. I think there's enough room to play oranges and lemons. There will be a treasure hunt, of course. I've done the clues already and Mrs Peyton has said we can use her rooms as well as our own. And she has offered us use of the gramophone for musical games.'

Matron nodded approvingly, as having fun came as high on her Christmas list as presents and food. 'I know some of the presents in that pile contain games. One new one is called "Blackout" and another "'Vacuation". We must find time to write our thank-you letters.'

Then her face clouded. 'I can't help but think about the soldiers in France, and how their families will be missing them. I do hope the gift we sent reached its rightful destination.'

Everyone in Britain had been encouraged to send a present to a serviceman, containing magazines, jam, darts, razor blades or something similar. Some of the girls' pocket money had been extracted for the gift.

'Is Mrs Elliot still holding a Christmas party for the girls?' Miss Sheppard asked.

'Yes, that will be on Saturday, the day before New Year's Eve,' Matron replied.

'The girls have got a lot to look forward to, haven't they?'

Suddenly an icy wind howled as it found its way in under the door. Sister Briggs shivered as it enveloped her. With lighting in the room already dim, she took a calculated risk and peeked out through the heavy blackout curtain.

'Matron,' she said joyfully, 'I think it's started to snow.'

11. The Royal Road

It is true, even people with painful childhoods . . .
grow up to be more interesting people. So, there's
always a positive to a negative.

Barbra Streisand

'Quickly, girls, come and report to me,' called Sister Briggs.
There was a flurry of activity as girls appeared from inside
the house and from the immediate grounds. Chores were
swiftly abandoned but the girls had no time to feel a sense
of relief, as they normally would. When she registered that
their upturned faces were attentive, Sister Briggs issued a
set of clear, concise instructions.

'Now, Queen Mary is visiting the princesses at Englemere House,' she began, bringing forth a murmur of
expectation from her audience. 'We will cross the road and
make a guard of honour when she drives away. Remember
your curtsies . . . and remember to smile!' Using her two
forefingers, she drew a big beam across her own face, to
illustrate what was expected.

The widow of King George V, Queen Mary's ramrod-
straight figure was hardly seen in public after his death.
During the war she was evacuated to Badminton House in
Gloucestershire, but when she visited her son and granddaughters at Windsor she would often take the opportunity

to see Louie and Thora, who belonged to the same generation of royals as herself. To them she was known as 'May', reflecting the month of her birth. On this occasion it seemed the royal trio had happened upon another way in which the girls could be made to feel special.

For the girls it was yet another quirk of this new lease of life: greeting the country's former queen as she left one of the neighbourhood's finest houses. In preparation there were some speedy self-administered spit washes while creases in skirts were vigorously hand-ironed as they assembled, crocodile-fashion, to cross the road to Englemere House.

As the large black saloon finally nosed its way past them at a sedate pace, they dropped into curtsies that came much more easily now, after their practice at the start of every knitting circle.

This time the bowed heads bobbed up a little quicker than usual to see the gloved hand of the seventy-three-year-old royal waving through the car-window glass. Her face bore a Mona Lisa smile.

It wasn't the only time their paths crossed with Queen Mary. On one occasion when they were making their way back from school, her car slowed to a crawl alongside them and they were rewarded with recognition and another royal wave. She later professed she was delighted to have spotted 'Louie's girls'.

Princess Marie Louise wasn't the only woman from Englemere House to figure in the girls' lives and sure enough they all discovered there was more to Lady Weigall than first met the eye. She was married to Sir William Ernest George Archibald Weigall, a former governor of

South Australia and, having spent two years there, Lady Weigall chose to entertain her young charges with talk of the wild animals of the outback. As she called like a kookaburra even the most reticent child could not help but laugh hysterically.

'Not so loud, Gracie,' Princess Marie Louise would call from the next room, although she was well used to her friend's theatrical ways.

'Sorry, Louie dear,' Lady Weigall replied, while winking at the children.

In their youthful eyes she cut a distinctive, even eccentric, figure, a striking presence, with piercing blue eyes and plenty of make-up. But age had taken its toll. By now her voice was throaty and she wore a wig to disguise the thinness of her hair.

For years she had been confined to a wheelchair, getting gradually more incapacitated after refusing to have an operation to correct knee cartilage damage sustained in 1928 in a riding accident. The death of her eldest daughter Kathleen, better known as Kit, in the First World War on an operating table under anaesthetic, had left her fearful.

With years of experience now behind her Lady Weigall was adept at speedily swivelling around her palatial home. One of her wheelchairs even had a glamorous gilt finish. She didn't permit her disability to hinder her fashion sense either, and she was immaculately dressed and bedecked with ropes of pearls. On her fingers she wore an array of large and glittering rings.

'Arch-eeee!' she called, high and long, as the specially installed lift doors opened. 'Arch-eeee, are you coming to see the girls?'

Then she produced knitting needles from the bun fixed on top of her head and continued to knit a garment that never appeared to be finished. Lady Weigall was personally committed to producing rectangular tabards made from rug wool on extra-large needles, which she said were for the boys on the minesweepers. They were sturdy squares worn over the chest and back by sailors subject to freezing weather, with the knitted pieces held in place by ribbon. Such hefty garments taxed the strength of her thin, sinewy arms.

Out of earshot her apparent lack of progress with the knitting became an affectionate joke among the girls. With her group of small girls to attend to, the knitting needles stayed in her bun for the time being.

'Help me with this, dear, would you?' Lady Weigall had unravelled a dark jumper that belonged to her husband to reuse the wool. Now she wanted to make the ball into a skein so it could be soaked to get the kinks out. She had Jenny sit with her arms outstretched and palms facing one another, with one thumb holding the fraying end in place.

As Lady Weigall began winding the wool round Jenny's arms she began talking about the history of the house. 'Of course we didn't always live here,' she explained. 'Englemere House once belonged to a man called Field Marshal Frederick Sleigh Roberts. Have you heard of him?'

Despite their youth, all the girls had heard of Lord Roberts, a hero among their parents' generation. Born in 1832, Frederick Sleigh Roberts became a legend of empire, serving in the army at the time of the Indian mutiny – alongside Ivor Peyton's army officer father John – through campaigns in Abyssinia and Afghanistan through to the Second

Boer War in South Africa. Before his death he was one of the most recognized faces in Britain, appearing on calendars, cups and tins. Both he and his son won Victoria Crosses.

His was indeed an extraordinary and full life but it seemed tame compared to the compelling story of Grace Weigall, the present tenant at Englemere House. She had four children by different fathers and divorced in a sensational court case that made headlines around the globe. She knew wealth beyond most people's wildest dreams. Yet here she was, consorting with Maurice girls.

Born Grace Emily Blundell Maple in 1876, she was the eldest and only surviving daughter of furniture magnate and Conservative politician Sir John Blundell Maple. When he passed away in 1903, her father left £2 million generated through the well-known furniture store Maple & Co. to her, with a few wisely drawn-up caveats.

At the time she was married to a German embassy official called Baron von Eckardstein, who was the father of the ill-fated Kit. He was known for his military bearing, a walrus moustache and as a high roller in the gentlemen's clubs of Edwardian Britain. Although a government employee rather than a soldier, he favoured the uniform of the Brandenburg cavalry, from the glittering helmet with its fluted spike down to knee-high jackboots. But it seemed the baron had married for money. After ten years of marriage Grace started divorce proceedings, a move that scandalized a society where a woman divorcing her husband was a rarity.

The baron flatly denied the allegations of cruelty and adultery and tried to persuade the divorce hearing that his wife was not fit to control her affairs. But a jury hearing the case at the Royal Courts of Justice on the Strand favoured Grace's torrid account of their marriage and she was granted a separation and then a divorce, with custody of their daughter. Still, the case left her enveloped in a cloud of scandal. Grace compounded this by having several affairs during which she had another child, secretly fostered. Cricket-loving Archie – whose mother was a niece of the Duke of Wellington – married her when she was pregnant with her third child, although he was not the father. In 1914 Grace and Archie had a daughter, Priscilla Crystal Frances – Grace's fourth child.

In Australia she was asked to speak at a charity that housed unmarried mothers. If anyone knew the pain that illegitimacy could bring, it was Grace. Although cushioned from the worst effects of public shame she nonetheless knew the spear-through-the-heart anguish of giving up a newborn.

'I hope the married mothers in this home will put aside any feelings of reproach or scorn that they might feel towards these women,' she told the audience. 'Christ's example is the one to follow. He never kicked a woman when she was down. He lifted her up. The woman who has sinned should be helped by her more fortunate sisters. She should be shown kindness when she expects kicks. I do not want any such woman to be scorned here. I want her to be helped because her shame is often not quite her own fault.'

So the girls without mothers from the Maurice Home soon won a place in her heart, particularly Jenny. When at first Jenny had been ferociously opposed to joining Lady

Weigall's group, the scowl that flashed across her face had not gone unnoticed by Lady Weigall. She saw that Jenny was much smaller than most of the others and how pale she looked. When she walked across the room with a skein of wool in her hand, the child's movement was unnaturally awkward.

Grace Weigall knew all about the difficulties of living with disability and her heart went out to Jenny. With abundant wealth behind her, Lady Weigall had long possessed a lamp at her home for light therapy, widely used at the time for a variety of ailments, including tuberculosis, anaemia and varicose veins. She also knew that doctors dispatched children who were underdeveloped through lack of vitamin D for light treatment.

The first ultraviolet lights had been used at the turn of the century and had won their inventor a Nobel prize. At first they had been like closed 'baths' that people lay inside. Now large bright lights were held aloft on a stand and directed at the patient below.

With the help of her live-in nurse, Lady Weigall used the lamp to ease her aching joints. Now she wondered if treatment might help Jenny, still struggling with poor health after her uncertain start in life. Rather than risk being overheard by the girls during one of the knitting circles, Lady Weigall wrote a note to Matron, suggesting that Jenny would benefit from regular spells under the lamp. With Jenny's frailty frequently uppermost in Matron's mind, she instantly welcomed the idea.

So soon Jenny became a regular visitor to Englemere House for reasons other than knitting. After donning distinctive flier-like goggles, she enjoyed treatments under

Lady Weigall's sun lamp, with Lady Weigall's nurse in charge of the sessions. Jenny relished the warmth of the lights on her translucent skin and being singled out for special attention in equal measure. Before long, the nine-year-old plucked from rural poverty thought nothing of sauntering into this impressive house, finding her way to the treatment room and cheerfully greeting Lord or Lady Weigall if she met them en route.

And so eight adventurous months of evacuation continued for the girls, who were revelling in the countryside and meeting princesses. The anticipated air raids didn't materialize and people began joking about the 'Bore' war, with British troops entrenched and immobile along the Belgian border. Evacuees felt they could return home with confidence and people often left their gas masks at home when they went outside. However, it turned out that Hitler and his forces had been waiting for better weather. And when their operations got underway, the consequences for everyone at Englemere Wood would be momentous.

12. Missing

The primary obligation of any prisoner is to escape.
Whether that means actually leaving or simply figuring out
a way to handle things so you don't go crazy is up to you.
George Orwell, Nineteen Eighty-Four

When the girls filed into church on Sunday, 26 May 1940 the atmosphere was leaden.

Ahead of the group, Matron wore an expression of grim fortitude. But it was the taut face of Dorothy Peyton that commanded their attention. With tension twitching in her jaw and eyes that were not tearful but certainly looked glassy, the girls knew something of enormous importance was unfolding.

At the time most people heard the news headlines via the eight million wireless sets distributed around Britain, read it in the daily newspapers sold on street corners or saw footage in short broadcasts as part of a cinema programme. The girls were aware that Dorothy's eldest son John was away in France, fighting with the British Expeditionary Force (BEF), and they had heard wireless broadcasts about the events unfolding there. Across the English Channel the Battle of France was now raging, with encircled British servicemen racing to meet rescue ships. Where was John Peyton now?

A Sunday visit to church was usual in any event for the residents of Englemere Wood. But on this occasion it was in response to a call from King George VI, who'd asked the nation to join him and the rest of the Royal Family in a day of prayer. If Britain was to fight on in the war, it needed its army back and there seemed little else anyone on the home front could do for now, other than pray. He and the queen had left Windsor for London, and were at Westminster Abbey with numerous dignitaries, their solemn gaze captured by the news cameramen.

The government, now led by Winston Churchill, was being constantly updated on a rapidly deteriorating situation. Troubling words appeared in public broadcasts like 'withdrawal' and 'regrouping'. Officials told a worried public that Dunkirk was 'powerfully entrenched', which chimed with a generation that had got used to trench warfare during the four long years of the First World War.

On the same day the nation turned to prayer, Field Marshal John Gort, the commander of the BEF, told the British government, 'I must not conceal from you that a great part of the BEF and its equipment will inevitably be lost even in the best circumstances.'

Luftwaffe bombers had destroyed the port and blocked its entrance, so the Royal Navy's big ships couldn't get close enough to the men that needed saving. First, the navy telephoned boatbuilders around the coast to locate vessels that could negotiate the shallow, shelving beaches. But still more were needed.

Three days after the church service the BBC broadcast a call for help from boat owners and experienced hands, who were asked to contact their nearest registrar or Royal

Naval Reserve (RNR). A fleet of small craft assembled, including fishing boats, paddle steamers, lifeboats, barges and ferries. Most were privately owned and with a shallow draught, the most diminutive being an 18-foot open fishing boat called *Tamzine*. And while men from the RNR were at the helm of some, owners and civilians also joined the effort. Not all of them would return.

Initially the best hope among politicians was to save 20,000 men. After five days there was triumph as 338,000 British and French fighters were safely brought to south-coast ports. Headlines crowed incredulously about a miracle that they saw unfolding as the ships docked. Mourning the loss of the *Gracie Fields*, an Isle of Wight ferry, broadcaster J. B. Priestley dubbed it an 'excursion to hell' with the plucky sailors 'snatching glory out of defeat'.

Retreating British soldiers had got help from another unexpected quarter. Confident in the ability of the Luft-waffe to contain the British army as it seeped to the French shores, Hitler had held his hitherto rampant Panzer divisions at bay – giving columns of men time to flee an eroding front line and board boats bound for the UK.

But of John Peyton there was no word. It soon became clear that he was not among the early returnees. Typically, no matter how weary or wounded, soldiers wrote to their loved ones as soon as they docked at the south-coast ports. Swift postal services in a country that relied on the speed of its mail for communication meant good news arrived within a day, or two at the most. Even as prayers were being fervently muttered that Sunday, men had started to be returned by the thousand. But there was no rattle of the letterbox bringing good news for Dorothy

Peyton, although neither was there a telegram, which was most likely to announce a death.

Four days after the church service, as Dorothy headed unobtrusively for her favourite corner of the garden, she was intercepted by Matron, voicing the concerns of Maurice Home staff and children alike.

'Any news?'

Yet she already knew the response from Dorothy's ashen-faced appearance.

'Nothing yet . . . but there's still hope,' said Dorothy heavy-heartedly.

Matron nodded and withdrew, understanding the older woman's need for contemplative peace.

For Dorothy the ominous silence was maintained until 3 June, a Saturday, when John's name appeared for the first time on a Ministry list, marked down as 'missing'. Missing meant his fate was unknown. Could he be wandering around French lanes, injured and dazed? Was he being hidden from German patrols by kindly French farmers in an outhouse? Or was his lifeless body being pulled in and out of the shallows with the tide on the beach at Dunkirk, a death as yet unrecorded?

Dorothy stared at the words on the official notification, willing them to tell her more. But all she knew with certainty was that his body had not yet been fished out of the sea and identified.

Operation Dynamo, the iconic rescue mission that captured the nation's imagination, had almost concluded when that list was issued, and the country was vibrant with the heroics at Dunkirk. That joy wasn't shared at Englemere Wood.

In response to the news that John Peyton was missing, the girls were even quieter than normal when they played outside and crept past the doors of his mother's quarters, for fear of disturbing her. After so many months the war suddenly seemed real and personal to them. Mrs Peyton's pain was shared by them all, although there was little they could do to help. That wouldn't stop them trying, though.

To mark their host's birthday on 19 June, the girls made a cake and bought some chocolates. Barbara was by now the eldest of the girls and she presented the cake, which had been decorated by Nurse Sheppard. Jenny, still the youngest, carried the sweets. Sitting in a sunken garden in the shade of an elderly oak tree, Mrs Peyton was visibly moved by their gentle consideration. But the kind gesture couldn't take away the nagging anxiety that she was experiencing, during every waking hour.

It was six long weeks later that the list was amended and a new notification revealed that John had fallen into enemy hands and was now a prisoner of war. The relief for Dorothy was immense. She'd already borne the bottomless grief of losing one son. At least John was alive, although she didn't know initially if he was well. Only much later did she find out the details of what had happened, when she discovered he was among the earliest soldiers to be captured.

A full week before the girls from Englemere Wood crowded into the church with the rest of the congregation at the behest of the king, John had been crouching in the flimsy shelter of a Belgian pigsty, aware it was probably only a matter of hours before he was found by Germans. When he was finally cornered it was still days before the name 'Dunkirk' became etched on the consciousness of the British nation. As the girls kneeled and prayed their hardest for his welfare, John was already a prisoner.

Like the rest, he had been nonplussed by a sudden surge of enemy soldiers that left him marooned from his men and uncertain about his direction. Every instinct told him to escape the impending onslaught, but he didn't know how to plot a route to freedom, nor did he even have much time to consider his next move.

A German army that was fast and fluid put paid to any hopes that the naive strategy drawn up to defend France might work. Along with countless others, he never made it to those oil-blackened beaches on the French coast, having been overtaken by the swiftly moving first wave of German soldiers who, he noted, 'had the air of men who understood what they were doing, knew that they were winning and were enjoying themselves'. His war was over before he made it out of Belgium.

Until the pigsty became his refuge, there had been flashes of hope. On one occasion three RAF fighters – deemed absent from the skies over the Low Countries at the time – shot down a German plane, to the cheers of the assembled British soldiers. Yet there was overwhelming confusion, rooted in poor communication. Some early reports had British forces in the ascendancy – which left them all baffled by the subsequent order to withdraw.

Mystified, John listened to a BBC report of a monumental tank battle taking place at Louvain in Belgium, some fifteen miles east of Brussels and in the same neighbourhood. John was sure the only tanks in the area belonged to the Light Brigade of the 1st Armoured Division – and he could see with his own eyes that they were not in action at all. Nor was it an onslaught of Panzers that he and his men feared. At this time the greatest threat to tank crews seemed to be hit-and-run attacks by Germans on motorcycle combinations. Agile and deadly, the motorcycle riders screeched to a halt while passengers fired a short burst of armour-piercing bullets at targets before accelerating into the distance. British tanks did not fare well in Belgium and France. When the last vestiges of the 1st Armoured Division returned to Britain in June 1940 it was without a single vehicle.

John may not have been ferried home on the ships mobilized to fetch the remnants of a beaten British army so it could fight another day, but he knew he was luckier than some. He had already witnessed charred bodies pinned under burnt-out vehicles and streams of desperate refugees trudging hopelessly ahead of the German advance. In fact, it was slow-moving refugees with prams, bicycles, cars and carts precariously laden with goods snatched from their homes that stalled the movements of defenders like John. Yet at times they all moved as one, diving for cover before being strafed by rapid fire from a low-flying Luftwaffe fighter.

On 18 May, shortly before his capture, John had watched powerlessly as John Livingstone-Learmonth, a troop leader in his regiment, was killed by a shell that seemed to move in slow motion before it landed squarely in the chest of the ill-fated second lieutenant. After that shocking incident John's recall is hazy. He became separated from his motorcycle and sidecar and joined a group of other soldiers running in what they fervently hoped was the direction of the coast.

The chaos that engulfed the BEF, and those other forces dispatched as reinforcements, came as no surprise to John Peyton who had already observed first-hand many of the shortcomings of the British army in the immediate aftermath of the declaration of war. He had chosen to leave Oxford University and join the army after Hitler occupied Prague in the spring of 1939, as it seemed to him from then that conflict was inevitable.

At first university life had suited him. John ate well, enjoyed horse racing and gambled excessively, while avoiding the rigours of sport. He dipped his toe in the water of university politics to no great effect. But when Neville Chamberlain returned from Munich in 1938, waving a piece of paper and declaring 'peace in our time', John was sceptical. In the same year his father Ivor had tumbled on to a railway track and John had given evidence at the subsequent inquest. Although they were not close, there were jarring unanswered questions festering at the back of John's mind about a father who even in death remained a distant figure. Other than a military heritage, they shared little else.

By the summer of 1939 John was in uniform and heading for York to join his regiment, the 15th/19th Hussars. On his first evening there he sat next to Mary Wyndham, danced with her afterwards and fell in love. At the time he had no idea how long it would take for this relationship to blossom. For now they parted with promises.

After the outbreak of war there was a long period of inaction, dubbed the phoney war. John was facing a different war to the one his father knew, with another array of frustrations. British tanks performed poorly in the field, he observed, with enough sharp edges and metal spikes inside to do serious injury.

Before being sent to France he was comprehensively taught about the dangers of gas warfare but forgot most of what he learned as he kicked his heels at various UK-based barracks. He was lectured on the strength, length and depth of the Maginot Line, built by France after the previous war to repel any German incursion, but noticed with unease the undefended gap in defences around the Low Countries. He found officers officious and instructors inept. Perhaps for the first time John began to understand the sadness and disappointment his father experienced.

An estimated 5,000 men died during the retreat to Dunkirk. A further 220,000 men remained in France at the conclusion of the Dunkirk evacuation. These men made their way to other ports, including Le Havre, Cherbourg and St Malo in the north, as well as Brest and St Nazaire in the west, in the hope of repatriation.

While they ducked and dived around French country-side, John was installed in a German prisoner of war camp. He first spent time at a transition camp in Brussels before he and fellow officers were transported to Warburg, to a new camp in north-west Germany, although the recently opened accommodation was far from adequate. John was assigned a hut that had more than a hundred occupants who slept on straw mattresses on high wooden bunk beds.

Under the Geneva Convention officers were not required to work, which meant there was little to occupy their time. In common with prisoners of war across the Reich the food was poor, consisting mainly of thin soup and black bread. Thus the days were dominated by boredom, hunger and dreams of escape as one month merged with the next.

On several occasions he was allowed out of the camp, either to watch a film show or to gather fuel in nearby woods. A letter he wrote after one outing reveals the profound effect a spell in the countryside had on him. 'It was an exciting experience to find oneself alone for even a short time, to be in a wood again, to see the miracle of colour that exists in a single leaf. After even a short period of two hours the restraint and leaden inertia of the prison camp began to fall away. I found myself face to face with life and beauty; those things which for a long time have been matters of hope and belief were proved as facts before my eyes ...' The next portion of the letter was censored for reasons that at this distance seem unclear.

At times his thoughts strayed to Englemere Wood, where he correctly guessed the Maurice girls were in raptures about the lush spectacle that nature was providing. In his mind's eye he could see his mother drifting around her beloved garden, cutting flowers and greenery to spread around the house. She would be worried, he knew, and frustrated she couldn't do more for him. And he wasn't the only one sparing a thought for the plight of Mrs Peyton at that time.

His mother was sitting in her drawing room on the last Saturday in July, with John uppermost in her thoughts, when a volley of barks from the dogs told her the postman had arrived. Mrs Osborn brought in the post.

'I think there's a special one in there for you, ma'am,' she said before she left.

The letter in question was in a heavy-gauge paper

envelope. Mrs Peyton went to her desk to retrieve a letter knife and when she pulled out the note she immediately noticed the royal crest at the top. It had come from Buckingham Palace and was written by the queen's lady-in-waiting. Lady Weigall had told the Royal Family about how Mrs Peyton was sharing her home with evacuees, the letter said. 'The queen thinks it is indeed good of you to have given up a room [illegible] so much and Her Majesty feels sure that the gratitude and happiness of the children now living in your house will be a reward, if one may use the word in that sense, for your kind and generous act.'

Mrs Peyton sank back into the chair. She knew the sentiments were genuine. But it was the timing that made the gesture so special. It was, she suspected, as much to do with recent news of John's capture and incarceration as for her involvement with the Waifs and Strays Society. The queen was extending comfort to her in this thorny time. Nor were the newly forged family at Englemere Wood quickly forgotten by the Royal Family.

A month later, on Friday, 23 August 1940, the calm of a summer afternoon was broken by the clang of a bulky black telephone, the handle vibrating in its cradle.

'Ascot 433,' said Mrs Osborn. 'Yes, I'll fetch Mrs Peyton now.'

If they heard it at all, the girls took no notice of the distant ring, nor did they notice Mrs Peyton subsequently talking to Matron. But suddenly they were summoned from the garden and the dormitory.

'Quickly, get ready and look your best,' they were told by Sister Briggs. 'Something very exciting is going to happen.'

Almost immediately she corrected herself. 'It might not happen – don't be disappointed if it doesn't.'

No one had the courage to ask a question when Sister Briggs was struggling to make any sense. Mystified, the girls got cleaned up and changed into Maurice Home uniform, including hats and blazers. Given the way their lives were turning out in Englemere Wood, these days they felt ready for anything.

Most assumed they were heading to Englemere House as it was a knitting circle night. But this was far earlier than the usual appointed time and no one had asked them to pick up their knitting bags.

Suddenly they were aware of a group that had recently arrived in the garden. There were the recognizable profiles of the princesses from Englemere House and Dorothy Peyton. But there were others too, making sedate progress towards the Maurice Home's quarters, with something achingly familiar about the woman who led the way. In a split second, the girls understood who was visiting. As the sun poked out from behind rolling clouds, they saw the distinctive silhouette of the queen wearing one of her familiar pinned, brimmed hats, sitting like a crescent on her head. As she approached them, her features became clearer and they saw her warm smile. Instinctively the girls knew this was no time to let soaring exhilaration get the better of them. Feeling the eyes of the staff on them, the elated girls straightened up ready to curtsy.

With a typically endearing humility the queen's first words were an apology that the king wasn't there to see them as well. As the youngest in the home, Jenny was picked to shake hands with the queen, an immense honour. It was the stuff of dreams and the youngster nearly swooned.

The queen was one of the patrons of the Waifs and Strays Society, along with the king and his mother, Queen Mary, so her interest in the girls was a given. Within moments Princess Elizabeth and Princess Margaret – at thirteen and nine, both similar in age to the girls at Englemere Wood – came running up from the direction of the mere. Relaxed in the company of older relatives, they began asking questions of the girls, revealing a genuine curiosity about their circumstances. As the royal children didn't go to school, they must have been eager to hear details of daily life at Fernbank Road. The young princesses were committed knitters, so they had that in common with the Maurice girls. There was animated conversation and the moment was captured on camera.

'Line up, girls, let's record this special event with a photograph,' called Princess Marie Louise, knowing the girls felt less awkward with very specific instructions.

Too soon, the girls were once again assembling to go back inside while the royal party was heading back to Englemere House. The privilege they had been shown wasn't lost on them.

'I can't believe we've met the queen and the princesses,' said Barbara in wonder.

'Princess Elizabeth is so beautiful, and the queen was so kind,' Sheila burbled.

As soon as the queen was out of earshot, Jenny declared she would never again wash the hand that had been gripped by royalty. Sensing their excitement, Una barked and ran round their legs, but they were too preoccupied to pet her.

Matron and Sister Briggs watched the girls go back inside, for once distracted by their own racing thoughts rather than being alert to the girls' behaviour. To meet the popular royals in their own backyard felt dreamlike and whimsical. The Royal Family was revered by everyone; they were the figureheads of the national struggle. To have figuratively and literally rubbed shoulders with these icons was a singular moment that none would forget.

13. Reunited

Parentage is a very important profession; but no test of
fitness for it is ever imposed in the interest of the children.
                                                    George Bernard Shaw

The piercing whistle of a steam train told Queenie Clapton she was nearly at her destination. As the countryside melted away past the train window more slowly now, she felt apprehensive about what the future might hold. Her new home would be at Ascot, she was told, but she was given no further details than that.

'This is our stop,' announced Miss Toynbee from the Waifs and Strays Society, as the train jerked to a halt. 'Pick up your bag and let's go.'

Queenie's mind started racing. When she had first gone to the St Mary's Waifs and Strays home in Cheam, some five years previously, she hadn't been particularly fearful and her experiences there were mostly positive ones. Since then, she'd seen a different side to institutional childcare, and she felt her concerns burning a hole in her stomach.

It was the spring of 1941 and Queenie's schooldays were judged to be over. But what sort of working life could she expect in this country town? Then there was the anxiety of meeting new roommates. After a short walk, she and Miss Toynbee rounded a gateway into a drive. Queenie surveyed the scene. It wasn't the first mansion she'd been sent to by the society. The one she had been evacuated to in Frant was considerably larger than this. But she hadn't stayed long, then got sent to another home where she was miserable. There was no way of gauging whether she was going out of the frying pan and into the fire. Her step got heavier as they approached the door.

Hearing a rap, Matron Bailey checked the time, rose from her chair and smoothed her uniform.

When she answered the door she raised her chin and adopted a sombre expression. As she expected, she was met by the slight figure of a girl, recently turned fourteen and considered to be at a fork in life's road.

Her memory of Queenie was as a small pale figure swamped in bedclothes and fighting off a devastating illness. Matron had read recently drawn-up records, and still couldn't quite believe the child she recalled so fondly had grown into the inveterate troublemaker the reports made her out to be. But she knew this was no time for sentimental reunions. If Queenie was to be saved from spiralling out of control, then she, Matron, would have to be resolute in her dealings with the girl from the get-go.

'Queenie Clapton,' said Matron, fixing the young girl with a steady and compelling gaze, 'I hope you are going to behave yourself with me. Because if not, your next place will be borstal.'

Queenie's eyes widened – but not in fear. She remembered Matron Bailey from St Mary's Home in Cheam. At that time Queenie was finding her feet after being parted from her parents, while Matron was in her first post. She knew Matron Bailey would quickly thaw. For Queenie the overbearing sense of trepidation that had been weighing on her shoulders for the entire trip to Ascot vanished in an instant.

There were many introductions made – to Joan, Sheila, Barbara, Nansi, Peggy, Dawn, Enid and Jenny – as well as a volley of instructions, but the words that stuck in her mind came from Matron.

'You are a clever girl, Queenie,' she said seriously. 'You will be going back to school. In my opinion you should do very well.'

Queenie couldn't hide her joy and set about getting to know the rest of the girls in the home with optimism. As for Matron, she headed back to her office to consider her options. Queenie needed taking in hand, it was true, but she was confident she and her staff were equal to that task. In fact, she was already prepared to believe Queenie would be one of her success stories.

After leaving St Mary's in 1939, life had gone wrong for Queenie. Her sister Gladys had left the home aged fourteen and was now back living with their mother. Did Queenie feel abandoned by her family? Or had the calming presence of a sibling been sorely missed? Even now Queenie couldn't recall why she and a group of others had run away from Shernfold Park, where the St Mary's Home had been evacuated.

Aged just twelve and branded a ringleader, she was sent to a convent in Leamington Spa, Warwickshire. It was a religious community, not run under the auspices of the Waifs and Strays Society. She was there when neighbouring Coventry was blitzed on 14 November 1940, killing more than 550 people and causing chaos. Waves of bombers filled the moonlit skies, the throb of their engines striking terror into those below. Six people died in Leamington that night, as well as those killed in Coventry. It was a traumatic episode followed by days of deprivation that scarred the population of the Midlands.

Going to school in Leamington, the significance of the Coventry raid, which dominated the wartime narrative for some time, must have brought the war sharply into focus. That she remained more concerned with life at the convent – which she detested – reveals just how bad things must have been there. Nuns ensured that children began the day with a spell in the chapel followed by breakfast, which was spent listening to one of the nuns reading aloud from the Bible.

Those girls who didn't attend school stayed at the convent to make tin soldiers, which were duly sold. The toys arrived in flat packs and had to be clipped together at the nose, hands, legs and feet before heading for the shops. Some of the soldiers stood six inches tall while others were made to sit in toy cars. The work was done in silence.

Before lunch there was another service in chapel to attend and at dinner times in the evening there was again no talking, as a priest was in attendance. At night Queenie watched in disbelief as many of the older girls climbed out of windows to visit Leamington. Only much later did she realize they were probably young prostitutes, still plying their trade despite their incarceration.

With her formal education drawing to a close, it seemed Queenie was destined for a life making toy soldiers with the other girls, for the next few years at least. It was a horrifying prospect.

One day at school her best friend asked her, 'Why don't you run away? That's what I'd do.'

Queenie thought for a moment. 'What if they catch me? That's what happened before – and then I came here.'

The notion of being returned to the convent following a failed escape bid, with even fewer privileges than she had now made her shudder.

'You've still got a mother, haven't you? She'll help. Why don't you write to her?' While the other girl spoke with certainty Queenie was thoughtful. Her mum had not stayed in touch by letter, as some other mums had, and it didn't seem likely she had the wherewithal to intervene. But did she have any other options?

'Maybe writing a letter is the way forward,' Queenie agreed, and she tore a page from her school exercise book. Soon the duo's heads were bowed together as they sorted out the necessary words.

'Tell her she's got to come and get you.'

Queenie welcomed the advice, but privately she doubted that would ever happen and didn't want to say so. She sucked the end of her pencil and looked out of the window. At the bottom of the grounds there was a glassy lake.

'I know,' she said. 'I'll tell her that I'm going to drown myself if she doesn't do something.'

The letter was duly signed and sealed. But how would she post it when she didn't have the money for a stamp?

'Here, give it to me,' said her friend. 'I'll give it to my mum and she'll post it for you.'.

Queenie waited with a sense of unease. She had no idea if the letter had even been posted, let alone read. But finally, within a few weeks, there was a response.

Mother Superior found her and said, none too kindly, 'Miss Clapton, you go and get your belongings. Someone will be coming to pick you up and take you away.'

Miss Toynbee soon arrived. She told Queenie she was going back to the Waifs and Strays Society, although at the time Queenie didn't realize she had been under a different regime. Now here she was, reunited with Matron and filled with hope for the future.

At around the time Queenie was arriving, Sheila was preparing to leave. After pressure exerted via Ascot Heath School and Mrs Peyton, Matron had finally – and reluctantly – agreed that Sheila should attend a boarding school. It was an extraordinary step for a home girl, but if anyone was academically ready, it was Sheila. She had already passed a scholarship exam in Ealing and had long been championed for further educational challenge by the formidable Miss Cory, who saw just how capable she was in lessons at the Fernbank Road school. Miss Cory joined forces with Mrs Peyton, but they struggled to sway Matron.

Sheila was unaware of what went on behind the scenes but the debate about her education was so contentious that W. R. Vaughan, the secretary of the Waifs and Strays Society, visited Englemere Wood to help decide the issue. He had joined the organization as an office boy and was popular among staff and children. Whatever he said had finally been enough to convince Matron that Sheila's educational future lay outside the immediate neighbourhood. Her golden rule, that the girls should all be treated equally, was going to be broken. There was nothing more to be done than help Sheila as best she could.

After Mr Vaughan had left, Matron spoke to Sheila,

outlining the new arrangements. During termtime she would stay at school but in the holidays she would resume her place as a Maurice girl at Englemere Wood.

There followed a trip to London to get the necessary beige and blue uniform and other kit. Sheila stared wide-eyed at the firemen she and Matron encountered, with faces blackened by smoke, eyes red-raw with tiredness and sheltering in shop doorways following nights of bombing raids. Trucks rattled past her with deliveries of scarlet cylinders of gas to fill tethered barrage balloons that were protecting the capital from low-flying aircraft. The sand-bags, the smashed windows and the acrid smell of burning on the wind were all a world away from Ascot. *How lucky we left London when we did*, she thought briefly, before being distracted by the contents of the department store. Armed with 'three of everything', she came back with her sights firmly set on her new school. The money for the items came from supporters recruited to Mrs Peyton's Maurice Home committee.

Before she left Englemere Wood, Sheila was told repeatedly about the privilege that had been bestowed on her. 'You must appreciate how rare this opportunity is among home girls like you,' said Matron severely. 'Many people have gone to a lot of trouble so that you can go to this school. You must repay them by working hard.'

Sheila nodded, already painfully aware that other girls, including Monica, had already finished their education and, as 'house girls', were training to be kitchen, laundry, parlour or housemaids, even though they were clever enough to stay at school. But she wasn't afraid of hard work and relished the chance to learn. As term started Sheila departed and for a while the home seemed a quieter place without her. For a while at least.

Crash! A stack of dinner plates slipped out of Queenie's hands and smashed on the kitchen floor.

Queenie reeled in shock, not quite believing the crockery had slipped through her fingers at such speed and without warning. She looked down in dismay at the shards surrounding her feet, then looked up to find Matron striding into the room.

'I–I'm sorry, Matron,' said Queenie fearfully. Had this happened at the convent there would be a rumpus, followed by some harsh punishment.

But Matron looked at Queenie's ashen face and sighed. 'What's done is done,' she said. 'There's no point worrying about it now. Hurry and clear up the pieces. But go steady next time.'

Queenie had arrived at Englemere Wood with a red flag over her name. Now she was one of the most obliging of the girls in the home, even if she did have butter fingers. To her delight Queenie had returned to school, as Matron promised, where Miss Cory admired her writing. However, she did not have the same all-round academic skills that Sheila possessed and, by the end of the summer term, her schooling came to an end. Like most of the other girls at Englemere Wood aged fourteen and above she was to train as a maid.

After Queenie arrived at Englemere Wood she came across another familiar face. Before being sent to Ascot, Evelyn Siddons had lived at the St Anne's Waifs and Strays home, which was in the same road as the convent. At the time the girls had passed a few pleasantries. Now they became the best of friends.

The strong connection that linked the girls was based not only on shared experiences but hopes for a better future. For this reason few dwelt on their past lives or confided to each other what they had previously endured. Only Matron knew the challenges each had faced so far in their short lives, and she would never divulge the details. Queenie didn't find out what had happened in Evelyn's young life until decades later.

Born in Fulham in 1924, Evelyn had been brought up in north London by her grandmother. Her mother, a high-kicking dancer, was largely absent, either for work purposes or because she was in poor health. Evelyn's mother was married – but her waiter husband was acknowledged not to be Evelyn's father. It seems she was the result of a stage-door romance with a married man. Evelyn knew this because she was given his surname as a middle name.

Her grandmother scraped a meagre living as a cleaner. On the days she was employed, there was enough money to send Evelyn, armed with a basin, to a shop on the street corner to buy dinner. After parting with a few pennies Evelyn brought back jellied eels and mashed potato, at the time a traditional working-class takeaway. If she didn't have sufficient cash in her purse, her gran certainly didn't want the neighbours to know. So she'd fry a solitary onion and open all the windows, so neighbours would think that a nourishing meal was being cooked up inside the house.

The London streets were her playground and here Evelyn joined other children running after motorized fire engines, sounding their clanging bell, or cheering on boys who would shin up lamp posts to extinguish the flame newly lit by the lamplighter.

Her mother died from tuberculosis when Evelyn was seven. At around this time the youngster was taken into the care of the Waifs and Strays Society, being sent to St Anne's Home in Leamington Spa, one of thirty school-aged girls looked after there. Much later she discovered it had been at her aunt Marion's instigation, as she felt sorry for Evelyn, being looked after by an elderly and none-too-kind granny.

Not all her experiences in an institution were happy ones. An inveterate sleepwalker, she would wake up to find herself outside her dormitory, panicking in the pitch dark. For this she was slippered, while girls who wet the bed were punished by getting 'no extras' for a two-week spell. That meant no jam, cake or sweets. The worst 'offenders' had mattresses taken from their beds and were compelled to sleep on the metal springs.

The home's matron had some fixed ideas about the route to good health as well and they were made to drink a cupful of hot cabbage water after the vegetable had been dished up at mealtimes. And every Saturday there was 'the weekly purge', when the girls were given either Epsom salts with peppermint, senna pods with breakfast prunes or liquorice powder dissolved in water. It meant the home's four toilets were continuously occupied for the rest of the day.

But there were some good memories too, like long winter evenings passed in front of a fire playing charades and summer days playing in the home's large garden. In the autumn they munched pears that had fallen from the trees there.

Yet suddenly Evelyn was told she was being moved. With just one day's notice she was dispatched to Ascot.

She had been at St Anne's too long, she was told, and was getting too used to being there. To Evelyn's ear it sounded like shorthand for a punishment. She was known for wanting the last word in any discussion and behaviour like this wasn't tolerated.

In both Queenie and Evelyn Matron had girls who had won a reputation for being problematic. Rather than focusing on those character traits that other homes had decried, she built them up instead.

'You, my girl, are capable of anything,' she told each of them. 'Don't put yourself down. Be proud of yourself. Don't pretend to be someone else; you are quite good enough as you are.'

It was just the kind of encouragement Sheila had been used to hearing when she was at the Maurice Home. Things were different, though, at her new school, as she quickly discovered. Although no one mentioned she was a home girl to the rest of the pupils, the truth was quickly out.

'What's that label in the back of your pyjamas?' one girl asked snarkily.

'Oh, look, it says "Gift of the Canadian Red Cross". Can't you afford to buy your own clothes?'

'Is that why you don't know any French?' another girl asked, warming to the theme. 'Or biology, geometry or algebra?'

A third tormentor joined in. 'Is that why you can't do even basic ballet? Is that why you're smelly?'

Despite her prowess at games Sheila was the last to be picked for sports teams and frequently found her schoolbooks mysteriously went missing for days at a time. At night she discovered wet sheets on her bed and her protestations that her nightwear was dry cut no ice with others in the dormitory. She was branded a bed-wetter and the injustice of it all burned. The end of term couldn't come soon enough.

But with her return to Englemere Wood came a school report, and Matron was far from pleased with what she read.

'For French and Algebra it says "very poor". The English teacher complains you contribute little to the lesson. And it says here you are "unresponsive to the overtures of the other girls". This is very disappointing, Sheila.' Matron eyed her furiously. 'You have been given this most marvellous opportunity and it looks like you have just wasted it. What will Mr Vaughan say when he finds out?'

Sheila was berated for some further time before being allowed to rejoin the Maurice girls, having never felt more miserable.

Soon afterwards it was time for each girl's regular health check, carried out by Ascot's Dr Halley. A regular visitor to the home, he was a popular figure.

Sheila stood in the room in her underwear, more chilled by Matron's continuing disapproval than any draughts as she waited to be weighed. The clunky scales, with measurements taken on a protruding arm, creaked lightly as she stepped on them. When Matron called out the weight it recorded, Dr Halley frowned.

'Are you sure that's right, Matron?'

After straightening her glasses Matron double-checked the number before confirming it. Deliberately the doctor handed her the medical chart before turning his attention to Sheila and Matron's eyes widened when she saw the drop in weight that had been recorded.

With a kindly gaze he began to ask Sheila about her new life at boarding school. With a gentle smile he enquired, 'Are you happy there?'

Sheila started to say she was but, confronted by his evident compassion, she instead burst into tears.

'I hate it there. I hate it and I never want to go back again – ever.' Tales of the casual cruelties she had encountered all came pouring out and the two adults were horrified by everything they heard.

'Well, there's simply no point you going back if it's going to make you ill,' said Matron sadly. 'I'm sorry this hasn't worked out for you, Sheila. I think we've all learned some lessons from this episode.'

Sheila returned to school at Ascot Heath, the work seeming even easier than previously. Sometimes she caught Miss Cory looking at her from across the room, her forehead furrowed. At the time she didn't understand how the teacher feared that yet another of the bright girls from the Maurice Home would be dispatched to a life of cleaning and polishing, when they were capable of so much more.

But it did mean that Sheila could join a Saturday cinema visit led by Mrs Peyton and including all the girls.

There was a hubbub of excitement as they filed into the circle seats in what seemed a vast auditorium.

'It's huge,' said Jenny to no one in particular.

'Whoa,' cried Sheila as she sat down. 'This chair feels wobbly. I think I'm going to fall.'

The cinema was newly built with government money, but it had been constructed quickly and furnished with seats and other equipment from bombed-out cinemas in London. Although this was a timely make-do-and-mend approach, the seats sometimes fell over and the projector frequently broke down, inspiring boos and missile throwing from the (adult) audience. Nonetheless, it remained popular among children and servicemen alike.

The film was *The Four Feathers*, about a British army officer falsely accused of cowardice. Mrs Peyton had a special reason for wanting to see the film, as it featured her nephew, Derek.

Despite his father Montague's deepest fears, Derek Eldred Montague Elphinstone led an apparently charmed existence. After joining the Royal Navy he went on to be an actor and writer, featuring in the 1939 version of *The Four Feathers* and Noel Coward's 1942 film *In Which We Serve*.

The first Sunday of every month was earmarked for family visits. For some girls, like Sheila, no one made the journey to Ascot to check on her welfare. Like Queenie, she didn't even receive letters. Sheila still had no idea she had numerous half-siblings or that she was the product of an extra-marital affair. As a baby she had been given to her father's family, the Coxes, in Appledore, Devon. They had struggled to bring her up as long as they could, while her mother Ethel had moved away to find a new life. When Sheila transferred to the Maurice Home in Ealing, she had moved to within a dozen miles of Ethel, the woman who gave birth to her and gave her away; who was by now either divorced or separated and living with a building labourer.

Monica's mum did visit and when she appeared she would take her daughter and a friend out to tea. Jenny's dad was an occasional treasured visitor.

Thus the girls at Englemere Wood observed for themselves that sometimes blood ties weren't the ones that bound them forever. At Englemere Wood, Matron, her staff and Mrs Peyton offered everything a family might, and sometimes even more.

Sheila fitted back into the daily routine there as if she had never left. One day, as she polished the tea urn, Matron's face appeared alongside her own in the reflection. Her face was grave.

'There's a school managers' committee meeting this afternoon,' Matron told her, 'and I might send for you, so please smarten yourself up and stay inside where I can find you.'

Sheila barely knew about the workings of the committee that governed the school. She'd heard more about the two committees linked to the Maurice Home: one from Ealing, which continued to run the affairs of the home, and one formed among Mrs Peyton's Ascot friends, which organized treats and outings. It was, she thought, unusual for the school committee to meet at Englemere Wood, as they were on this occasion.

After finishing the urn and checking her short hair in its shiny reflection, Sheila fetched her knitting bag and sat at a suitable vantage point, wondering what would happen next. Quickly she became distracted by a rounders game that had started outside. She could just make out the running figures and hear the cheers. Despite her sporting skills, Nansi, one of Sheila and Monica's firm friends, had just been caught out. Surely that was Sister Briggs going into bat now, wielding the well-used wooden tennis racquet with which she could hit the ball high in the air. Dawn was preparing to bowl. Encouragement at ball games lavishly given by John Peyton when he visited had had its effect and everyone now took the field with more confidence.

The tinkle of cutlery on the tea trolley now had her attention. Tea was only served when the committee meeting was over and she was filled with frustration at missing the rounders match apparently for nothing. With one ear cocked she thought she could hear Madam's voice, but then Rev. Walton appeared in front of her, his hands behind his back and a thoughtful expression on his face.

'Hello, Sheila, I have some news. We – that is, the school committee – have decided to give you one more chance and allow you to make use of the scholarship you won back at Ealing. The director of education at Reading and the headmaster of the grammar school at Bracknell have agreed to give you a year's trial, to see if you can cope with the work. If you abuse the privilege or fail to reach the required standard, you will leave school at the end of that year and begin your training as a house girl. Is that quite clear?'

Solemnly Sheila replied that, yes, it was clear.

Rev. Walton visibly relaxed. The meeting had been a long one, and for once he found himself on the same side of the debate as Miss Cory. And unusually he was pitted against Matron, a determined adversary, it turned out. Matron's historic reluctance to permit one girl privileges that set her above the rest had been very much in evidence, especially given the unhappy time Sheila had experienced at boarding school. But central to the argument about Sheila's future was Mrs Peyton – and she had no doubts about where the girl's future should lie. Since moving to Englemere Wood two decades previously Mrs Peyton had heard nothing but good things about Ranelagh, the red-brick grammar school in Bracknell, which had first opened its doors in 1908 and was now an established beacon of educational achievement. It had taken all her powers of persuasion to change Matron's heart, but her pleas for better expectations of the Maurice girls had won support from the committee. Sheila would fit in well, Mrs Peyton was sure. Her faith in Sheila's ability reaped rewards for other Maurice girls and later Jenny, Marguerite and Peggy joined Sheila at the grammar school.

Before returning to the meeting, Rev. Walton offered to coach Sheila in Latin on Saturday mornings, to ease her path into the grammar-school life. In 1935 he had set up an Evening Institute for boys and girls aged fourteen and over in Ascot, to supplement their education while they worked, so he was used to the concept of extra tuition.

With Sheila's grateful thanks ringing in his ears, he returned to Mrs Peyton's side of the house and the cup of tea that awaited him.

Grammar-school pupils like Sheila still had to do chores, but now they had to squeeze in extra time for homework, perched at the end of a table where others were cleaning or crafting. Their frowning foreheads became a familiar sight as they wrestled with piles of precariously balanced textbooks. It wasn't easy but the rewards were huge. They would not be heading for a life in service, as other Maurice girls were, but might go into teaching, nursing, secretarial or administrative work. Thanks to Mrs Peyton, they were on the rise.

'Sheila, you must move these books now,' barked a busy Sister Briggs. 'Nanna is coming to visit and we need to clear this table, so she has room to sit down.'

Sheila felt a flash of despair. How would she ever get her homework done if she kept being moved from pillar to post? But the irritation soon ebbed away as Matron's white-haired mother was always a welcome visitor. A plump, homely figure, while Matron was small and slim, she was now sixty-five years old, yet still showed inexhaustible interest in each girl.

When she visited, she chatted with them all as she helped the youngest get ready for school. After realizing one girl had lost her gloves and risked cold hands, she spent the day knitting a replacement pair. She took special care with the most vulnerable and those apparently without relatives.

But despite the care and consideration shown to them all by Nanna, Matron, Mrs Peyton and the staff, the girls were still vulnerable to illness, and – not for the first time – Jenny was confined to the sickroom, after contracting a cold and sore throat. The room had recently been donated by Mrs Peyton and was designated for ailing girls. After her temperature surged, Jenny became oblivious to what was going on around her. She didn't hear the clang of the brass bell that indicated an air raid was imminent, wasn't aware of being carried down Mrs Peyton's main staircase – usually forbidden to the girls – to reach safety as quickly as possible. She didn't wake up until she was ensconced behind the protection of the largest of the kitchen tables laid on its side with its legs against the wall. Parched and eaten up with fever, she craved a drink of water. Then, as frail as a wren, she fell into an unconscious sleep that lasted days.

Her next memory was waking up, the sickroom dark but for the flames of an open fire. Lying beside her in a green woollen dressing gown on a camp bed was Matron – but Jenny had never seen her look like this before. Dark hair that was normally pinned in place was tumbling down her back. The glasses usually perched on her nose were missing, so the fretful expression was apparent even to young Jenny. It didn't matter how many times she sat by a sickly child, the worry always took its toll on Matron.

She sighed, as Jenny stirred. 'Thank God, you are back with us again.'

Much later, Jenny learned she had suffered from an earache that had escalated. Middle-ear infections like this used to be a significant cause of infant mortality until the arrival of penicillin. Dr Halley was on holiday at the time but his replacement pressed for her to be given some of this new miracle medicine, even though it was still only being trialled. Jenny made a slow recovery with visitors only permitted singly.

Spending days in the sick bay, Jenny turned to books and jigsaw puzzles to help pass the time. Matron, she discovered, was also a fan of puzzles and would regularly slip into the room to help.

'Matron, Matron,' Sister Briggs called from nearby. With a finger held over her lips, Matron would slip out of sight of the doorway so she could continue to fit pieces for a few moments more.

'Matron,' said Sister Briggs, bustling through the door. 'Here you are, I was calling you.'

'I'm sorry, I didn't hear,' Matron replied, throwing Jenny a conspiratorial look.

Matron wasn't Jenny's sole visitor. Barbara came by and taught her to knit using four needles rather than two. While

Jenny was still confined to bed Mrs Peyton would also pop in, on one occasion bringing a teddy that had belonged to her own sons years before. It was the first dark brown teddy Jenny had seen. Immediately she named it Mr Tommy, after Mrs Peyton's youngest son, whose whereabouts were unknown. For many months now she had been certain that, if she had to choose between Mr John and Mr Tommy, she would pick the younger of the brothers. Although she quickly noted to herself how much she loved Mr John as well. The teddy took pride of place on her bed, sitting alongside Margaret, the doll given to her years before in Ealing.

One Sunday Jenny was bundled up in blankets and carried downstairs to spend time with Mrs Peyton, Matron and the rest of the girls after tea. There was a heartfelt cheer when she appeared, something that left Jenny visibly awkward and self-conscious. Feeling loved and wanted, she squeezed Mr Tommy's paw hard, finding comfort in the yielding fur and the sense of joy that filled the house. Unfortunately the undiluted happiness that touched them all that day would be short-lived.

Girls from Grenville House on holiday in Cromer in the late 1940s.

Until Sheila was given the option of further education, all the girls at Englemere Wood were trained as housemaids. Dorothy Peyton was the staunchest advocate of higher education for the girls.

When Maurice girl Sheila married Eric Steward in 1952, the reception took place at Grenville House and she was given away by Col Eugene St John Birnie, the secretary of the Children's Society, seated right, next to Matron.

On a visit to Grenville House, Queenie stands by as Matron's mother holds Roger while Monica talks to her daughter, Joy.

Queenie and Monica often took their toddler children to Grenville House, where they would meet other old girls also there to visit Matron.

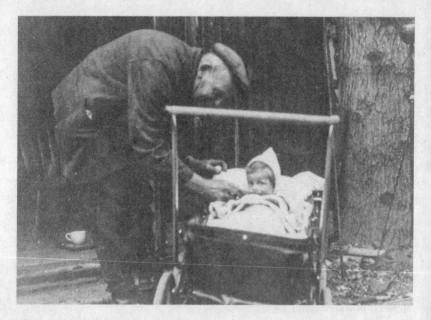

All the staff welcomed old girls and their offspring. Here, Mr Groves, the Grenville House gardener, shares a cup of tea with Roger.

The Grenville House pram came in useful when old girls visited. Queenie's son, Alan, is pictured in it here, while Roger sits in Mr Groves' wheelbarrow.

In 1949, Queenie was a regular visitor at Grenville House with her son Roger.

Queenie's son playing in the gardens of Grenville House.

When one of Queenie's sons got married, it was an opportunity for Englemere Wood girls to get together again, and Matron, third from the right, was at the top of the guest list.

After leaving Grenville House, Matron retired to North Devon, where she was visited by Queenie, accompanied this time by her daughter-in-law, Linda.

In Devon, Matron offered girls who had been in her care and their families the chance to stay at a seaside chalet and, although it was rudimentary, golden memories were forged there. Nansi Finch's two children, Rob – in school uniform – and Susan, are pictured with accompanying friend Nick Huggins.

Despite her golden curls and rosebud lips, Princess Marie Louise was dubbed 'ugly' by her grandmother, Queen Victoria, an anecdote that shocked the Englemere Wood girls.

The letter below provided comfort after Mrs Peyton's son John was captured in Belgium, prior to Dunkirk.

26ᵗʰ July 1940.

BUCKINGHAM PALACE

Dear Mrs Peyton

As I am here in waiting the Queen commands me to write & say that Her Majesty has learned, through Lady Weigall, that you have given up your dining room for the use of the Waifs & Strays now in your house.

The Queen thinks it is indeed good of you to have given up

a room you have in so much & Her Majesty feels sure that the gratitude & happiness of the children now living in your house will be a reward – if one may use the word in that sense – for your kind & generous act.

Yours sincerely

Katharine Seymour

After Mrs Peyton sheltered the occupants of the Waifs and Strays' Maurice Home from the Blitz, she received a letter of acknowledgement from the Queen: '26th July 1940. Dear Mrs Peyton, As I am now in waiting, the Queen commands me to write and say that Her Majesty has learned, through Lady Weigall, that you have given up your dining room for the use of the Waifs & Strays now in your house. The Queen thinks it is indeed good of you to have given up a room you [miss] so much and Her Majesty feels sure that the gratitude and happiness of the children now living in your house will be a reward – if one may use the word in that sense – for your kind and generous act. Yours sincerely, Katharine Seymour'

In the garden of their North Devon home, Queenie's son Roger embraces Matron, who he knew as 'Nanna', and Sister Adams, his 'Aunt Edie'.

14. Local Hero

Soldiers are citizens of death's grey land,
drawing no dividend from time's tomorrows.
Siegfried Sassoon, 'Dreamers'

Christmas 1941 seemed a dull, drab event. It wasn't just
the weather that made everyone feel that way: grey, windy
and without any promise of snow.

Following the Japanese attack on Pearl Harbor on 7
December, America was for the first time fighting alongside Britain. That was good news, as its manpower and
manufacturing would surely tip the balance of the conflict
in favour of the Allies. But for the moment British colo-
nies in the Far East were toppling like dominoes, thousands
of soldiers were being taken prisoner and Japanese forces
were set to press the British Empire through its back door,
India. The outcome of ongoing battles in the Atlantic and
North Africa remained uncertain.

Although the girls had been at Englemere Wood for
almost two and a half years by now, the number of outright
British victories celebrated during that time had been woe-
fully few. Crucially food shortages continued to affect
everyone, with German planes, warships and U-boats sending much-needed supplies to the bottom of the oceans. It
would be a more hard-pressed Christmas than ever before,

and there was even a shortage of paper in which to wrap presents.

Still, despite all this troubling news, there was a warming Christmas spirit illuminating Englemere Wood and everyone fell into its embrace. The focus of the girls was locked on to life in the house, where there was a special and unexpected treat in store.

Tommy Peyton was home, albeit on crutches. He had fractured his leg during training in rough country at Achnacarry in the Scottish Highlands earlier that month. Of course, his appearance set pulses racing among the young girls who considered him better looking than any Hollywood idol of the era. And Mrs Peyton was also overjoyed to see him, her boundless pleasure only tempered by a tiny twinge of guilt at her good fortune, knowing so many other servicemen would be apart from their loved ones at Christmas.

He was all smiles when he carved the Christmas chicken on behalf of the household. 'Sheila, how many slices for you? Twelve, is it, or fourteen?' he teased. 'Jenny, I think you're still the youngest at the table, so you have the wishbone.'

There were, as usual, charms and sixpences wrapped in greaseproof paper to be found in the Christmas pudding. The princesses and Lady Weigall came over to help distribute presents, requested by the girls by letter earlier in the month and paid for by Mrs Peyton's supportive Maurice Home committee.

Mrs Peyton opened an embroidered book cover made by Jenny while she was recuperating, with the names of famous authors and poets stitched on the back. Mrs Peyton was delighted with the gift and said so. For the first time eleven-year-old Jenny understood how the pleasure and pride of giving could far outweigh the joys of receiving a present.

When they were alone together in the drawing room, Tommy looked around approvingly at the greenery from the garden, artfully entwined on the mantlepiece. 'Fewer cards this year, Mother?'

Mrs Peyton smiled. 'I believe there have been difficulties finding enough postmen, as just about everyone is in uniform these days. And there's much less space to carry letters and parcels on the trains too.'

'The girls didn't seem to get very much by way of presents,' Tommy said, concern written all over his face.

'Don't worry,' said his mother. 'They have more presents to open yet. Matron prefers them to have the presents in stages. Anyway, what they will most enjoy is the party and the dancing – with you. Are you up to it?'

Tommy's face broke out into a grin, and he thumped his crutch twice on the floor enthusiastically. 'Of course,' he replied. 'And I've brought a new record with me. It's Glenn Miller's "Jingle Bells". I think we can have some fun with that.'

So there was music and dancing, and despite his injury Tommy twirled each girl round in turn, thrilling them with his attention. Yet at times over the Christmas holiday his dark smouldering eyes betrayed something of his anxieties, and his mother watched with a furrowed brow. There were moments when it felt like there was great distance between them, even when they were in the same room. Was there, she wondered, any way she could help ease his evident tensions? She felt a bit of him had been left behind that festive season, with the men he served alongside.

Part of an elite squad of men, all expert fighters and itching to see action, Tommy was indeed frustrated and anxious. Would this injury cost him his chance of seeing frontline action with the men he'd come to see as brothers? He couldn't confide his concerns, even to his mother. Operational secrecy was paramount.

When Christmas was over Mrs Peyton waved weakly at his retreating figure, as he hobbled away down the drive, a rush of unease filling her heart. Although he was barely out of his teenage years, he looked much older. One son remained incarcerated at a distant prison camp and now Tommy's immediate future was uncertain. But she knew he shared her iron-strong sense of duty and would be keen to serve.

Before the start of the war Thomas Grenville Pitt Peyton had completed his education at Eton and emerged from the Royal Military College, Sandhurst, to join the King's Royal Rifle Corps. Fresh-faced, handsome and full of youthful fervour, Tommy had inherited the military bearing of his Uncle William and was six inches taller and more robustly built than most of the men he served alongside. He was soon marked out for a different course beyond the regular army. After Dunkirk Churchill had demanded that a new detachment be created out of the army's most promising soldiers, capable of nimble manoeuvres and equipped to spring deadly ambushes. These new units were known variously as Combined Operations, Independent Companies or Special Service battalions. Ultimately the name that stuck was Commandos.

Numerous men stepped up for the challenge. With its commanders searching for abnormally high levels of intelligence, self-reliance and an independent frame of mind, Tommy must have impressed to win one of the coveted places. He joined an 'Independent Company' in July 1940, aged just nineteen, before becoming part of 2 Commando, formed in March 1941.

Physical training was rigorous. There was intensive tuition in arms and explosives and lengthy hikes that lasted for hours, taking place in all weathers, usually in the wilds of Scotland. During cross-country treks the men might be asked to problem-solve for imagined scenarios to ensure they remained alert. They also learned an array of survival skills and when they played war games it was with live ammunition. If commanders witnessed any issue with the attitude or accomplishments of any of the men, they were returned to their original units.

The Commandos wanted to roll up their sleeves and get involved, always hoping their actions and sacrifices would make a difference in the outcome of the conflict. For months they were held at heel. But as they waited, and were formed into smaller units, strong bonds were forged. Aged twenty and a lieutenant, Tommy found himself in close friendships with men he would not have ordinarily met. His captain was Michael Burn, known universally as Micky, and the pair were fast friends. In the thirties Micky had abandoned his studies to tour Europe. Through his friend Unity Mitford, Micky even met Hitler and for a while fell under the mesmerizing spell of the Nazi leader, lauded in many political circles at the time for wide-ranging economic successes. His esteem for Hitler was quickly eroded, however, after he visited Dachau, a new concentration camp where political opponents to the fascist regime were penned up. Another close associate was Morgan Jenkins, who had worked in a draper's. Drawn from different strata of society, they were now a tight, loyal unit.

In February 1942 2 Commando's commanding officer, Lieutenant Colonel Charles Newman, was called to the War Office to see Admiral Lord Louis Mountbatten, the newly appointed director of Combined Operations. A blueprint for an audacious raid – code-named Operation Chariot – was unveiled, revealing St Nazaire was the target. Specifically it was the Forme Ecluse Louis Joubert, which was both a lock permitting entry into the Loire River and a dry dock. Significantly it was the only dry dock on that lengthy section of coastline that was capable of servicing major warships.

If this berth was destroyed, it would vastly reduce the likelihood of Germany's last remaining battleship, the *Tirpitz*, wreaking havoc in the Atlantic. Also at St Nazaire were the concrete bunkers that housed U-boats while they were being repaired and serviced.

All the services had a role to play. The Royal Air Force was to stage a diversionary raid. The Royal Navy's role was vital, sailing the Commandos to France. The intelligence services had already contributed up-to-date plans of the facilities at St Nazaire, from which a model had been built.

Mountbatten told Newman he was 'not expecting anyone' to return from the operation. 'If we lose you all, you will be the equivalent of the loss of one merchant ship, but your success will save many merchant ships. We have to look at the thing in those terms.'

Figures for shipping certainly looked bleak, even without the *Tirpitz* roaming the high seas. During 1941 some 1,300 British, Allied and neutral ships had been sunk in the world's waterways. U-boats were the biggest predators, but ships also fell victim to aircraft, mines, agile raiders, warships and coastal defence forces.

Early in 1942 there seemed only a limited chance of Tommy being fit for service in the spring. But with characteristic grit he made this full recovery in time to be part of a grand plan still being kept under wraps.

Officers – the first to know about the destination of the raid – weren't told until 17 March, eleven days before it was due to take place. Tommy gasped when he realized the aims and implications of the plan. Boldness was clearly going to be the key to success. Like the rest, he was inspired by the thought that his mother – and the girls – would be fed thanks to the operation they were chalked up to do. In essence, the Royal Navy was going to ram the dry dock at St Nazaire with a doomed destroyer laden with time-delayed explosives while Commandos in accompanying craft leaped on to the dockside to wreak further havoc.

Plans to send the destroyer with eight motor launches were soon revised upwards, until sixteen were included. The flotilla would also include a motor gunboat and a motor torpedo boat. Micky picked Tommy and a dozen others to accompany him in *ML 192*.

Operation Chariot ran on an ambitious timetable but there was still time for rehearsals. However, on a trial run to the Scilly Isles many of the men were stricken with seasickness. And a mock landing at Plymouth degenerated into farce as the Home Guard collared the would-be attackers without undue exertion, after the motor launch pilots had been blinded by searchlights on the approach.

Shortly before the operation got underway Micky urged his men, now formed into Six Troop, to write letters home and to make a will. Bathed in early-spring sunshine, Tommy wrote his sitting on the planked deck of the *Princess Josephine Charlotte*.

Before putting pen to paper, his thoughts turned to Englemere Wood. During training he had been focused on every aspect of the operation. But afforded some spare moments, he thought fondly of his mother and the girls who now shared his home. He was the son of an imperialist, who'd had fixed ideas about Britain's rigid class system. Now Tommy was exploring current political thinking that would realign British society, giving working-class people better opportunities. Was it youthful optimism or the kernel of a dynamic new politics being drawn up for post-war Britain? Although his background had been cloistered by privilege, the British army in general and the Commandos in particular had given him a rare breadth of view. The presence of the girls – born with the fewest of life's advantages but so evidently thriving at his family home – played its part.

In fact, he wrote two letters to his mother, the first of which confided the ideals he'd fostered and for which he was prepared to sacrifice his life. Looking to the future, he hoped the war would result in a new age of social justice. But his greatest fear was that the men he was serving beside would be consigned to the scrap heap of unemployment at the conflict's end, becoming forgotten heroes. Instead, he hoped 'this war will achieve a better place and system . . . some new British Order.'

The second letter to his mother was written within hours of his departure for France and exposed his enormous personal courage. If he was reported missing, he urged her to believe 'that there is every chance that I will be at large in France'.

Should he die, he felt that no sacrifice was too great in the quest to defeat Hitler. He was, he said, among his greatest friends. Heartbreakingly he ended with: 'I have always wished that I could in some way show my affection for you and I would like you to think that we have gone into this fighting on your behalf.'

On the night before the operation Tommy sat among his closest friends drawn from every social order and once again addressed political imperatives of the day.

'Have you seen the new politics of the 1941 Committee?' Tommy was asking Morgan Jenkins, his fellow lieutenant but from a different background to his own. Jenkins was the son of a Welsh railway navvy who had moved to London during the Great Depression to find work. At twenty-six he was six years older than Tommy.

'Aye, I've seen it in the *Picture Post*, but it won't have an effect,' said Morgan quietly.

'But I think it could,' said Tommy urgently. 'J. B. Priestley has the ear of the nation with his radio broadcasts, after all, and he's at the head of it. Some of the men in it fought in Spain against Franco. They know what they are talking about.'

'OK, comrade.' Morgan prodded his pal with some gentle teasing. 'Politics in this country is a mess, I'll agree with you there. But what's the 1941 Committee going to do when we are at war that the government can't?'

Tommy wouldn't be thrown off the theme. 'I'm not saying there should be a revolution, just a bit more fairness in this world.'

Morgan, who felt he had heard it all before, grunted. 'Fools like us go off and get our hands dirty. And I bet you a week's wages the establishment will stay just where it likes to be, at the top.'

Tommy was thoughtful for a moment, looking around at the volunteers poised to risk their lives to conquer fascism. 'These are the finest men in the country,' he said finally. 'I couldn't bear it if, after the war, they couldn't find proper work, didn't manage to support their families – or weren't treated with the dignity they deserve because they didn't go to the right school. We need change.'

The debate went on into the night without reaching a conclusion. The following afternoon, Thursday, 26 March, the vessels slipped anchor and on a calm sea they formed into ranks and headed south-west.

A night of storm and fury lay ahead for the Commandos and the 264 Royal Navy crew involved, while at Englemere Wood the girls, who still frequently talked of how they danced with Tommy, were safe in their beds and sleeping soundly.

The next day Matron told them a daring Commando raid that was dominating the news headlines had surely involved Mr Tommy. The men concerned were being called heroes. Collectively the girls took a sharp intake of breath. From the lines of concern etched on Matron and Madam's faces, they could see Tommy's fate was unknown. They continued with chores as best they could, eaten up with anxiety as a pall set over the house.

But suddenly the mood lifted. Mrs Peyton's face transformed into one of joy after news reached her that Tommy had survived the raid and was among those who'd returned. It was surely only a question of time before he made his way home, up the gravel drive and through the door into his mother's arms.

In response she and Matron immediately agreed to an impromptu dance just like the one the girls had enjoyed a few months before with Tommy in attendance. Mrs Peyton came in to operate the gramophone that usually spent its days in the corner of a room covered with a dust sheet.

Girls partnered up to quickstep to hits of the era and there was a lightness to them as they whirled around. 'Let's Call the Whole Thing Off', a song written by George and Ira Gershwin for the 1937 film *Shall We Dance* was a favourite, with everyone singing the words loudly. They enjoyed weak orange squash from a previously hidden supply and nibbled on biscuits surreptitiously stored for an occasion such as this. There was a stream of visitors calling at the door, and on the telephone, keen to congratulate Mrs Peyton on her family's good fortune. When they went to bed that night every tired girl was filled with secret happiness, knowing the tall, handsome soldier who lit a spark in each of them would soon be home again.

Tommy's survival seemed to fit perfectly with the wartime narrative the girls understood. People had died, they knew that, as names of the dead from Ascot were read out during Sunday services. But they were by nature cheerful and positive and nothing that unfolded during the war had so far dented that optimism. Earlier that same month, during 'Warships Week', they were among pupils from Ascot Heath

School who had been taken to the Hermitage Cinema to see *Forever England*, the 1935 black-and-white film based on a C. S. Forester novel, brushed off to endorse patriotism among the cinema-loving public.

The next day, a Monday, dawned with plenty of promise. A brightness of mood after the previous day's good news was still in evidence and Easter was approaching. If there was a shortage of chocolate during the war years there would be no limit on the number of games the girls could play in the garden during the Easter weekend if the weather was kind.

Suddenly there was a rap on the door. Some of the girls doing work at the house might have heard a short muffled exchange on the step. Anyone in the road would have seen the slight figure of a General Post Office telegram boy, his lapelled uniform belted and his cap pushed back on his head, pedalling fast away from the house.

Mrs Peyton stood with the official notification limp in her hand. It wasn't Tommy who had returned safely from France, as she had been led to believe, but another man, whose name sounded the same but was spelled differently. David Paton was one of the medical officers and he had survived the treacherous operation. Tommy was missing.

It was a nightmare she had endured before. Again, it would be weeks before the real story emerged. Government bureaucracy served to prolong the agony, with an aching official silence blanketing the human cost of the operation. And typically there were miscommunications that fogged the events of that night.

The first news of the fate of a missing Commando from 2 Commando came in a broadcast by William Joyce, also known as Lord Haw-Haw, on 1 April. Later hanged for high treason, Haw-Haw gave propaganda radio broadcasts on behalf of the Germans. No one was banned from listening in Britain, where his exaggerations and lies were treated with disdain. But on this occasion the naming of Arthur Young as someone taken prisoner at St Nazaire was a welcome intervention. Some of the missing Commandos had survived, and Young was one who had served alongside Tommy.

Dorothy was soon in regular communication with Micky's parents, who'd likewise been informed their son was missing. His father Clive Burn was well connected and used every channel at his disposal – official or otherwise – to find out more. He spoke to one of the journalists taken to witness the raid, who was confident that Micky, Tommy and their men had made it ashore. The reporter even predicted both had a fifty-fifty chance of survival. But tantalizingly he'd spoken in terms of 'a beach' – and there was no beach at St Nazaire docks – so suddenly his words seemed to carry less weight.

More than two weeks after the raid Clive Burn and his wife Phyllis were sent a copy of a German newspaper, with a picture of British troops being marched into captivity. In it was their son Micky, who was walking with his arms up at gunpoint, and nonchalantly making a discreet 'V for Victory' sign with his fingers.

There was, though, no word of what had happened to Tommy. All Dorothy had, alongside the telegram, were the final letters he'd written, which had been forwarded by a fellow officer. They were, she said, 'full of comfort & the very highest ideals'. She had a nagging feeling that Tommy's fate was already well known and she would be the last to hear. Two months after the raid she wrote to Clive, saying: 'I have heard nothing at all . . . I do just wonder what is happening.'

Tommy's twenty-first birthday passed at the beginning of June, with Dorothy not knowing if he was dead or alive. No one remarked on the show that the rhododendrons gave at Englemere Wood that spring. The freshness of new leaves on the trees went unnoticed. Everyone was fixed on Tommy's unknown fate.

It was a further ten days before his name finally appeared on a casualty list – and Dorothy's worst fears were confirmed. Two days later, his death notice appeared in *The Times*, with the announcement by Dorothy ending: 'Please, no letters.'

In truth, she did want letters – not those filled with mawkish sympathy and well-worn words but from people who could fill in the facts about how he had died. In the end a letter sent from captivity by Micky helped to fill in some of the missing pieces.

Tommy was in the first launch to be crippled by German firepower. Two heavy shells, probably from the shore-based battery, hit the starboard side of his motor launch at about 1.30 a.m. Until then the flotilla making its way towards St Nazaire under cover of darkness had encountered few issues, convincing German lookout posts it was friendly. Tommy crouched with the others, on the deck of *ML 192*, within touching distance of two 500-gallon drums of fuel. Men had queried the presence of something so combustible when they would surely come under fire, but they were told in no uncertain terms the vessels could not get home without fuel.

Once it was hit, the boat careered out of formation, heading straight for the dock while being raked by machine-gun fire.

Commando Arthur Young was first to reach the dock steps and hauled a drenched Micky Burn in his wake. Weighed down with kit and ammunition, both men wobbled for a moment when they got to dry land. As they steadied themselves, they looked down and saw Tommy's body floating past in the current. They couldn't tell if he had been burned, shot or had drowned.

Months of training served to subdue their first inclination, to haul his body from the water and try to revive him. Micky knew they had to make headway if Tommy's death wasn't to be in vain.

Fuelled by grief, he climbed on to the dockside where he found a German defender inert on the ground. Wielding the butt of his revolver Micky rained quick blows on the head of the soldier. If he hadn't been dead beforehand, he was within moments. Micky moved off to complete his objective, although he finally arrived at the nominated target, a bridge, entirely alone. In addition to Burn and Young, just three other Commandos from *ML 192* swam to shore. Eight Commandos, including Tommy, and four of the crew were dead.

Other motor launches were also set ablaze. Men that got ashore set about their objectives as best they could. With satisfaction most saw the booby-trapped destroyer embed itself into the lock. It exploded much later, long after the Germans thought the attack had finished. Of 612 sailors and Commandos who set off from Falmouth, just 228 returned. Tommy, and Morgan (who'd been in *ML 268*), were among 169 casualties, while a further 215 men, including Micky Burn, became prisoners of war.

As the picture was pieced together it gave scant comfort to Dorothy, especially when she realized Tommy, the youngest officer to die, had perished before the fighting started. He hadn't made a pivotal contribution to the war effort, as he'd hoped.

When she next wrote to the Burns her grief was raw. 'I shall not see Tommy again. He meant so very much to me . . . life has taken on a particularly lonely phase without him.'

For her there wasn't even a body to bring home. Her next painful task was to write to her eldest son, John, who was still held by the Nazis. Inside the envelope she tucked a photograph of Tommy, standing tall with his shoulders thrown back, in the grounds of Englemere Wood. As she did so, her tears began to fall again.

John received the letter just after an escape tunnel that he and others had spent seven months digging had been discovered by guards. Inside the tunnel, air was being circulated in a pipe made of Canadian milk-powder tins sent to prisoners by the Red Cross. A guard had speared muddy ground with his bayonet and heard the sound of metal against metal, betraying the existence of the 250-feet-long escape route.

When they couldn't find its precise path the Germans dissected the area round the hut with a ditch and filled it with the contents of the latrines. As he wandered round the perimeter fence, deep in thought, John pondered his mother's endurance in the face of repeated heartbreak and felt he might drown in misery.

Although she didn't relish the idea, Dorothy agreed to have a memorial service at All Saints in Ascot conducted by Rev. Walton. The princesses and Sir Archibald and Grace Weigall were among the mourners, and, for the first time, she met Micky's parents.

Back at Englemere Wood, the atmosphere was leaden and, for once, Matron Bailey struggled to hide her feelings from the girls. Tommy's death was reminiscent of her brother's years before.

Her every instinct was to offer comfort and support to Mrs Peyton. However, that proved impossible as the older woman disappeared from view. Mrs Peyton chose to wrestle with her emotions behind closed doors, unwilling to share the colossal burden of her loss.

In the house the girls walked as if on eggshells. In nightly prayers they remembered both Mr Tommy and his heartbroken mother. Yet in the gloom Matron was already shaping an idea that would further cement the bond between them all.

She gathered the girls together in the dining room as the last rays of the midsummer sun set over the garden mere.

'Girls, Mr Tommy is dead,' she told them gently. 'He died a hero and he died for us, so that we can live freely. There is no greater sacrifice.'

Some of the girls were holding hands, while others rested their heads on the shoulder of the girl next to them. When Matron stopped speaking the sound of her words was replaced by their choked sobbing. Their stomachs were knotted, their throats were stinging and their hearts ached.

'But there's something we can all do to pay tribute to Mr

Tommy,' Matron continued. 'We should live as he lived: bravely, nobly and with kindness. From today I want each and every one of you to be inspired by him. Although he is gone, he can still improve our lives.'

They were, she explained, to become living testimonials for Tommy Peyton. He was just one man among many who had died in the ongoing conflict but he was the handsome, happy young man who had touched all their lives. Now they were charged with keeping his spirit close and embodying all his best qualities as they did so. Later there would be a song that celebrated Tommy's life, which united them all in an act of remembrance every time they sang it. For now Matron stood alongside the girls as they took a pledge that had Tommy Peyton at its heart.

'We will, as a family, build by our very lives an unseen memorial to the memory of this gallant Christian gentleman and in so doing we will remember all others unknown, who made the same sacrifice.'

15. Food for Thought

If you have the chance to do something to give hope,
and you think it's impossible, do it anyway. Try it.
                                          Micky Burn

After she'd been at the home for some time Evelyn was allocated a bed in a small room at the top of the house, additional space given by Mrs Peyton and a reward for older girls like herself. It meant she enjoyed the rare luxury of personal privacy, but felt she could also roam the premises, unobserved.

One evening she lay on her bed daydreaming about a cake in a tin on the larder shelf. Cakes were a rare treat. She could see it clearly in her mind's eye and almost taste the moist sponge. From under the covers she checked the face of her alarm clock and watched the minutes creep by.

At 10 p.m., when she knew everyone would be asleep or tucked away in the staff sitting room, she tiptoed downstairs barefoot, with the sweet treat in her sights.

There was no fridge at Englemere Wood. Food was stored in the outside larder, kept cool by air that came in through a grille. That larder lay beyond the kitchen door. Moving silently through the darkened house, she was pleased to see the light had been left on in the kitchen, making her progress a bit easier. Evelyn made her way past the shelves stacked with plates to retrieve the larder key from its hook on the kitchen dresser, then she headed outside. After stepping cautiously through the back door Evelyn gently shut it behind her and turned her full attention to the larder – and her prize. She wiggled the key in the lock and with some satisfaction felt the latch grind back. All the obstacles in her path had been cleared – or so she thought.

She had just put her hand inside the tin when she froze. Matron's voice sounded from the kitchen. 'Sister, who left this kitchen light on?'

The next thing Evelyn heard was the handle of the kitchen door being tried. 'Sister, you've forgotten to lock the back door.'

Then came the scraping sound of the key turning in the kitchen-door lock, filling Evelyn with foreboding. She'd been locked out. Her route back to the safety of her bedroom was now blocked and she was, as far as she could see, doomed. Even if she survived a night under the stars in just her nightie, she knew she would have to face Matron sometime and explain why she was outside.

Her thoughts raced and she came up with the most plausible story she could muster. Closing the cake tin without taking so much as a bite, she shut the larder door and bided her time. Then she began banging frantically on the kitchen door until Matron opened it wide.

Forcing out tears, Evelyn claimed she must have been sleepwalking – a habit she had once been known for – and woke up to find herself outside. Matron and Sister Briggs were horrified to hear it and swiftly installed her back into bed with a hot-water bottle and a cup of sweetened milk.

It looked like she might have got away with it until Matron and Sister Briggs did their rounds – and found the larder key outside. It didn't take them long to work out what had happened and, in less time still, Sister Briggs was by her bed for a second time in quick succession, but this time with all semblance of sympathy gone.

'Out of that bed, madam. Bring your mattress and bedding with you; we'll have you where we can keep an eye on you.' She spent the rest of the night on the floor of the youngest children's dormitory, under the gaze of Nurse Sheppard who was on duty that night. The indignity of it remained with her for a long while.

When Matron's face was marked with a frown, it wasn't the time to voice the thought that was haunting them all. The limited quantities of plain food set in front of them each day just weren't satisfying enough. Vegetables weren't rationed. However, sometimes shortages left holes on the dinner plate. Onions were so rare during the war they were used as raffle prizes. Only much later did Monica pluck up enough courage to tell Matron they were hungry.

'I know you are hungry,' responded Matron. 'But what can I do? There is only so much food to go around and I must treat you all equally.'

'What happened in the last war, Matron?' Sheila asked. 'Were you hungry then too?'

Matron paused for a moment, before she thought of the National Kitchens that were established to ensure people could eat properly when there were food shortages.

'There were dishes like soup, roast or boiled meat and vegetables, and a meal like that cost six pence,' she told them.

To the girls the money seemed a ludicrously small amount.

'A tanner would only buy you half a pound of potatoes these days,' remarked one.

'Puddings and cakes were cheaper still, at about one penny, the same as it cost to post a letter,' Matron continued. 'The first National Kitchen was opened on Westminster Bridge by our very own Queen Mary. And all kinds of people ate there. It wasn't just clerks like me but city gentlemen and workers, as well. We all sat side by side on long tables, a bit like we do now on our tables.'

Subsidized kitchens were not a new idea. Previously charities and trades unions had provided food for the hungry in a communal setting. But this time it wasn't just the poor and needy that the kitchens were aimed at. Office workers like Doris were target customers as the government sought to eliminate any whiff of pity about the scheme. It's why the meals were cheap but not free. As First World War food shortages became more acute, many dropped by the National Kitchens for cooked potatoes, for example, to bolster their own evening meals.

The Ministry of Food provided financial grants and the capacity for bulk buying and National Kitchens flourished; they numbered more than 300 at their peak, until government funding was withdrawn in 1919. The girls loved to hear Matron's memories and came up with as many questions as they could. However, for the girls at Englemere Wood, the diet of plain food would continue for some years to come. They were not the only ones to know the grumble of hunger.

As the anniversary of Tommy's death approached, Matron came across a subdued Mrs Peyton in one of the hallways.

Despite her grief, she had joined family life at Englemere Wood once more.

Matron began with a quiet question. 'How is John?'

'Just the same,' said Mrs Peyton wistfully. 'He's studying now, which helps pass the time. There are some fine legal minds with him in the camp and that's a terrific help. But from what he tells me, he's still hungry most of time.

'Still, he's been fortunate up until now. A kind Dutch woman is sending him food parcels. But he is asking her to stop because he has heard the situation is terrible in Holland too.'

John had indeed benefitted from the kindness of strangers. Jacoba Alida de l'Ecluse was a teenager working in a department store in the Netherlands when the war started. Called Co for short, her heart went out to the prisoners of war held in Germany. When she discovered she could send supplies under the auspices of the Red Cross she and her family packed up a parcel of chocolate, nuts and tobacco. At random they were given a prisoner number (424), the one by which John Peyton was now best known. Afterwards John received regular care packages including luxuries like fruit, soup cubes, marzipan, biscuits, condensed milk, fish paste and peppermint. He sent back prison postcards giving his thanks. Initially he didn't realize that electricity and gas were rationed in the Netherlands from 1941, with Co and her family now dependent on food stamps.

'I cannot tell you how much I appreciate your kindness at a time like this,' he wrote. 'But if things get too hard for you, I hope you don't hesitate to stop sending parcels.'

The situation continued to decline in the Low Countries. When she received his postcards she could at least take them to the store, where they earned her extra rations. But by the middle of 1943 he was sure her outlook regarding food was worse than his own. Now he was more emphatic. 'I realize how hard it must be for you to fill those parcels, so please don't worry about them any more. I hope that things are not too difficult for you. For myself I am quite all right and can still work. Again, very many thanks for your past kindness.'

He was right to be concerned. Worse still lay ahead for de l'Ecluse who, like other Dutch people, was reduced to eating tulip bulbs and animal feed in the harsh winter of 1944 after the Germans punished the Dutch with a blockade. Nazi authorities had been angered by a rail strike orchestrated by Dutch train drivers in support of the Allies.

As her pain slowly eased, Mrs Peyton focused on the plight of her last surviving son and the hunger he related in letters home. In response she threw herself once more into the war effort, by delivering Women's Voluntary Service supplies, including milk powder for babies, in her car. Chauffeur George Moore and his family had moved on so he could take a greater role in the ARP, and now she got behind the wheel herself.

Meanwhile, Queenie also had reason to be thankful to passing strangers. She'd spent a short time at school before joining the older girls in learning how to keep house. Training was structured so that each girl gained in rotation experience as a parlour, scullery and kitchen maid as well as working in the laundry. Between 1.3 and 1.6 million women were in domestic service during the interwar years. It was typically low paid, low status employment, with long hours. When the girls reached sixteen, Matron would find them work locally, within reach of the support network that had been built at Englemere Wood.

As parlour maids they wore distinctive black outfits with aprons and were taught to serve food at the table, practising on home staff. It was their job to wash up the cutlery and lay trays for tea in the afternoon. There were two housemaids who spent their days cleaning windows, polishing floors, dusting or putting a shine on the bathroom. As well as washing clothes, laundry girls had to tackle the ironing and distribute the clean items. The scullery maids worked in the kitchen, preparing vegetables for meals, then washing all the pots and pans afterwards. The task of putting food in the outside pantry also fell to them, as well as washing the dishcloths and tea towels.

It was at the end of a long day working as a scullery maid that Queenie got into difficulties. After a prompt start in the morning she had been preparing vegetables before lunch and washing pots and pans afterwards. Shopping had been stacked in the pantry. Washed tea towels were hanging on the line, which was tucked away at the back of the house, and laundered clothes had been checked and mended.

With the tasks of the day behind her, she had allowed herself a few moments' reverie in the winter evening's gloom. Then she remembered the tea towels, still fluttering outside on the line even though dusk had descended. Her work was not yet done. Nor did she want to announce her silly forgetfulness to the household. Unobtrusively she slipped out of the back door wearing just a cotton uniform, without telling anyone where she was going. The washing line was sited off the tradesmen's entrance in a secluded part of the garden.

If there was a sharp chill in the air Queenie didn't notice. She was determined to redeem her mistake as quickly as possible before she became the subject of some good-natured teasing, and she strode purposefully down the path into the garden on a route she had taken many times previously.

Busily she unpegged the cold cloths, focused only on how she wanted to drape them on the warm range inside before anybody noticed they were missing. When she had liberated the last one from the line she turned back towards the house. Only the house – large as it was – seemed to have vanished into a black pit. Looking left, then right, she could not detect a pinprick of light in the thick darkness.

Like every home in Britain, Englemere Wood had been subject to the blackout laws from the day the girls had arrived, and Mrs Peyton had ensured the job was done properly. Not a chink of light escaped from the windows at night.

There were no street lamps on the nearby road for fear of assisting the Germans nor were there stars in the sky. Moreover, the garden was enveloped in silence.

Queenie took a few tentative steps one way, then another, but she was by now utterly disorientated in the obsidian black. She plunged around the grounds, getting more confused as every long minute went by. When she finally came to a halt, in the grip of growing panic and still holding an armful of laundry, she heard a familiar sound, faintly at first but growing louder with every second. It was the comforting sound of British army boots hitting Tarmac.

A platoon of soldiers billeted in Ascot's racecourse stands were marching along the nearby Bagshot Road.

'Help,' she cried faintly at first.

'Help, help.' She was louder this time. If she didn't make herself heard, she realized she could be stranded in the garden all night long.

Immediately a cry considerably more robust than her own rang out. 'Platoon, halt.' As the sound of marching feet stopped a man's voice rang out. 'Where are you?'

'I'm here,' she shouted back.

'Where?' came the disembodied voice.

'Here,' she shouted louder still.

She made out the sounds of people coming towards her. With apparent ease two soldiers located her – she had wandered out into the road – and returned with her to the sergeant in charge.

Queenie explained where she lived and what had happened and, together, they all made their way to the house. The sergeant headed towards the front door, the preserve of Mrs Peyton and her guests.

'Let's go round the back,' Queenie implored.

When they arrived at the back door she made a half-hearted attempt to say goodbye and thank you. But, as she suspected, the soldiers wanted to see her inside. After they knocked a perplexed Matron Bailey appeared on the step.

At seeing Queenie among the soldiers her response was one of surprise and concern. She bade goodnight to the soldiers and turned her full attention to Queenie. In the warmth and security of the house, the youngster was overcome with conflicting emotions. She felt relieved, foolish – and more than a little concerned about the retribution that might await her.

As she burbled her explanations Matron responded swiftly. 'Well, that will teach you a lesson you won't forget in a hurry . . .'

Then her expression softened. To her horror one of her charges had been outside at night, lost and alone. The child had clearly been terrified and Matron felt no desire to compound her troubles.

With one arm round her shoulder Matron led Queenie gently into the kitchen. Still listening to the fractured account being given, she made a drink of hot milk. She knew Queenie was not a fan of the drink but the overriding concern was that she slept well that night to recover from the ordeal.

There was no telling-off for Queenie that night or the day after – but no one was allowed to leave the house alone after dark again. It was one of Queenie's last memories of Englemere Wood.

In her mid-teens, with her house training complete, Queenie left to return to her mother's address in London where her sister Gladys was still living. For Queenie it was a sorrowful day that had come all too soon. She said a sad farewell to girls she had come to see as siblings and to the woman who had been like a mother to her.

Matron watched her go down the Englemere Wood drive, until she was out of sight. Queenie possessed all the gifts that Matron considered necessary for a happy life: she was kind, considerate, hard-working and good-humoured. There was only one thing that bothered her. Would Queenie's mother now recognize and appreciate all the qualities her daughter had? Previously she'd encountered mothers who were all too keen to have their daughters back home once they were able to command a weekly wage.

Matron was right to be concerned. Although they were related by blood, there was little that bonded Queenie to her mother and she struggled to find common ground with either her mother or her sister Gladys. Immediately Queenie joined the staff of one of the wartime nurseries, established to help working women whose husbands were in the services. When children arrived first thing in the morning at the site in Balham they were dressed in nursery clothes, to save mothers the task of laundering for their children. Children were bathed and fed there too, before being collected by weary mums, typically after a long day inside a noisy factory.

Each day Queenie clocked on at 7 a.m., ready for her eight-hour shift. After a bite to eat, she usually chose to stay at the nursery for a few more hours. Not only did she love her work, she had little inclination to return home. And when Queenie finally did turn up at the end of the day, it wasn't to a cosy hearth and a hot meal but to the privations of the local air-raid shelter. Hitler's V-1 and V-2 bombs were causing terror as they rained down on London. During long and often sleepless nights spent in the damp, dark shelter, cheek by jowl with neighbours, her thoughts strayed to Englemere Wood and she longed to enjoy the closeness of the family life that she had known there again and the comfort of Matron's presence.

Yet for some girls, Matron's winning ways were not immediately apparent. The school log shows that one girl,

Vera, ran away twice in quick succession. Police were called in to find her on the first occasion. She was, apparently, a difficult case. Yet just weeks after the second incident the same school log shows Vera won a prize for writing, indicating Matron had won her round. It seems Vera had settled into the home's warm embrace, started to enjoy school and was thriving.

Lois was also a reluctant resident. One of five children, her family life ended abruptly with the death of her mother. Everything about her new home irked her: the rigid controls on food, the rigorous cleaning rota, the rules she considered petty and the routines that left her numb. She yearned for a loving hug – and there were none to be had at Englemere Wood. Matron still believed hugging individual children would make them all think she had favourites. Lois wondered if she had done something terrible, to land up in a home, even though she was accompanied by a sister. A promise to 'be good' made to their mother on her deathbed, still haunted her. Children like Lois presented a major challenge for staff at Waifs and Strays homes up and down the country; bereft by bereavement or damaged by negligence. The sole option was to ensure those remaining childhood years were tolerable, or even joyful. Only years later, after having children of her own, could Lois acknowledge that her childhood – although not perfect – was comfortingly secure.

Girls continued to come and go, with Barbara leaving to work for Princess Marie Louise, and sisters Gloria and Joyce joining the Maurice Home. But the knitting circle remained a constant in the girls' lives. When new girls arrived in the place of those who had started their working lives, the royal knitting circle protocol was painstakingly learned. Joyce, who replaced Jenny as the youngest in the home, practised hard before leaving the security of Englemere Wood for the 'white house'. Everyone was convinced she had mastered the necessary manners so no one was prepared for what happened next.

As she stepped forward to greet Princess Marie Louise, she bobbed down as she had been drilled to do and uttered: 'Good evening, My Highness.'

The heads of the older girls swivelled, then all eyes fell on Princess Marie Louise to see her response. A highly charged hush was swiftly broken.

'How delightful,' the princess cooed. If she had noticed the deathly silence that had fallen over the room, she was certain she didn't want Joyce to be aware of it.

'From now on you must all call me "My Highness". That's absolutely the right thing to do,' she told them with a smile.

With the production of woollens for the troops at such a high rate, the girls felt like part of a special regiment devoted to the war effort. After they were on one occasion awarded small enamel pins to mark their role as volunteers, they set about new pieces of clothing with renewed vigour.

In addition to the satisfaction of helping British soldiers beat Hitler and the thrill of meeting royalty, there was another reward for the assembled girls that occurred to them only much later. The weekly date was rarely broken, a fact that ultimately became clear to the girls. That commitment by the princesses and Lady Weigall elevated their status from abandoned children to valued companions, and made them understand the merit of keeping one's word.

One Friday at the start of June 1944 a column of girls left Englemere Wood at the appointed hour, heading for Englemere House. They expected to stop as usual at the road, which was always busy with military vehicles, to wait for a gap in the traffic. Today there wasn't a car, truck or motorbike in sight. The girls exchanged glances and Enid called out, 'Where has everyone gone?' Matron and Mrs Peyton couldn't be sure of the answer, so said nothing. But four days later, the newspapers revealed the Normandy landings had taken place. Allied troops set foot in occupied Europe for the first time in four years and soldiers from local bases were part of the fight.

Although Germany continued to put up stiff resistance, it became obvious that the Allies would win the war. The progress of British soldiers was triumphantly monitored, although the deaths of local men were still being announced in church every Sunday. Still, there was an undercurrent of optimism around the place.

In the spring of 1945 two women who had spent the war years together, enjoying good times and enduring terrible ones, were seated in the drawing room at Englemere Wood, sipping tea from china cups.

'I've been thinking about the future,' Dorothy Peyton began cautiously. Matron nodded but said nothing. Her gratitude for the safe, stable environment of Englemere Wood during troubled times had already been roundly stated.

'John will be coming home at some point, of course,' Mrs Peyton continued. 'He will need the tranquillity of Englemere Wood to help him recover from this awful ordeal he is going through. We will need our home back.'

If Matron felt a lightning bolt of concern at the words,

nothing was betrayed by her face. In fact, she had already calculated that the harmonious arrangement between them would end when the hostilities did. By any measure, she felt her host had gone far beyond the realms of public duty, with all that she'd yielded up to the staff and children of the Maurice Home. Nonetheless, there was a niggling concern about what lay ahead for her girls now. She knew the premises that used to house the Maurice Home, in Mattock Lane, Ealing, was derelict and probably couldn't be used, at least not yet. But Mrs Peyton wasn't finished.

'The girls have fitted in so well in Ascot and everyone in the town has grown quite used to having them around,' Mrs Peyton continued. 'The girls at the high school are doing well; it seems a shame to disrupt them. And I know everyone on the Maurice Home committee is keen to continue.

'I've been speaking to Mrs Elliott on the subject. As you know, she lives across the road at Sandridge House. I used to live there and I know just how large it is – far too big for her now. She is hoping the Waifs and Strays Society will take it on, so you could all move across the road into that house, from this one, while she moves into the Coach House.'

A beam erupted across Matron's face and Mrs Peyton couldn't help smiling herself. She had delivered the girls from peril when London was under threat from German bombers but, in return, they had been her salvation after Tommy was killed. With John in distant incarceration, the girls became her reason to carry on – and it wasn't something she was ever going to forget.

After an arduous campaign through France and Germany, Allied troops were finally victorious and 8 May was declared VE day to mark the triumph in Europe. It would be another four months before Japan surrendered.

Peace brought a series of changes to those at Englemere Wood, now in its final furlong as a children's home before returning to a family residence. Most memorably VE day was marked by a telephone call from John Peyton. The first bonfires of the VE day celebrations were being lit as his flight into Aylesbury touched down. It wasn't, however, a moment of unfettered joy.

When he spoke with the RAF station commander's wife, just before making the call, it was the first woman's voice he had heard in five years. Then more new experiences left his nerves jangling: eating with china plates, sleeping in a bed, travelling by train, using a ceramic toilet, enjoying a bath. He met people who had spent the war without experiencing danger. Others he encountered had been in major battles in which they were commended for their courage and achievements. Neither matched his experiences.

Dorothy had been anxiously waiting for news of his return. But when it came the telephone conversation was short and delivered in monotones. Both had been irrevocably changed by the conflict: he by years of incarceration and she by the presence of the Maurice Home and the loss of a much-loved son. Together she and John were united in numb grief. But reliving the tragedy was not a unifying experience.

John found he didn't want to go home, as his mother had hoped he would. Reluctant to discuss the prison camp years, he knew they would both find Tommy's absence upsetting and suspected it would drive them apart rather than bring them together. Furthermore, Mary, the woman he had met and fallen in love with on the eve of heading to France all those years before, was about to marry someone else. His mood was low.

When he visited Englemere Wood, the girls saw his thin, drawn figure walking the grounds and sensed a gulf between his wartime experiences and their own.

Dorothy felt the harrowing detachment and hoped it would disappear with time. Once she had been a mother to three robust boys. Now her brood was reduced to one and the pain never left her. In her heart she hoped her surviving son would never experience such grief. Even now, three and a half years after Tommy's death, it was difficult for her to articulate what she felt.

Although she approached the celebrations of the conflict's end with mixed feelings, Mrs Peyton nonetheless provided a victory tea for the pupils at Ascot Heath School on Thursday, 17 May. The children had already enjoyed a two-day holiday from the school the previous week to mark peace in Europe.

Four days later, there was more excitement to come. The gates of Englemere Wood were flung wide and small groups of excited girls were beckoning cars in. It was Whit Monday, 21 May 1945, and a scaled-back race meeting was being held at Ascot Racecourse, which Princess Elizabeth was attending. Mrs Peyton had suggested her capacious drive could be used for parking, with the car parking charges going to the Waifs and Strays Society to help with the expenses of the move. The girls soon produced a hand-painted sign for the occasion, saying CAR PARK 10 SHILLINGS.

Like other illustrious sporting events, Ascot had been

cancelled for most of the war. Now there was a huge appetite to attend, and cars poured through the gates: Standard tourers, Lagonda Coupés, Triumph Dolomite Roadsters, Sunbeam-Talbot Saloons and even the occasional Hillman Minx. British car production had largely been given over to military purposes in the early forties and for most it was a first opportunity to take the dust sheets off their prestige vehicles.

Before the war it had been an occasion for high fashion. As a nod to the continuing war effort in the Far East, people dressed down this time, wearing bowler hats rather than top hats. But women still used flowers and feathers on their hats to their best advantage, and smart clothes that had survived since 1939 in the backs of wardrobes seemed pristine against the drab outfits that had characterized the war years.

The younger girls lined up at the windows to watch events unfold. 'Oooh, look at her,' said Joyce, as a willowy woman with a matching suit and bag stepped out of a car, a hat decorated with osprey feathers perched on her head.

'I prefer that one,' said Gloria, pointing to a boater, its rim heavy with fresh blooms. Before long a group of girls burst into a popular music hall song already more than fifty years old.

Where did you get that hat? Where did you get that tile?
Isn't it a nobby one, and just the proper style?
I should like to have one, just the same as that!
Where'er I go, they shout, 'Hello!' Where did you get that hat?

'Look at her lipstick and her rouge,' said Peggy, pointing out another new arrival.

'A woman's first duty is to her face,' said Gloria, having glimpsed a recent newspaper advertisement.

They turned suddenly at the sound of Matron's voice.

'Why attempt to improve on God's handiwork?' she asked them quizzically, with eyebrows slightly raised. They had no response but went on to admire the creamy pallor of the racegoers' faces more quietly than before.

Outside Sheila was selling fresh buttonholes from flowers cut from gardens in the neighbourhood. Although she enjoyed seeing the fashions and the faces she only just about disguised her awkwardness at being so conspicuous. It felt, she thought, like being the little match girl in Hans Christian Andersen's cautionary tale about poverty and pity.

She looked over at Barbara, now a maid working for Princess Marie Louise, who was also busy in the drive, helping to welcome visitors. They exchanged a grin before continuing with their respective tasks. Sheila didn't notice the much longer look shared between twenty-year-old Barbara and the princess's chauffeur, smartly dressed in a peaked cap, tie and gloves. In fact, it took many moments for Barbara and Harry to drag their eyes away from one another.

Inside the gates Major Fyson, now the chairman of the Maurice Home committee in Ascot, was directing vehicles with military precision. Once they were in position, and their owners heading the short distance to the racecourse, the girls patrolled the rows to ensure nothing happened to the cars while they were in the custody of Englemere Wood.

At the end of the day the owners of the cars and their passengers returned, with those who'd bet shrewdly keen to share their good fortune. At the sight of Matron in her neat uniform on the steps of the home they plucked notes from their bulging wallets and pressed them in her hand.

'Here, this is for the kiddies. Get them something nice,' they boomed.

Sometimes, racegoers gave coins and notes directly to the girls; Sheila was presented with a five-pound note. There was no thought of heading triumphantly to the sweet shop, though. All money went to Matron, who kept a cash box and an account book that mapped the income and expenditure associated with each girl. The money they took to All Saints for church collections came from here, as did the cash to buy stamps for letters home. The rest went into National Savings Certificates, a scheme started in the First World War to help cover conflict expenses. Everyone had been encouraged to save money that could be used on the war effort and would pay dividends when the conflict ended. The project continued in peacetime and returned in the next war when the government told people: 'The things we are saving for are the things we are fighting for: freedom of religion, justice for all and a better life for the future generation.'

With national savings drives a frequent occurrence around the country, the imperative to save money didn't change with the declaration of peace, and there was no resentment among the girls at being parted from their money.

Plans to move from Englemere Wood were accelerating. Still, Matron found time to read aloud a letter from Waifs and Strays Society secretary W. R. Vaughan. 'Gather round, everyone,' she instructed her staff. 'Here's a letter from head office, from Mr Vaughan himself.'

The staff had met Mr Vaughan when he visited Englemere Wood to discuss Sheila's education. They were impressed by his dignified manner and were thrilled to hear from him, even if the words were intended for all society homes.

After clearing her throat, Matron began to read his words aloud, praising the response of the staff during the conflict. 'It says here: "The society stood as a buffer between the worst effects of wartime conditions and the children who stood to lose the most." Goodness me. In five years the society accepted almost 9,700 children, with more than 5,000 of those under the age of five. It became the protector and guardian of more under-fives than any other organization in the country.'

Miss Hutchings broke in. 'Thank goodness for the war nurseries. And what marvellous people there were, to give their homes to the society so that so many nurseries could open.'

Matron resumed with the letter. 'Mr Vaughan calls it "the conquest of common sense over chaos". And he goes on to say that matrons "added to their duties by writing personal letters of thanks for everything received and sent frequent news of the children to their unseen friends overseas and this helped to maintain a friendly link with the donors".'

Matron lowered the letter with a furrowed brow. 'Well, as if we would accept the kind donations we had, without writing a letter to say thank you. There may have been a war on, but we still had our good manners. I simply don't understand why we should be thanked for this, doing what we should be doing and what anyone would do, but there we have it.' She finished the letter with all its praise but couldn't help feeling misunderstood by the powers that be.

Staff continued to work hard, to eradicate as many difficult childhood memories as they could among their young charges, and tried to put the war behind them. But one day they were confronted with one of the worst legacies of the conflict in a surprising way.

'Matron,' called one of the girls, rushing into Englemere Wood in the autumn of 1945, 'there are boys playing football on the racecourse in their pyjamas.'

Turning slowly to greet the questioner, Matron's thoughts were racing. The boys playing on the racecourse had been liberated from Belsen and other concentration camps and flown to Britain to start the long road to recuperation at Woodcote House. As the British government refused to finance a refugee scheme the Central British Fund – the same organization responsible for the Kindertransport that had spirited 10,000 Jewish children out of Europe before the war – paid for hundreds of children to be re-habilitated in Britain for two years.

They'd had numbers, much as girls in the Maurice Home did, but theirs were tattooed on the papery skin of their arms. While Ascot had mourned the loss of soldiers like Tommy Peyton, that day's football players had lost their entire families in concentration camps and the scale of their suffering had been immense. These Belsen boys were bone-thin with thread-like hair, hollow cheeks and grey skin. But mostly they were happy to be alive – and it showed.

Matron had already heard that they used their distinctive concentration camp shirts to distinguish their team when they played against local boys. They were proud survivors, content to talk about their dreadful experiences and looking forward to a brighter future that had been denied to so many young Jews throughout Europe.

For a moment Matron feared she would be left floundering for words to reflect the atrocity that came into such sharp focus as the war in Europe ended. Before the conflict finished, Matron had listened in horror when BBC reporter Richard Dimbleby told what the British Army found when they liberated Belsen in April 1945, with bony, emaciated survivors barely clinging to life. Since then, she had seen the film shown in cinemas about the concentration camps, just as the government suggested. It started with scenes of the grass-covered graves at Belsen. Grave No. 2 had 5,000 bodies in it, Grave No. 3, a similar number, Grave No. 8, 1,000 and in Grave No. 10 there were an unknown number. It would be difficult to convey the scale of killing that had taken place.

'Girls, remember how we lost Mr Tommy during the war?' Matron looked expectantly at the girls around her. Those who had lived at Englemere Wood for several years nodded keenly.

'Well, he died because there are some wicked people in the world who want to do harm to other people. Hitler didn't like those boys and their families because they were Jewish. I don't know why that was,' she said quickly, as one girl appeared ready to jump in with a question.

'Mr Tommy went to war so those boys could be saved. There was nothing fair about it, but there it is. Now we must hope those boys live a good life, just as we must. Remember the promise we made?'

Most of the girls nodded, although a few of the newer arrivals looked uncertain.

'I know,' said Matron. 'Let's say the promise again together now.' And her voice joined the chorus that followed.

'We will, as a family, build by our very lives an unseen memorial to the memory of this gallant Christian gentleman and in so doing we will remember all others unknown, who made the same sacrifice.'

Matron viewed them with satisfaction. A plan drawn up to comfort grief-stricken girls three years previously looked as if it would continue to wield a good influence.

16. A New Era

Moving house is always stressful, but to their immense relief Matron and her staff were given the luxury of time, so the switch wasn't immediate or rushed. The owner of Sandridge House, Mrs Elliott, often travelled abroad, leaving Matron and her staff the chance to plan their rooms before the move. Afterwards it was renamed Grenville House in honour of Tommy Peyton.

The official opening, on 27 July 1946 by Princess Marie Louise, was consequently a low-key affair, as it was impossible not to once again be immersed in the grief of his loss. But following the ceremony there was a get-together, the kind repeated many times afterwards as Matron realized the boost that a party brought. Not only were all the residents there but numerous old girls came along too.

Mrs Peyton watched proceedings, thrilled that the home had found more appropriate accommodation despite the circumstances. She smiled warmly at the girls who had until recently been living under her roof and still called her

'Madam'. When it came to old girls, she asked how they were and what they were doing – and marvelled at how well life was treating them, even in the global tumult.

To Grenville House she gave a portrait of Tommy, which took pride of place in one of its hallways. Rays from a skylight poured down on it during the daytime. At night an electric light was switched on, so his face was never in darkness. The girls who had been at Englemere Wood in the early years of the war needed no reminder about his death. But Mrs Peyton knew his values and everything he stood for would now be at the core of this new household, and that gave her some solace. Alongside the portrait was a cross made from wood salvaged from St James's Church in Piccadilly, where Dorothy and Ivor had wed, after it was bombed on 14 October 1940. Evelyne Evans, a friend of the home, godmother to one of the girls and long-time friend of Matron, had previously presented it to Mrs Peyton.

Sheila was by now a sixth-former – and she was given a room of her own. With more space than ever before, Matron could afford to allocate bedrooms to older girls that offered them the same kind of privacy that other girls their age knew. After almost a decade in her care, Matron was delighted that Sheila was to benefit, although she was careful to mask her feelings for fear it would be interpreted as favouritism. However, Sheila was instantly carried away with this unexpected good fortune. After Matron had delivered the news as she went to explore Grenville House for the first time, Sheila went bounding up the stairs to the third-floor box room without a backwards glance.

'Well?' Matron said sternly to her swiftly departing figure.

'Thank you, Matron. Thank you very much,' gasped out Sheila, her joy undented. The war was over and many of the girls she grew up with had moved on, but Sheila's dependence on the home continued as she strove for a career.

She took in the black iron bedstead, the Victorian wardrobe with its mirrored door and a table that would act as a desk – and hugged herself with happiness. After her first night in the room, she realized she didn't miss the companionship of other girls or the symphony of sleep noises one bit.

Mrs Peyton was also getting used to a quieter life. When the Maurice girls were gone and with her son making independent steps in the post-war world, Englemere Wood would once again seem cavernous and unappealing. She wanted less living space but was still very attached to the house. She maintained her links with the girls, as the same committee that looked after the needs of Englemere Wood girls would switch its support to Grenville House. Thanks to her, there would still be a sense of aspiration attached to Grenville House, just as there had been to Englemere Wood, with some girls going to Ranelagh School. She helped find work for those destined for more menial work, often providing employment in her own household. And she kept in contact with many old girls by letter.

Matron was still in charge of the home, bringing steadfastness, security and comfort to girls whose lives were chaotic. For although the war had ended, the problem of unwanted or unmanageable children continued and Grenville House would see just as many challenging children come through its doors as Englemere Wood had. At the time the lure of London's bomb sites proved too much for many children, who preferred clambering over towers of bricks and delving into exposed cellars to the rigours of reading and writing. But if London and Europe beyond it were in turmoil, the same disciplines that once held sway at Englemere Wood now governed Grenville House.

Gladys Raffell, ten, and her eight-year-old sister Vera were among those who skipped school to play hopscotch on the pavement, marbles in the gutter or to swing on ropes hung from the tops of gas lamps in the street.

When they arrived at Grenville House on Friday, 18 April 1947, at 5 p.m., Matron's first act was to usher them into the dining room where the other girls were huddled round the wireless, listening with rapt attention. The programme being broadcast was *Children's Hour*, compulsory listening for anyone between the ages of five and fifteen.

At the same time every day the programme beamed enchanting fiction into homes across the empire, including the *Just So Stories* by British author Rudyard Kipling, creator of *The Jungle Book*, as well as Sherlock Holmes, Worzel Gummidge, Toy Town and Winnie-the-Pooh. This time the drama was about the fabled Cocos Island treasure, Spanish gold hidden on the uninhabited Pacific island in the nineteenth century. With talk of ruthless pirates and a seven-foot-tall solid-gold Madonna lost to a desert island's shifting sands, all the girls were wide-eyed and silent.

The producer of this dramatic story was Derek McCulloch, also known as 'Uncle Mac', whose sign-off line of 'Goodnight, children, everywhere,' became particularly poignant following mass evacuation during the war years. *Children's Hour*, which started in 1922, was a radio stalwart until 1964, when it stopped after losing most of its audience to television.

Gladys and Vera slipped unobtrusively into their places in the semi circle, soon forgetting to be self-conscious as the story caught their interest. There was a familiarity about the show that put them on a level pegging with the girls they were meeting for the first time. As it ended, they fielded a few questions from curious girls.

'Where are you from?' demanded one, her eyes narrow.

'London,' said Gladys with a toss of her head. She was used to speaking on behalf of her younger sister.

'Where's your mum?' Another girl calculated the question would pierce the bravado of this new girl.

'London.'

Her mum, suffering from degenerating sight, was indeed still at home with her other siblings, although the girls had been deemed too much of a handful. Gladys decided that was enough information to give away for the time being, particularly as they were all being beckoned into the playroom for tea.

Afterwards Matron took them up a sweeping staircase, past numerous doors left and right, to a cupboard on a landing filled with clothes. She held up garments against them; these were second-hand but not scruffy. The girls selected the best fits for skirts, dresses and shoes before the garments were marked with their numbers, Gladys being nine and Vera six.

Until this point the girls hadn't given clothes a thought. Every day they had put on the same well-worn outfit, caked in city dirt and too shabby to be patched. Now they had a full ensemble of clothes: jumpers, skirts, school uniforms, socks and shoes. Although they fizzed with pleasure they hid it behind blank expressions, behaviour learned in their younger years.

Next it was back to the playroom for a haircut. All the girls in the home who were of school age wore the same short bob. Vera's hair was already cropped but Gladys was sat down to be given the ubiquitous style. As the long scissors started snipping, her eyes wandered between bookcase, lockers and the polished wooden floor, then fell on the dolls' cots in the corner. This new home began to show promise! There was a piano, she could see that, but also a sewing machine, something unfamiliar that would only be operated by staff when they repaired sheets and clothes. Tall glass doors revealed the garden had plenty of shrubs and flowers but also fruit trees and vegetable beds. It didn't take long before the task was finished and Gladys felt an unfamiliar breeze round the back of her neck as she fingered the ends of her hair, now just below her ear lobe.

As they crossed the main hall a striking head-and-shoulders portrait of a young man in soldier's uniform attracted their attention. Sunlight was pouring down on to the picture. Even at night it was illuminated by an electric bulb, and it was difficult to pass by without comment.

'Who's that?' Gladys asked Jenny. The older girl was helping her to navigate the seemingly endless corridors.

'That's Tommy Peyton. Mr Tommy we called him,' said Jenny sadly. 'He lived at the house where we lived during the war. Now he's a symbol for us of all the young men who are now gone, so that we might live in a peaceful world. After he died in the St Nazaire raid we all made a promise to live better lives to honour him. And you will soon, I expect.'

Gladys gazed at the strikingly handsome face for a few moments before heading to the bathroom at the end of a green-painted bedroom with six beds. After a bath, the sisters were shown where they would be sleeping. Gladys looked round sharply to see if her sister was nearby. No, Vera was being taken to a different bed in the same room. Unexpected excitement surged through her. For the first time in her life Gladys would be sleeping in a bed of her own.

Stretching out on the mattress after the lights had been turned out felt strange and luxurious. But suddenly she felt a familiar warmth cuddling in on one side. Vera had tiptoed across the dormitory and wriggled her way under the covers.

'What are you doing?' Gladys whispered.

'I can't get to sleep by myself,' said Vera quietly. As they lay together in a familiar pattern of interlocking arms and legs their eyes began to close and instantly it seemed as if they were back home in London, fighting for space in the bed with their brothers and sisters. Had they dreamed the trip to Grenville House? All the conflicting emotions about leaving their home vanished for a moment.

But in the morning came the soft voice of one of the home's sisters. 'Vera, you must get back into your own bed now.'

Grenville House was real enough and both girls would soon learn to live within its regulations – and take pleasure in sleeping alone in a single bed.

At first, Gladys grappled with the unfamiliar house rules. She wasn't allowed to go off to play until a variety of chores had been completed. For now the home seemed a maze. There was a bedroom for the older schoolgirls, known as the blue room, and one painted pink for the school-aged girls. Gladys and Vera were in the green-themed nursery above the quiet room so they could be assured of always getting enough rest. Sited furthest away from the green room was the bedroom where the house girls slept, as their tasks started early and continued long after the youngest children were asleep. Although she was nineteen, Sheila now occupied an old-girls' room when she came back from her teacher-training course during the holidays. She always got a warm welcome. Her conversation was mostly with Matron Bailey and staff, but the younger girls were thrilled when she spoke to them. To them she seemed impossibly glamorous.

When it came to the door of the bedroom belonging to Matron or one of the sisters, the girls had to creep past quietly so as not to disturb them. It was made clear Gladys was unlikely to see the individual bedrooms at the top of the house, not for the time being anyway. But somewhere up there, she was told, apples and pears were being stored after the autumn harvest so there was the promise of tasty pies.

Coats and boots were kept by the back door, but once again the clatter and chatter when coming in from the garden had to be kept to a minimum, as Matron's office was next door. Girls arguing over whose turn it was to clean the shoes were quickly put right, with the task often being wielded as a punishment.

That first weekend flew by, marked by communal singing, a long walk in the countryside and a church service, with Gladys and Vera getting to know routes around their new home and garden. They drank tea drawn from a cumbersome brass urn, not realizing the beloved workhorse had been brought from Ealing and had been used every day since. For Sunday breakfast they enjoyed fried bread spread with dripping.

Outside, both looked up in wonder at the fir tree that dominated the garden, its lower branches touching the ground and creating a hideout by the hefty trunk. When Vera ran towards a large boat-like pram parked by the wall, hoping to find yet another doll inside, she was told it was only used by older girls when they ran errands in the town. (Later it came in useful when old girls visited with new babies.)

By now the society had been in existence for more than sixty-five years and cared for at least 70,000 children. Many, like Gladys, had been habitual truants and she was dreading the day she would be returning to the classroom.

The next day, Monday, Gladys awoke to the sound of a small bell, with a sinking feeling in her stomach. 'It's seven fifteen,' one of the sisters called into the room.

'Gladys, you're new, aren't you? First you must wash your hands and face, clean your teeth and go to the toilet. Then make the bed – with "hospital corners", mind. Don't worry, you'll have an older girl to help. After that I'd like you to help sweep and dust the bedroom. Breakfast is at eight ten. And no talking.'

With Grenville House much more spacious than Englemere Wood, there were a greater number of rooms to clean. Girls busied themselves with the daily tasks allocated to them. Gladys's head buzzed with the volley of instructions until another bell sounded, this time at 7.45 a.m. Now it was time to wash hands, change into school uniform and line up to have their nails inspected. Before she had time to object, she was washed, dressed, had cleaned the bedroom and was filled with porridge before being funnelled into the crocodile of girls making their way to school. Still not a word had been uttered among the girls.

Accompanied to and from school by staff, there was little opportunity for Gladys to bunk off. However, school had an alarming familiarity about it. The letters on the pages of textbooks jumped around in front of her while the maths made no sense at all. In truth, Gladys could not even write her own name. Too overawed to ask a question, she doodled, ran her fingertips across the ridges of the wooden desk and daydreamed about her life in London. Yes, she had often been hungry, and it could be cold on the London streets, but in retrospect it wasn't so bad after all. She hatched a plan.

At 5 p.m. that night Matron was passing when the phone rang.

'Hello, Grenville House,' she said. 'Matron here.' Then she listened carefully as the stationmaster from Ascot told her how a small girl with a telltale haircut had turned up a short time before. The girl hadn't bought a ticket, but clearly had every expectation of catching the next London-bound train as she wandered under the station's frilled canopies.

When she put the phone down, Matron quickly established

the girl at the station was Gladys. She'd suspected as much. Gladys wasn't the first girl to abscond from Matron's care and probably wouldn't be the last. Keeping reluctant children in the fold was a difficult task but an essential one. She fought an initial instinct to rush to the station to retrieve her wayward charge. Instead, she summoned Jenny, now sixteen, and dispatched her to the station instead.

It was a short distance to the station from the home and Jenny arrived before the London train was due to depart.

'Gladys,' she called from the station entrance. Shoulders slumped, Gladys trudged towards the older girl, understanding the game was up for now at least.

The silence between the pair was broken by Jenny as they made their way back to Grenville House.

'Look, I'm not sure why you tried to run away but you need to think about this. Matron's not a bad sort. I think you can see that already. I've been in the home since I was younger than you are now and, honestly, there are much worse places to be. There's a lot to be said for having everything laid on for you when you need it. Doing chores isn't so bad. Actually, I like it much better having everything neat and clean. And I know you don't feel like you want to go to school now but it can't all be jam. What do you want out of life, Gladys?'

Gladys contemplated the question. Undeniably there were aspects of her new life that seemed to hold promise for a better future: warm clothing, regular meals and a bed all to herself.

When they arrived at Grenville House, Gladys flinched when Matron bowled towards her.

'Goodness me, child, did you think I would smack you?' Matron asked, looking deeply troubled rather than angry. 'There's none of that sort of thing here; there never has been, has there, Jenny?'

Jenny agreed and they both looked at Gladys, who for the first time understood what the weight of expectation felt like.

Gradually Gladys found that, after she learned to make friends, she liked school a little better and finally began to tackle educational challenges with enthusiasm. She mastered letters quickly and found she loved writing. She also triumphed over basic maths. Swiftly she pushed memories of her former shambolic lifestyle to the back of her mind.

Gladys was the sixth child of a London couple, born two years before the war started and who had been evacuated from Seven Dials with her family to Marlow, Buckinghamshire. But when German raids didn't materialize they didn't stay away for long. That put them in the line of German fire during the Battle of Britain when slum-clearance programmes that had been planned prior to the conflict were completed by Luftwaffe bombers.

The Raffell flat had two rooms and a box room. There was no inside bathroom. Domestic routine was frequently interrupted by bombing raids, which then entailed a trip to a nearby bomb shelter.

At five years old Gladys was already truanting from school, even when she was accompanied to the school gates by her mother, hobbled by diminishing eyesight. Before the older woman opened the front door on her return, Gladys was already inside the family home. Chased out by her mother, she failed to head back to school but roamed instead among weed-ridden bomb sites or splashed in the fountains at Trafalgar Square, running among the feral pigeons that flocked there. Her ambition was to scale the lion statues that guarded Nelson's Column and to this end she devoted some considerable effort. However, the one time she succeeded in mounting the bronze beast she tumbled, injured herself and was taken to hospital by an American GI.

Even without taming the lions, there was plenty to do outside. Games of hide-and-seek, leapfrog and skipping with ropes sprang up everywhere. She picked up and pulled apart the dog-ends of cigarettes to liberate the last remaining scraps of tobacco. These could be swapped for empty cigarette packets – collectors' items of the era – or other treats. When she was feeling particularly brave, she might cling unseen to the back of the horse-drawn coal merchant's cart for a free ride.

When the V-1 and V-2 bombs began raining down on the capital in 1944 she spent a few months on a farm in Wales before moving back to London, this time to Shepherd's Bush. But Gladys continued to play truant, tempting her younger sister Vera down the same path. They drove their mother – almost blind at this point – to distraction with their behaviour.

Eventually the girls' Aunt Em intervened, and it was she who signed the papers that had them sent to a children's home, something for which Gladys thanked her emphatically in later life.

Gladys soon got used to the notion of lessons every weekday in Ascot – she felt she had no choice but to put up with it – but it was the weekends she particularly relished.

On Saturdays there was an assembly in the main hall at Grenville House. The girls gathered in a semicircle, with one choosing a hymn and another being chosen to sing a verse solo. Gladys soon learned she had a fine singing voice and quickly began vying with the others for the privilege. Like all the girls, Gladys and Vera got to know the music and lyrics of 'The Grenville Song', an anthem to all those who lived in the house, specifically recalling the heroism of Tommy Peyton and drawing them closer together in his memory.

Saturday-morning singing was rousing and invigorating, and gave the girls renewed energy for their afternoon activities. Often the girls went for a walk, either to Virginia Water or Windsor Great Park. The format had changed little over the years. Girls carrying their picnic and a small square of waterproof cloth to sit on walked through the racecourse, found the same area covered with tree trunks to sit on, walked or ran for miles through grass and bracken and played the same games that children who were by now old girls had known.

The faithful Una had died, to be replaced by Susan, a black mongrel puppy retrieved from a dustbin in Ascot and unwanted until she received an enthusiastic welcome at Grenville House. Trotting behind them now, Susan was so obedient she didn't need a lead.

In the summer the Grenville home went to Cromer for the third successive year for picnics, paddling and wind-blown walks. By now they were known by local people, including famous lifeboatman Henry Blogg, who saved 873 lives in an illustrious career with the Royal National Lifeboat Institution. They even went to Sandringham in the hope of seeing Queen Mary on their first holiday in Cromer, after the war – she had recognized them and waved as she drove away from the royal home.

At Christmas there were presents engineered by Matron and the Maurice Home committee in the usual way. When Gladys and Vera received nothing from their mother they assumed they had been forgotten. But caught up in the excitement of stockings from Father Christmas, a Christmas lunch and parcels under the tree, they didn't dwell on the lack of contact. There were, as always, a series of parties and a panto at the theatre in Windsor to look forward to as well.

For Jenny 1948 would be a memorable year for all the wrong reasons. It started brightly enough. Carol Carter, who wrote 'The Grenville Song', had known Matron Bailey since her days spent working in London. It wasn't the first piece of music she'd written for the girls. Inspired by the ties being formed at Englemere Wood, and a radio broadcast to the nation by Princess Elizabeth in 1940, she wrote a musical nativity play called *The Prince of Peace*.

The princess's speech had included the words: 'And when peace comes, remember it will be for us, the children of today, to make the world of tomorrow a better and happier place.'

In the musical children sought a better world in the future and it ended with Jenny – much younger then and in a starring role – giving her treasured Brownie uniform to the newborn Prince of Peace – the most valuable item she possessed.

The play was deemed such a success it was performed in churches and village halls around Ascot. With each performance the children gained confidence. And Miss Carter had enough conviction in her work to write other plays, including *The Land of Other-Where*, which was performed by the girls in the garden at Englemere Wood, this time for Mrs Peyton's birthday. But perhaps the greatest moment for the young actors and the prolific playwright came after one specially written Easter play was performed. *Consider the Lilies* was so popular that word of it reached the ears of the king. One gardener, whose identity has been lost through time, was so impressed that he mentioned it as the monarch took a stroll around the castle gardens. Before long an inscribed invitation arrived from the Royal Family, asking the girls to perform at the Royal Chapel in Windsor Great Park. On Sunday, 9 May 1948 the girls were in the spotlight, fighting nerves to give the performance of their lives. Matron's words were ringing in their ears as they took to the stage: 'Backs straight. Head up. I want to hear every word.'

Afterwards they shook hands with the king, Queen Elizabeth, Princess Elizabeth and her fiancé Philip before the audience departed for the Royal Lodge. For Jenny, once again in a leading role, it was a bright spot in a darkening personal vista.

Trailing in her studies after missing so much time through illness, Jenny had been delighted when local man Frank Booth offered her coaching to help her catch up. Living at an Ascot hotel, his daughter was a friend of the Maurice Home. Twice a week, he would tutor her in the great works of English literature, either in the quiet room of Grenville House or in the lounge of the hotel where he lived. On those occasions 'Uncle Frank', as she knew him, would accompany her back to Grenville House on the bus, before returning to his small hotel room.

Uncle Frank was already popular among the girls, as he regularly took small groups of them out for tea in Ascot. Perhaps when he began to ask that Jenny was included in all these groups, Matron's concerns were raised. For other girls there might have been no concerns. With Jenny's background in mind, however, she was watchful. She was further alarmed when he produced two tickets, for himself and Jenny, to see *Macbeth* at the Aldwych Theatre in London.

Uncle Frank was about the same age as Jenny's father and the youngster saw no dilemma in their relationship. But one day she was called into Matron's office for a difficult conversation. With a solemn air Matron pointed out that a close relationship with a man was inappropriate and might have consequences. Although those consequences were left unspoken, Jenny flushed with foolishness and was worried that she might have embarrassed Matron, her friends at the home, Uncle Frank and, finally, herself — although she still wasn't sure how or why. Meetings between the older man and herself dwindled until they eventually ended altogether.

As her school term came to an end she narrowly missed being expelled, not so much for stealing another girl's sandwiches when she was hungry but for the lies that followed the theft, as she tried to cover her tracks. Although the misdemeanour was relatively slight, rationing was still in force and food still had great currency. It was Matron's disappointment that was hardest to bear. The incident was immediately followed by a bout of mumps. For so long the youngest in the Maurice Home, she was now seventeen and the oldest girl in Matron's care.

Months had passed since she last heard from her beloved father, but an unknown couple visited Grenville House in July, close to Jenny's eighteenth birthday, bearing a leather toiletries case from him. She was delighted by the gift; he had not forgotten her after all. In the flurry of preparing for the annual holiday at Cromer, she put a lack of explanation about the luxury gift to the back of her mind.

Cromer was bracing and beautiful, and letters sent by relatives were distributed after being checked by Matron in the usual way. One August morning Matron gave out the post but held one back and asked Jenny to join her in a side room.

Hesitantly Jenny closed the door behind her.

'Jenny, I have some bad news for you, lass,' Matron said quietly. 'Here, sit down.'

Tears began rolling down Jenny's cheeks as she learned her father had died four days after her birthday.

Patiently Matron waited until an initial wave of frantic sobs had passed. She had known this moment would come eventually. The letter she held in her hand had taken away any time she might have liked for preparation. But Jenny was nearly an adult. It was time to share with her difficult facts about the family life she had left years before. Matron had always known the shocking story of Jenny's upbringing and spent years censoring letters, trying to shield her young charge from the terrible truth. Now she hoped the armour-plating of a secure childhood in the home would protect Jenny from the worst of the emotional tsunami that was about to break over her.

'I've a letter here from your mother,' said Matron quietly. 'She thinks you should now know the facts about your family.'

Warily Jenny looked up. Could there be any worse news than what she had just heard?

'As you know, your father was sixty when you were born,' Matron continued.

Jenny looked up. She knew he'd been older than other fathers and used a polished cane for support when he walked, although his advancing years hadn't stopped them enjoying great and, for her, memorable outdoor adventures together.

'You have an older brother and a younger brother with the same parents, as you know. I think you know already that your mother and father did not get married.'

Jenny nodded, blushing furiously with the shame that illegitimacy habitually brought to her.

Matron hesitated. 'Jenny, it was impossible for them to marry. The other men in your family, who you have always thought of as half-brothers, are also your half-uncles. Your father was father to them all – including your mother.'

Jenny began crying once more, tearing rigid fingers down her face in misery. Matron stood in sad silence while the heart-rending sobs were unleashed. Until now only she had known that Jenny had been taken into care to save her from the peril of sexual abuse at the hands of her own father. Incest was a recurring issue for children's homes everywhere. As for Jenny, her thoughts were racing and confused, with a lifetime of love behind her for a father who, it turned out, was nothing short of a villain.

'Oh, this is shameful. I feel like the lowliest person,' she said through palms by now running with salty tears.

'Well, you certainly are not that,' said Matron. 'You are a kind, thoughtful and lovely person who has done absolutely nothing wrong. I am sorry to hear the sad news about your father. But you, lass, have nothing to be ashamed about, nothing at all.'

Jenny emerged from the side room with raw eyes, a red nose and puffy cheeks. Every so often her body was wracked with another sob. Matron asked Sheila and Nansi, older girls who'd returned to the home for the holidays, to walk along the shoreline with her before they joined the rest of the group. But although Jenny's tears subsided, the ache inside didn't end and confused emotions were making her head spin. Her father had done a terrible wrong, yet all she really knew was that now she had no one to talk to who understood her quite so well as he did.

Jenny's misery was compounded when she returned to Ascot to find she hadn't achieved good enough exam results to attend college, as she had planned. Instead, she became a house girl at Grenville, before becoming a parlour maid for Mrs Peyton. Then Matron found her a job as a nanny in nearby Sunningdale via Dorothy Peyton's network of contacts.

For Jenny there was a measure of resentment. Times had changed at Grenville House and girls were no longer destined to always become domestic workers. Sheila had gone on to be a teacher and Jenny, who believed herself to be academically advanced as well, had dreams of doing something similar. During quiet hours at her new job, Jenny's thoughts turned in a different direction. She became curious about her remaining family, and she resolved to renew a relationship with her mother, a woman she barely knew.

When she shared her plans for a visit with Matron, the older woman offered to accompany her but was detained at the last moment. Jenny went alone and found her mother on a smallholding in the country with three more sons, aged eleven, ten and eleven months; her stepfather was a thatcher. Jenny was immediately in love with the bucolic lifestyle. When they seemed pleased to see her after the long absence, she decided to move in.

She returned to give in her notice – and almost instantly had a call from Matron, asking her to visit Grenville House.

Despite her calm exterior, Matron was struggling for words. Had she done the right thing by allowing the terrible family secret that was now obviously haunting Jenny to be shared?

'Please sit down, Jenny,' she said kindly, trying to ignore the sour expression on Jenny's face.

For a few moments the conversation was about Jenny's job and her employers, but for Matron it became harder to hide her concerns. 'I must say how disappointed I am that you've stayed at your job in Sunningdale for just eight months. Things were going well, were they not?' Matron looked directly at Jenny, who said nothing.

Matron searched for new ways to persuade Jenny, trying to put herself in the youngster's shoes. 'It must seem like a dream come true to find a loving family living in the heart of the countryside. But you must remember, Jenny dear, that your mother never visited us at Englemere Wood or here. And she was always welcome. She didn't come even when you were dangerously ill. I'm not sure the bond between you is as strong as you would hope.'

Mutinously Jenny stated again that she wanted to live in Hampshire with her extended family.

Matron continued to press her. 'Can you at least consider rethinking your decision? I wonder how you might feel at the end of all this.'

'I'm eighteen now and I think I'm old enough to know just what I want,' said Jenny with a stormy expression.

'I wish I had come with you to see your mother,' Matron continued in frustration, as much to herself as to Jenny. 'Then none of this might have happened.'

'Well, I think it would have done,' retorted Jenny, irritated now. It was perhaps the first time she had seen Matron getting flustered and she was watching with a curious detachment.

Matron groped for a more powerful message. 'And what do you think Madam will say?'

'Who cares what Madam says!' yelled Jenny, turning her back on Matron and heading for the door. As she slammed it behind her, Jenny was emphatically breaking the link with the only family she had properly known. Matron heard fast footsteps heading for the front door and silently cursed herself for what she considered was a clumsy approach driven by emotion rather than rationale.

It wasn't the only problem Matron had on her plate. When she received a letter from an old girl she read the contents to Miss Hutchings with increasing horror.

'Enid became pregnant,' she told her. Enid had lived at Englemere Wood for two years. 'She's not married and she's decided to keep the baby, but her mother threw her out, and so did her landlady. She's found a place to live with another of the girls from the Maurice family, thank goodness. How could a mother do such a thing, just when her daughter needs her most?'

Miss Hutchings frowned and shook her head slowly. 'What can we do to help?'

'She's always welcome to come and see us here,' said Matron. 'And I must write and tell her so immediately. Unfortunately she can't live here with us. But I'll also write to some people I know, to see if I can find her a live-in post with the baby. The last thing I want is for her to feel shame. I have every confidence this was not her fault.'

And Sheila found she was not too old to be taught a lesson by Matron too. Having secured her first job at a rural boarding school in the Cotswolds she realized a bike was essential for transport and borrowed money from Matron to buy one, on the understanding the loan was repaid by Christmas.

As her twenty-first birthday approached at the start of 1949, Matron asked what gift Sheila would most like. Sheila asked for a suitcase to replace the trunk that had accompanied her through her Maurice Home years, something that would also make travelling back to Grenville House much easier. In a letter Matron told her the wish had been granted. But when she turned up just after Christmas for a birthday visit she made the mistake of wearing a new coat, bought out of her first pay cheque.

After Matron presented her with the case Sheila was delighted and remarked how it matched her new coat.

Matron took in the smart garment and enquired, 'Who bought it for you?'

With some satisfaction Sheila said she had bought it herself. Then she noticed a change in Matron's expression.

'And what about the eight pounds you borrowed for the bicycle? Have you got that?' Matron asked with severity.

Sheila was left floundering. She had put the debt at the bottom of her list of priorities and suddenly felt full of shame. She didn't have the money. 'I–I'm sorry . . .' she stuttered.

Matron moved in swiftly, took the suitcase from her hand and said meaningfully, 'Debts take precedence over self-indulgences; to help you remember that I am taking back this suitcase and we shall ignore your birthday.'

Afterwards, when she related the incident, Sheila told her friends from the home: 'The problem was, I knew in my heart of hearts that she was right.'

At Grenville House strenuous efforts were made to ensure the residents felt at home rather than part of an institution. Girls were encouraged to help decorate their bedrooms, choosing colours and fabrics. Pudding-bowl haircuts were also relegated to history, and hair could be kept in plaits, ponytails or cropped short, as long as it remained tidy.

It was not only Matron Bailey's aim to keep the rooms homely; it was also an avowed aim of the Children's Society, the new name for the Waifs and Strays Society. In its 1948 handbook the aims of the society were to 'give the children . . . the best possible substitute for a normal happy family life and to ensure, by fostering a true understanding of Christian ethics, that the children will leave the shelter of the branches [of the Children's Society] with the self-reliance and judgement necessary to enable them to lead a good life. The children should be treated as individuals and independence fostered in every way.'

It meant the durable green and orange floral dresses made years before by the Maurice Home staff for every girl in their care were out of fashion in more ways than one. Women in a group known as the Golden Needle League now undertook to sew individual garments for children to help them avoid stigma.

The handbook said: 'Uniformity in the clothing of the children must be avoided so that they are not differentiated in any way from other children in the locality. This particularly applies to the provision of best coats and hats, which the children themselves should be allowed to choose so as to avoid any possible suggestion of uniform. Children during their holidays or leisure time should be provided with play clothes but they must never be allowed to wear ragged or untidy clothing.'

Decor in homes was to change from pre-war standards too, a principle Matron and her staff had already embraced. 'The greatest care must be taken to avoid anything that savours of an institution. The building and the life in it should be really home-like. Such things as light, cheerful colours for the walls, curtains and coverings, suitable pictures, flowers in the living rooms and on the dining tables, all help to create a right atmosphere.'

In the same year the National Health Service was created, offering free high-quality health care for everyone. Its universal aims chimed with those expressed by Tommy Peyton in the letter written just days before his untimely death. He had hoped the war would result in equal opportunities for working people, what he had termed as 'some new British Order', to upend the class-ridden society he knew.

Matron soon had personal experience of the new set-up when her mother, Emily, became ill. Grief at her eventual death, aged eighty-three, rippled through the home, with older girls readily recalling the kindnesses shown by 'Nanna' Bailey down the years. However, there was a silver lining to the dark cloud, as a new member of staff joined the home. Edie Adams had been a nurse at St Peter's Hospital in Chertsey, Surrey, having spent the war years nursing Blitz victims in London and supporting her sister Clare, a young mum who was widowed when her Royal Navy husband was killed at sea. After her mother was hospitalized in Chertsey, Matron Bailey was so impressed by Sister Adams that she wanted her on the staff.

There was only one problem. Sister Adams was a Catholic and the Children's Society was an Anglican organization. Indeed, everyone within its walls followed the doctrines of the Church of England. Today it seems a small matter, surely two like-minded women could work harmoniously together for the benefit of disadvantaged children. Yet there was still evidence of long-standing anti-Catholic feeling in the country, one that had pervaded British society since the Reformation. Every year effigies were burned on bonfires representing Guy Fawkes, the Catholic who had tried to blow up the Houses of Parliament in 1605 in the Gunpowder Plot. The 1701 Act of Settlement, which said any member of the British Royal Family who married a Roman Catholic would have to renounce the throne, was only altered in 2013.

At the time Matron Bailey fought to secure a role for Sister Adams at Grenville House, religious intolerance remained a brooding issue, although it had not yet ignited into conflict in Northern Ireland. But nor had there been any official stamp of approval to a growing ecumenical movement. That didn't come until 1960 when Geoffrey Fisher, the long-serving Archbishop of Canterbury, visited Rome. Using sound sense and gentle persuasion, Matron coaxed a relaxation in the stiff rules at the Children's Society and Sister Adams joined the staff in 1950.

Every Sunday Matron led her girls to church in one direction while Sister Adams cycled to her service of choice in another. To the girls it was a living example of how prejudice could be dismantled on a domestic level and she was just as much of a hit with the Maurice Home old girls as with the residents at the time.

Many of the girls visited Grenville House to introduce husbands-to-be or new babies. Each name and significant date was noted by Matron in a book that followed the fortunes of girls she had had in her care. There were regular newsletters too, connecting the widespread family.

Despite the stability brought about by the presence of Sister Adams, Matron was still troubled by the rift with Jenny. Suddenly, out of the blue, came a letter. Although several years had passed, Matron recognized the writing and she didn't open it until she was behind closed doors.

'Edie, dear, I've heard from Jenny,' said Matron in the privacy of the Grenville House staffroom.

'She's apologized for everything she said. She became ill when she was with her mother, jaundice this time. Jenny was always such a poorly child.' Matron sighed, remembering the lengthy bedside vigils she had maintained when Jenny was much smaller.

'Now she's had her twenty-first birthday and she's working as a cook, which suits her very well. She calls her mother jealous and vitriolic, and I'm not surprised to hear it. How she could stay away when Jenny nearly died that time was quite beyond me.'

Although she hadn't met Jenny, Edie was visibly relieved, knowing how much the argument had weighed on Matron's mind. 'It's marvellous news that she's back in touch.' She watched as Matron retrieved her writing compendium and began to frame a reply.

After Jenny's letter had been answered, the next step was a telephone call, and the prospect of making it filled Jenny with trepidation. Matron's letter had been full of references to their past relationship. Did she really want to welcome Jenny back after her headstrong outburst? When Matron's familiar warmth came flooding down the telephone line, Jenny knew beyond doubt that she was loved and did belong.

In 1952, the following year, there was a major event taking place at Grenville House. Sheila had met and fallen in love with husband-to-be Eric. Without a family to call her own she had resigned herself to being virtually alone on her wedding day. Matron saw things differently.

After the happy young couple visited Grenville House, Matron wrote to Sheila who, thanks to her stint at college, had lived at Grenville long after all the other girls of her era had moved on.

'As this was your home for so many years, we should

like you to be married from Grenville House,' the letter said. 'The staff and I, with the society's permission, would like to give you a white wedding and a reception in your own home.' It meant Sheila could get married across the road, at All Saints in Ascot, the backdrop for so many nativities throughout her childhood, all of which she could still recall with clarity.

On the night before the ceremony she slept in Matron's bed at Grenville House, and used the staff bath the following morning as she got ready. These small gestures made her feel weak with happiness. Barbara was there, still working for Princess Marie Louise, packing clothes for her honeymoon in tissue paper. The case caught Sheila's eye. It wasn't the battered trunk she had arrived with, but the silk-lined valise presented to her on her twenty-first birthday by Matron and swiftly taken back in response to an unpaid debt.

Downstairs the rooms were filled with flowers and foliage. Colonel Eugene St John Birnie, a noted soldier, mountaineer and explorer, was now secretary of the Children's Society and it was on his arm that Sheila made her way to the altar, clutching a bouquet of white freesias. One of her bridesmaids was Joan, who also grew up in the Maurice Home but was now a sister in a busy London hospital. In the congregation was Princess Marie Louise and it was she who signed the marriage certificate. Sheila, whose birth certificate lacked a father's name, had wedding documentation bearing a royal signature. As she made her way down the aisle, Sheila remembered the lessons given so many years before, and stopped to curtsy to the princess. Like Matron, Mrs Peyton stood as proudly in the congregation as any mother might. Her son John had been elected as MP for Yeovil the year before. It had been a decade since Tommy's death and the clouds of grief had parted. He would, she mused, very much have approved of everything that had occurred at Englemere Wood.

Afterwards Grenville House was filled with people who had meant so much to the girls at Englemere Wood: their teacher Miss Cory, cook and soprano singer Miss Hutchings, Dr Halley, Major Fyson and his family, and many more. Rev. Walton had moved on from Ascot in 1946 but another minister, familiar with the home and its ethos, officiated.

A few months later, a young woman pushing a bike loaded with small cases made her way towards Grenville House. Despite receiving an invitation to Sheila and Eric's wedding she chose to stay away, fearing her presence would cast an awkward pall on the event. She'd arrived via the station and it wasn't a long way to push the bike, but the walk gave Jenny enough time to consider the fences she had to mend during the homecoming.

It wasn't just Matron but also Elizabeth, a younger child with whom Jenny had been paired to guide and inspire. Jenny had also turned her back on Elizabeth when she had walked out, and she knew she would have to apologize. And then there was Mrs Peyton, who had taken such obvious pride and interest in the girls even when she had mourned the loss of her son. By abandoning the job found for her by Mrs Peyton, by leaving a family high and dry, she had been intolerably rude. Jenny's heart went cold as she realized the devastating effects of her impulsive actions years before.

As she turned into the Grenville House gate Jenny looked up. Lines of tension vanished and there was soon relief and pleasure written all over her face. There in the doorway stood the Matron's distinctive frame. She was a little older but the smile lines on her face were just the same. The reunion was an emotional one for both women, and Jenny joined the Grenville family again with calm waters closing over the dispute as if it hadn't happened.

Armed with a heartfelt apology, Jenny visited Mrs Peyton. Englemere Wood had now been converted to four flats, the biggest of which was Mrs Peyton's. Afterwards Jenny even filled in as a cook there while Mrs Peyton awaited a new housekeeper, and served Princess Marie Louise when she came to lunch. After both women doted on her, she walked away from the table as if she was walking on air.

During this spell at the home she made some life-changing decisions. When she shared her plans, Matron voiced some misgivings, rooted in concern about the long-term ill health that had dogged Jenny since childhood. It wasn't so evident these days but Matron remembered all too well how precarious her well-being had been. But when Jenny headed off to join the services, she had Matron's blessing. Jenny found a place in the Women's Royal Air Force, marched proudly in her uniform and quickly became an officer.

During the mid-fifties Grenville House remained a busy home. There were the girls directed there by the Children's Society and frequent visits from old girls and their families, who were always welcome. There was room too for Tina, Evelyn's eldest daughter.

After leaving Englemere Wood Evelyn went into service in Rake, Surrey, working as a nanny. Her future husband worked nearby. Evelyn worked upstairs, over an archway, and from below he would serenade her. Every week he bought her flowers, a habit he maintained until her death.

The couple had married in January 1947 in Milland Church, and daughter Tina was born in December. Evelyn and her farmworker husband lived in poverty. He used to work seven days a week to earn sufficient money for the family. Pet rabbits went in the pot when times were hard. They didn't even have sheets on the bed. Their bedding consisted of army blankets with coats on the top.

Aged eight, Tina had pneumonia twice in nine months, as well as tuberculosis. She spent a considerable amount of time in hospital. Matron Bailey was contacted by the family GP who requested the convalescence.

A frail small child, Tina was put on a train in the care of a guard and was picked up in Ascot by Matron. Her stay got underway with a head inspection to ensure nits didn't come into the home. At the time it was standard practice in schools so Tina thought nothing of it.

On this occasion she spent more than a year at Grenville House, long enough to join the school when she was sufficiently recovered, to be taught by Miss Cory. Tina even spent Christmas there, finding a stocking on the end of her bed in the morning. There was an enormous Christmas tree in the hallway, almost within touching distance from the galleried landing, and she joined the others in singing carols outside Matron's bedroom door early that morning. When she was well enough she was put on the rota for chores.

When she returned home she was always in a smart outfit. Doctors also discovered Tina, almost paralysed by shyness, suffered from curvature of the spine. It was Matron Bailey who took her to leading doctors to receive medical care.

Even when Tina was at home with her mother she felt the warmth of Matron's care across the miles, thanks to packages of second-hand clothes sent for her and her four sisters.

Tina accompanied the other girls on a summer holiday at a cottage in the grounds of Holkham Hall, a Palladian mansion in Norfolk, along with two other children of old girls and two children from a school in Maidenhead whose head teacher requested a place for them because they had never before seen the sea. Once there, napkins filled with a picnic lunch were numbered for resident children while visitors like Tina were always identified by their names. But other than that, all the girls were treated just the same. During all the months she spent at Grenville Tina doesn't recall Matron once raising her voice.

And Tina wasn't the only summer-holiday arrival. Matron's niece Vickie, born the year the war started, was a regular visitor to both Englemere Wood and Grenville House. Sometimes accompanied by her mother Mary – Matron's younger sister – but often undertaking the railway journey from her home in Colchester, Essex, alone, Vickie would also take holidays with the rest of the girls. For her it was a welcome reprieve from a difficult family life. At home her father refused to allow her to play with children from neighbouring council houses. Once she was under Matron's care, her loneliness vanished. And she, like Tina, was treated like every other child at the home. If she was naughty, she was sent to bed without supper. But mostly she thrived in the company of others under Matron's watchful eye and relished her holidays at Cromer.

In 1957 it became clear that Grenville House's days were numbered. But there was another matter occupying Matron's mind, the fifteenth anniversary of Tommy Peyton's death at St Nazaire. She hadn't forgotten the oath she took in the black days following his demise, and she knew the girls of Englemere Wood hadn't either. She was immensely proud of those girls and felt the pledge they made that day played no small part in the way they had grown up.

Now many more girls had joined 'the family' and it was time to bring them into this circle. In March that year she wrote a letter to old girls from Englemere Wood, referencing the day Tommy died as 'a vivid memory'. 'The older girls of our family made, with the staff, a solemn promise and dedication. Can we make it again, this time drawing in a still greater family, including the grandchildren who are old enough to understand?'

The promise was, she wrote, firmly and reverently made. And she paid tribute to the girls who made the vow. 'To those dear members of our family who, standing in the dining room at Englemere Wood, looking on the sunset over the mere on that Sunday evening, we give our thanks for their determination and their vision for it is they who . . . dug out the foundation of our family life here . . . If a few girls could do so much because they believed and were sincere, what then can the greater family do now if, when reading this letter, each rededicated their life to the highest service? Let us prepare in our minds for this special day . . . by the same spirit of courage and fearlessness to truth and honour as shown by Grenville Peyton.'

To those who wanted to contact Dorothy Peyton she advised them to send a carefully chosen flower card, with a message of remembrance. 'We all know Mrs Peyton so well, and her dislike for any acknowledgement but just a few words might be all right and she would be blessed by your thoughts, and encouraged.'

Jenny returned 'home' with some monumental news. While in the WRAF she had met Michael, who had proposed with a ruby ring. And when it came to her wedding Matron once again insisted that Grenville House should host the occasion.

When Friday, 17 May 1957 dawned, Grenville House was once again bedecked with flowers. As well as those made by the staff, to smother banisters and balconies, there were sprays of apple blossom, pink rhododendrons, white clematis, lilies of the valley and carnations donated by one of the friends of the home. Matron once again gave up her room to the bride-to-be, a touching sign of motherly love, and Jenny was also helped to prepare by Barbara, who had once, long ago, used newspaper to dress her as Bo Peep.

As she walked down the aisle the congregation sang

'Praise My Soul, the King of Heaven' just as they had at Sheila's wedding five years earlier. It was a hymn that had often resounded not only at All Saints Church down the years, but also at Englemere Wood and Grenville House. Jenny made her own dress and Elizabeth was bridesmaid, the bond between them repaired and as strong as ever.

Princess Marie Louise had died the year before. But Mrs Peyton and Colonel Birnie were there to wish her well, as were many friends of the Maurice Home.

When she got back to Grenville House after the service, Jenny was overcome with emotion. After greeting all her guests with a smile that was making her cheeks ache she made her excuses and escaped from the celebrations. In the hall she collapsed on to a plush red-velvet chair, intending to compose herself for a few moments, and her gaze fastened on the portrait of Tommy Peyton. So much had been lost during the war years, she thought. And yet, for a group of girls who began with so few of life's gifts at their disposal, so much had been gained. Matron's kindness, compassion and common sense had brought her, Jenny, a girl with the most uneasy start in life, to this celebratory point. Mrs Peyton's graciousness and good-hearted generosity had also been a major factor. Working in harmony, the women had shaped her destiny and been her salvation. Not that many years ago, she'd thought her family lost and grieved for it. Now she knew with conviction that she had found her real 'family' when she'd arrived at the Maurice Home in Ealing eighteen years before. From childhood she'd had everyday lessons in resilience, consideration of others and the difference between right and wrong. Jenny's face broke into a smile and she flushed with a moment of higher understanding. None of it had been lost on her, she realized. She'd thrown off a bleak legacy and won life's glittering prize.

17. Bright Futures

To the world, you may be one person,
but to one person, you may be the world.

As the framework for institutional care evolved in the post-war period, so Grenville House was slated for change. The property stayed in the Children's Society fold but in 1960, it became a nursery. Now its rooms echoed with the cries of much younger children and a different set of staff was charged with satisfying their pressing needs. Yet 'the family' that had come together, both there and at Englemere Wood, remained as close as ever. With newsletters, birthday, anniversary and Christmas cards Matron ensured its beating heart continued long after the doors of the home were shut for the final time.

Tommy Peyton still figured in her thoughts. In 1959, although she was concerned by the impending closure of Grenville House, Matron was determined that the promise made in his honour would stay alive and wrote in her newsletter: 'For the remaining months, however many they may be, an effort will be made to conclude, in a fitting manner, this great and glorious memorial to a gallant gentleman.'

She said she was sending each girl a Christmas card, but added: 'Please keep unopened, so on Christmas day, the day when we have all at some time been so happy together, we may again unite in a great family bond and give thanks for all the joys of the Grenville family, remembering the ideals for which we all stand.'

In 1966 she had marked the anniversary of the Nazaire raid with a letter to Queenie, written from Devon. 'Monday is the family's special day when Mr Tommy was killed . . . and the seed was sown for our family life, which to me is so wonderful, and such a miracle.'

Five years later, Queenie and others were returning to Ascot for a golden wedding anniversary party in honour of the Fysons, long-term supporters of the home, although Matron couldn't make the journey.

'The day you are at the reception, it will be with the shadow of a great family behind you,' Matron wrote. 'Please have a special word with Mrs Peyton. Never have I longed to be anywhere as I do to be in Ascot, so I could shake her by the hand and assure her, her son's life was not in vain.'

After the Ascot premises became a nursery, Matron, accompanied by Sister Adams, went to north Devon to open a home that looked after elderly people. The property had been donated and they didn't do it for money, rather to look after people who were struggling to look after themselves. By this time both were in their late fifties.

In the garden of the house, close to the glorious vistas of Saunton Sands, there was a chalet where they invited all the old girls – and their young families – to stay, in return for a peppercorn rent. It comprised one room containing beds and a gramophone, with a washroom outside and the toilet some distance away, but no one minded the primitive surroundings. It meant the next generation of children, who knew Matron as Nanna, had fabulous summer holidays when they might otherwise never have set eyes on sun-spangled waves or felt warm sand running through their small fingers.

When visitors, with tinged skin and peeling noses, arrived back after a day spent paddling or exploring the dunes, there would be a home-cooked meal or a freshly baked apple pie waiting for them on the step.

Known as Nanna to the children of 'her girls', she wrote to them regularly, and sent parcels. One, dispatched to Nansi's two children in November 1964, contained two ornamental cats. 'One puss cat has its tail broken off, so have put in three shillings and wonder if Daddy would get some tube of [glue] and see to this for you,' Nanna wrote. 'They are a jolly pair and I think that you will like them.'

Among other items, the parcel also contained pencils, a pencil sharpener in the shape of a car, a pair of bookends also in need of repair and a red scarf. 'These small things have come to me from a friend who is moving, and she is one of the few in the world who has lots and lots of things, and I want to share some with you,' Nanna explained.

Although Matron and Sister Adams tended to just a handful of elderly guests, their own advancing years meant this endeavour finally had to end. The pair retired to a home in West Buckland in the heart of the Devon countryside. However, the passing years could not peg back their caring natures. They collected clothes and toys for children in eastern Europe, money for a dispensary in India, stamps to help a mission in Africa, where they financially supported two orphans, and silver paper for a children's hospital in Britain. Matron also supported London charities for the homeless and cancer patients. Furthermore, she took pride in being a good neighbour, one of the best, in fact. When she was compelled to use a frame she would carry hot home-made soup to neighbours she considered worse off than herself in a Thermos flask slung round her neck.

At Grenville House Matron had hosted gatherings to mark significant events. There were three weddings in all, as well as parties for the departure of girls who went to live overseas or when they started new careers. Her pleasure in reunions was always undimmed, and at every invitation her past charges would flock to her side.

It was a welcome opportunity for the girls to see one another too. Living at such close quarters as children, they had observed one another minutely, sharing the pain of mundane tasks and rejoicing in wartime triumphs as rivals, co-conspirators and counsellors. Torment and teasing there may have been, and from time to time torrents of tears, but the deep well of affection among the girls never ran dry, with mistakes and mishaps quickly forgiven. If anything, personal shortcomings had become a badge of honour now worn with pride.

Such parties were now, it seemed, consigned to history, but nonetheless Matron didn't forget the girls she knew so well. She was a regular in the congregation of St Peter's Church in the Devon village where she now lived, often devoting her prayers to the girls. Beside her in the pew was the chunky personal record book that contained the names and birthdate of all the girls she had cared for and their expanding families.

Down the years husbands had been welcomed into the fold and there was rejoicing each time a baby was born. (A

Grenville christening shawl was passed among them.) Names were promptly inscribed into this book so no one would be forgotten when it came to birthdays and anniversaries. The hand that penned the names may have become increasingly shaky but her spirit was firm.

The bonds between Matron and the girls remained robust, so much so that a reunion held at West Buckland School in Devon just prior to her ninetieth birthday was a busy, vibrant occasion. The school's head, Michael Downward, was a neighbour who couldn't help but be impressed by Matron's extraordinary commitment to good causes. John Peyton and his wife Mary were also guests. Special prayers were written for the event, with words that meant everything to girls who were by now pensioners themselves.

'For those who have been an inspiration to us; for those who by their warning counsel have kept us from mistakes we might have made and sins we might have committed. We thank thee for the homes we have shared in times past.'

They each closed their eyes and dwelled for a moment on the steadying influence who had smoothed their path from traumatic childhood to stable adulthood. Thanks to the emotional resources Matron gave them, they were women who could escape life's pitfalls, which had earlier swallowed up their parents, and go on to have jobs, families and children of their own.

At the service, when someone remarked about the strong links between herself and her 'girls', she felt she knew where credit was due. 'It's just them,' she said of the girls who once had been in her care. 'They have done it all; they would do anything for anyone.'

For her their success was rooted in the pledge they all made following the death of Mr Tommy, and her faith in the Grenville family never faltered. Tommy is remembered at All Saints Church in Ascot with a plaque dedicated to him and the men he fought alongside, which was installed by Dorothy and his brother John. Furthermore, his name is engraved on the back of the gravestone jointly dedicated to Ivor, Dorothy and little Henry. The memorial includes the words 'All you had hoped for, all you had, you gave to save mankind.' The quote is from a poem, 'The Supreme Sacrifice', written by Sir John Stanhope Arkwright, which later became the words of the hymn 'O Valiant Hearts'.

Like other men whose bodies were never recovered, his name appears on the military memorial in Brookwood Cemetery, Surrey, a cemetery created in the Victorian age to cater for the escalating numbers of London's dead, sited just ten miles from Ascot.

When Matron finally died at Bideford Hospital, on 23 June 1995, there was an outpouring of grief. To the girls she had cared for, she really was the angel of Englemere Wood.

Among a cascade of tributes to Matron Bailey was this one from Dawn, who wrote to Queenie about 'our Angel', saying: 'Although we didn't realize until we were grown-up, she put qualities into each and every one of us, in so many different ways: the rules and regulations; [learning] loyalty to each other, even though we didn't see it at the time; the sharing and caring, in good times and bad.'

Nansi summed it up like this: 'Looking back I think we must have been a very happy group of girls. We had our ups and down, but then who doesn't? We were not perfect specimens of humanity by any means. But the teaching and example of Matron, Sister and the staff was that we should think of others and what would give them most happiness before thinking of ourselves and I feel the advantages we had compared with the majority of children were tremendous. We had Christian staff who were interested in things like honour, loyalty and truth. I think it must have been the four years I spent at Ascot that moulded me into the person I try to be and for which I am deeply grateful to Matron, Sister Briggs and other staff members. I hope as she looks down, she knows we have tried to keep our [Grenville] promise [from] so long ago.'

Another Maurice girl, Shirley, reflected on the loss she felt after Matron's death. Although she was by now a senior citizen, she grieved as if it was her mother who had passed away. 'She was such a comforting help, always, not just when I was sad but sometimes, I suspect, when I was getting too complacent. By her example I learned so much about life. It seems ironic that an elderly spinster who didn't travel far and wide could give so much sound advice, comfort and joy to so many other people.'

One woman, who commented anonymously in the Children's Society magazine in 1996, paid tribute to Matron's contribution to her upbringing. 'Actually being wanted was a wonderful feeling. To have a bath, hair washed and clean, nice-smelling clothes and to go to bed (a bed to one's self) with actual white sheets and pillowcases was just out of this world.'

Valerie, at Grenville House between 1952 and 1958,

wrote: 'We were taught the rights and wrongs, how to give and not just to take. We were all equal. It was a real family atmosphere for me – the memories will always remain.'

For years afterwards another girl, Veronica, organized Christingle services every year to raise money for the Children's Society. 'I feel I owe the society something. That is why I want to give all I can back to them, in memory of my dear Nanna, the mother I didn't have. I miss her very much, like we all do.'

John Peyton shared with the girls some memories of his own. 'We all of us will remember her as someone who had very clear views about what was right, who held to them always and who was at pains to implant them in those who were in her care. Her best memorial, and the one she would value most, is the mark she left in the hearts and minds of those who first came with her to Ascot . . . no longer perhaps her "girls", but still in some way belonging to her.'

'None of us were angels all the time,' reflects Queenie. 'It was all about forgiveness, starting again and doing better next time. That's what we were taught.

'I have tried to live a decent life and bring up my children in the same way I was brought up by Matron. I don't think I would have been here today to tell this story without that courage she instilled in me. She encouraged all of us to do things beyond duty and expectation. This book is to tell how fortunate we all were being brought up by Matron and her staff, who showed to us the power of unconditional love.'

With grief raw for many months afterwards, they took solace in each other and shared memories of their time under Matron's care. Queenie became the hub for communications and the Grenville family continued to exchange news through regular letters. But what of the girls that called Englemere Wood and Grenville House home in the forties and fifties?

Sheila Stewart became a teacher and owned a nursery – the first of its kind to be recognized by the Ministry of Education – and later started a career in writing. When she wrote an autobiography, published in 1967, she dedicated it to Matron Bailey who, she acknowledged, 'would not approve of it at all'. In a personal note Sheila added: 'Hoping you will forgive me for bringing out your light from under its bushel and shining it in the public eye'. Afterwards Sheila's career soared. As well as being an award-winning scriptwriter, she penned books about the disappearing fabric of rural existence in Oxfordshire and the life of women on canal narrowboats. She died in 2014.

After reaching school-leaving age, Monica left Englemere Wood, returning to Tonbridge and her mother. Matron was disappointed that Monica turned down the opportunity to be an apprentice milliner and instead went to work in Woolworths, for the sake of better pay. The milliner was paying seven shillings and six pence, compared with a pound a week at Woolworths. And it turned out Matron knew Monica better than she knew herself. She was quickly dissatisfied with a shop job and cast around for a different career. However, at sixteen she turned down her dream job as a trainee nurse because the route from her home to the hospital lay through a field of cows. Despite the rural surroundings she grew up in Monica never got over a fear of cows. Instead, she became a nanny before a spell working at a wine merchant. Eventually she joined the Wrens, then met husband-to-be Bill at a fairground. He was a D-Day veteran and recipient of the Légion d'honneur. Monica was married at eighteen and a mum by the age of twenty-one. She remained fast friends with many girls from Englemere Wood, including Queenie. On a visit to Monica's home in Wembley Queenie met Bill's brother Dennis and they fell in love. Now sisters-in-law, Queenie and Monica would often decide to spend the weekend together 'at home'. By home they meant Grenville House, where they knew Matron was happy to provide a bed, a meal and a catch-up. In return they pitched in with food preparation and washing-up.

Queenie continued to work with children before having a family of her own. Later she became an auxiliary nurse at a hospital close to her London home, then worked a further ten years as a doctor's receptionist before retiring aged seventy-two.

Nansi and her husband Stanley took advantage of financial incentives offered by Australia after the war to immigrants. Down Under the influx were known as £10 Poms, reflecting the amount they paid for the fare. They stayed nine years before returning to the UK with their family. After her marriage, Jenny had two children before emigrating to Canada. As she was making plans, her thoughts drifted back to Ascot Heath School and the geography lessons she had there. Jenny always had a passion for education, but never thought she would see these wonders for herself.

Barbara and chauffeur Harry's romance flowered and together they went to work for other members of the aristocracy, including Lord Luke, whose father, the son of a butcher, founded the Bovril empire.

Aged sixteen, Gladys left Grenville House and went to

work for Constance Spry, the renowned society florist who ran a domestic science school with cook Rosemary Hume at Winkfield Place in Cranbourne, Berkshire. Its clients were mostly young women from wealthy families. Starting work at 7 a.m., she put in an eleven-hour day to earn £1 5 shillings a week. Unable to settle here or at a nursing job she returned to Grenville House to work part-time for Mrs Peyton. After that she worked for evangelist Tom Rees, although she still considered Grenville House as home. Even after she married, she kept in close contact with Matron, who frequently sent parcels of clothes and other items that were beyond the financial reach of her family.

Today Doris Hurford Bailey's many triumphs may seem low-key, with the changes she made largely going under society's radar, but put simply the formula fashioned at Englemere Wood and later at Grenville House helped make the world a better place.

Inevitably the cast of characters from Englemere Wood had already diminished even before Matron's death. After the war Dorothy Peyton continued as chair of the support group for Grenville House until she resigned in 1956. At the time she was spending increasing amounts of time abroad, driving to her favourite European destinations with friends. She continued to live at Englemere Wood in one of four flats created from the original house. Gladys Walton, the wife of Rev. Walton and also now a widow, lived in another. Mrs Peyton kept in touch with many of the girls who lived with her during the war until her death in 1977.

After the war John Peyton became a lawyer, then went on to become an MP. He was transport minister in

Edward Heath's government between 1970 and 1974 and even ran against Margaret Thatcher for leadership of the Conservative party, although he came bottom in the poll. He gave up his Yeovil seat in 1983 after thirty-two years and was subsequently made a lord. Mirroring his parents' nightmarish experience, he lost the youngest of his three children. The death of five-year-old Charlie during a routine operation was devastating for the family. Ultimately his marriage failed and, following his divorce, he wed Mary – the woman he had danced with before leaving for war – in 1966.

His commitment to the girls at Englemere Wood never faltered and twice he entertained former residents at the House of Commons. He was also closely involved with getting suitable housing for Gladys when a new estate in Hampshire was built. After his death in 2006, his son Tom continued the philanthropic work associated with the family.

The older generation linked to the Grenville family had long since passed on.

Princess Marie Louise died in 1956, aged eighty-four. Her sister, Thora, had died eight years earlier and both were buried at St George's Chapel in Windsor.

Grace Weigall died on 24 November 1950 and, like Dorothy Peyton, was buried at the Priory Road cemetery in Ascot, where she is recalled on a small obelisk with husband Archie, who died two years later. In her will Grace left £296,934, its value approaching £10 million today.

Sister Adams, called 'auntie' by both the girls she cared for and those she got to know from previous eras, cared for Matron until her death. Afterwards she returned to her

London roots and lived at a Catholic-run home, where she died in 2001. In the same year Sister Briggs died aged ninety-six.

This chapter of history has almost closed, with the loss of almost all the women who featured in it. Englemere Wood remains a set of private residences. Grenville House is deserted.

Yet unexpectedly Queenie has found herself back at Englemere Wood twice in short order in the recent past. Years before, Sheila's bridesmaid Joan Waters emigrated to New Zealand and spent her adult life there, although she never forgot her formative years at Ascot, where she learned life's lessons in fun and laughter, wisdom and fortitude, caring and compassion. Joan had made it known that, following her death, she wanted to come 'home'.

So, after she died, her three daughters came to the UK with half of Joan's ashes, which, in accordance with her wishes, were scattered at Englemere Wood. Queenie had been an older girl assigned to care for Joan in the home and was there to witness the occasion. And she also came to witness the cross that had spent so long next to Mr Tommy's portrait at Grenville House being installed at All Saints Church.

Years before, a memorial in the Lady Chapel to Tommy had been fashioned under the guidance of his loving, grieving mother. The cross that had stood by his portrait at Grenville House had been given by Matron to a girl who'd married a woodturner, knowing he would take special care of it. He had died and the cross was in need of a new permanent home. To Queenie, All Saints Church in Ascot was the obvious choice. Tom Peyton, the son of

John Peyton and nephew of war hero Tommy, was there too on behalf of his family.

Gazing at Englemere Wood's glorious façade – the place Queenie had always thought of as home – she knew it would fall to her that day to beckon the past, when she and Joan were children, from its greying shadows. It wouldn't be easy. Queenie wasn't given to big speeches or grand gestures, let alone ones that simultaneously put a world war and the elation of youth into perspective. Nor had she made notes. But thinking about Matron and the twinkle that would be in her eye on such an occasion, Queenie drew a deep breath and took the floor. Speaking from the heart, she told of bonds unbroken and of shattered lives rebuilt. There was no secret to Matron's success, she realized as she spoke, and anyone could achieve the same gleaming results if only they tried. All the well-worn epithets that applied to their upbringing could be summed up in two words: be kind.

Her speech over, Queenie was escorted towards the main house by Tom, who was slightly in awe of this new-found prowess at public speaking. Although he had known Queenie for decades, it was a side he hadn't seen before.

At the bottom of the steps she hesitated and Tom looked at her enquiringly. Her face broke out into a grin. It was some sixty years since she had first turned up at Englemere Wood, her unspoken fears for the future falling away when she had encountered Matron. The house seemed smaller now, but that wasn't the only change. The most momentous was about to unfold.

She giggled. 'This is the first time I've ever been through the front door.'

'The Grenville Song'

Sweet as the flowers of Spring, this time of gladness,
Bright as the sun in Heaven, this happy day,
Bring we our song of thanks to God, our Father,
Whose love has gently led us all the way.

Gone are the days of darkness and of terror,
Gone are the days of danger and of fear,
Here on the threshold of a glad tomorrow,
Sing we of joy and gladness, shining clear.

Sing we of one to whom we came for shelter,
Sing we of all the love that has been ours,
Grant that we may not fail in grateful wonder,
Give in return, our consecrated powers.

Sing we of one whose life was nobly given,
Sing we of him whose name we proudly bear,
Grenville for God, Grenville for King and country,
This is our pledge, and this our earnest prayer.

Here in this happy home we'll build a future,
Here we will serve each other, trust and give,
Here we will practise joyful love in action,
Here we will strive to conquer, nobly live.

So we will sing of mercies past and present,
So welcome we the tasks the years may bring,
So pray we that God's blessing on this household,
May come through those who lift their hearts and sing.

Bibliography

A Home from Home
By Sheila Stewart, published by Longmans, 1967
Commando to Colditz
By Peter Stanley, published by Murdoch Books, 2009
Everybody's Children
By Mildred de M. Rudolf, published by Oxford University Press, 1950
Remembering Wartime: Ascot, Sunningdale and Sunninghill 1939–1945
By Christine Weightman, Cheapside Publications, 2006
My Memories of Six Reigns
By Her Highness Princess Marie Louise, published by Evans Brothers Limited, 1956
Without Benefit of Laundry
By Lord John Peyton, published by Bloomsbury, 1997

A List of Sources

The National Archives, Kew
The Children's Society Archives
Archivists Ian Wakeling and Richard Wilson
The Berkshire Record Office
Genealogy
Emma Tucker
The 'Belsen boys' who moved to Ascot, BBC News, 6 May 2018
The Grenville Story
Unpublished memoir
My Life, by Gladys Raffell
Unpublished notes

With Special Thanks To

Queenie Clapton

Monica Harmer

The Hon. Tom Peyton

Sally McGuinness

Jean Forbes

Vickie Bonner

Tina Siddons

Rob Small

He just wanted a decent book to read ...

Not too much to ask, is it? It was in 1935 when Allen Lane, Managing Director of Bodley Head Publishers, stood on a platform at Exeter railway station looking for something good to read on his journey back to London. His choice was limited to popular magazines and poor-quality paperbacks – the same choice faced every day by the vast majority of readers, few of whom could afford hardbacks. Lane's disappointment and subsequent anger at the range of books generally available led him to found a company – and change the world.

'We believed in the existence in this country of a vast reading public for intelligent books at a low price, and staked everything on it'
Sir Allen Lane, 1902–1970, founder of Penguin Books

The quality paperback had arrived – and not just in bookshops. Lane was adamant that his Penguins should appear in chain stores and tobacconists, and should cost no more than a packet of cigarettes.

Reading habits (and cigarette prices) have changed since 1935, but Penguin still believes in publishing the best books for everybody to enjoy. We still believe that good design costs no more than bad design, and we still believe that quality books published passionately and responsibly make the world a better place.

So wherever you see the little bird – whether it's on a piece of prize-winning literary fiction or a celebrity autobiography, political tour de force or historical masterpiece, a serial-killer thriller, reference book, world classic or a piece of pure escapism – you can bet that it represents the very best that the genre has to offer.

Whatever you like to read – trust Penguin.